MEASUREMENT IN PUBLIC CHOICE

In the same series

Edited by Peter Bohm and Allen V. Kneese
THE ECONOMICS OF ENVIRONMENT

Edited by Jan Herin, Assar Lindbeck and Johan Myhrman
FLEXIBLE EXCHANGE RATES AND STABILIZATION POLICY

Edited by Steinar Strøm and Lars Werin
TOPICS IN DISEQUILIBRIUM ECONOMICS

Edited by Steinar Strøm and Björn Thalberg
THE THEORETICAL CONTRIBUTIONS OF KNUT WICKSELL

MEASUREMENT IN PUBLIC CHOICE

Edited by

Steinar Strøm
University of Oslo

The proceedings were originally published in
The Scandinavian Journal of Economics, Vol. 81, 1979, No. 2

First published in book form 1981 *by*
THE MACMILLAN PRESS LTD
London and Basingstoke
Companies and representatives
throughout the world

ISBN 0 333 27767 8

Printed in Hong Kong

CONTENTS

INTRODUCTION

Each year, *The Scandinavian Journal of Economics* produces a special issue in which we gather Scandinavian and non-Scandinavian experts in a field of economics of current interest. This issue is devoted to "Measurement in Public Choice".

Public choice "can be defined as the economic study of nonmarket decision-making, or, simply the application of economics to political science".[1] There is already a considerable amount of literature on the theory of public choice. Until recently, however, little interest has been shown in testing empirically the various hypotheses in this field of economic theory. The term "measurement" in the title indicates that the emphasis of this special issue is on problems in the field of empirical public choice. The reason is that we felt there was a need to bring the economic theory of public choice closer to application. All of the articles are aimed at achieving this goal.

The contents of this issue are organized under the following headings:

I. Estimating Willingness to Pay for Public Goods
II. Public Good Decision Mechanisms
III. Inequalities and Income Distribution
IV. Econometric Models of Government Behavior.

Estimating the willingness to pay for public goods is discussed in Part I. *Peter Bohm*'s article treats a set of conditions which demand-revealing mechanisms must pass in order to be politically acceptable for real-world applications and real-world experiments. The paper by *A. Myrick Freeman* constitutes a survey of the theoretical basis and assumptions required to *estimate* the willingness to pay for environmental amenities such as air and water quality. A similar problem is dealt with by *Melville McMillan*, who uses hedonic prices in conjunction with a system of budget share equations to examine the demand for environmental goods and housing characteristics. The topic of the last paper in Part I, by *Gregory Hildebrandt* and *Timothy Tregarthen*, is the demand for school quality and other local public goods. The efficient level of public goods is estimated by means of a weak complementarity approach.

Part II deals with public good decision mechanisms. In the first paper, *Vernon Smith* compares three public good mechanisms which differ with

---

[1] Mueller, Dennis C., "Public Choice, A Survey", *Journal of Economic Literature XIV*, no. 2, 1976, p. 395.

respect to free-riding behavior. *Ted Bergstrom*'s analysis is based on an article by Bowen from 1943 and it is shown that Bowen's model can be extended to demonstrate that majority voting and an appropriate tax system lead to Pareto efficient provision of a public good. Using the solution concept of dominant strategies, *Jean-Jacques Laffont* and *Eric Maskin* discuss how to implement the solution obtained from maximizing a social welfare function which incorporates ability to pay instead of willingness to pay. A negative conclusion is reached, but it is suggested that other solution concepts would provide more optimistic results, although these are not explored in the paper.

Inequalities and income distribution are the topic of Part III. Based on an experiment using a sample of students, *Louis Gevers, Herbert Glejser* and *Jean Rouyer* arrived at the very interesting conclusion that envy is highly common in affluent income situations, but that inequality aversion predominates when the income situation is closer to more actual circumstances. The next paper by *Vidar Christiansen* focuses on the system of child allowances used in Norway to redistribute income in favor of families with children below a certain age. The welfare weights revealed to be implicit in the Norwegian system of indirect taxation are discussed and, given these weights, it is shown that the allocation of child allowances used in Norway is inconsistent with these revealed welfare weights. An issue frequently dealt with in the literature on public finance concerns the distributional consequences of government expenditures. Under reasonable assumptions, *Aanund Hylland & Richard Zeckhauser* reach the conclusion that government projects should be designed without taking any distributional aspects into account and that redistribution should be accomplished solely through the tax system. An article on how to measure poverty by *Amartya Sen* is also included in this section on inequality. He argues that the measurement of poverty is not an ethical exercise, but primarily a descriptive one. His discussion results in a poverty measure which is a function of more common measures such as head-count ratios, income-gap ratios and the Gini coefficient. The main point is that rather than working on one measure of poverty, classes of poverty measures can be defined in accordance with what the measures are trying to capture.

The three papers in Part IV on econometric models of government behavior focus on the question of what economic conditions determine the popularity and re-election of governments. The macroeconomic indicators used in order to explain popularity include unemployment, inflation, growth in real income, etc. *Bruno Frey* views the government as having a monopolistic position and maximizing its utility subject to re-election constraints. Voters evaluate a government's performance with respect to the success of its economic policy. Empirical research from several countries is presented. *Martin Paldam* raises the question of an electional cycle. Based on comparative studies of national accounts, he proves that a cycle does exist and finds that there is a policy-generated cycle in the OECD countries. The paper by *Lars Jonung* and *Eskil*

Wadensjö begins with a survey of earlier Swedish studies on the relation between economic conditions and election outcomes. On the basis of polls conducted during the period 1967–78, they show that unemployment and inflation have a strong influence on government popularity. The growth in real income has a much smaller impact on the popularity of the ruling party.

The Editor

ESTIMATING WILLINGNESS TO PAY: WHY AND HOW?

Peter Bohm

University of Stockholm, Stockholm, Sweden

Abstract

The main purpose of this article is to advance a set of conditions which demand-revealing mechanisms must pass in order to be politically acceptable for real-world applications and—to begin with—for real-world experiments. Without such non-laboratory experiments, real progress seems unlikely to take place in this field. So far, there are few indications that these conditions can be met with respect to the proposals made in the literature on public goods. One possible example of a mechanism that meets the "acceptability" conditions is given here. In addition, we present some comments as to why demand-revealing mechanisms constitute an important economic problem, a view which has recently been questioned.

I. Introduction

Recent technical developments in two-way communication, e.g. using cable TV, have made it possible to conceive of people participating directly in public choice decisions in the near future. Whatever one's attitude to using present and potential arrangements of this kind, it no longer seems to be the purely technical or administrative problems that hold us back from involving people in individual policy or managerial issues in the public sector. The main stumbling blocks are—aside from the ideological aspects—the theoretical and empirical problems connected with eliciting people's true preferences.

During the last decade considerable research efforts in public economics have been devoted to problems of estimating demand for public goods. A major part of this research activity has concerned finding a mechanism for direct questioning of consumers whereby incentives to misrepresent preferences would be absent. The existence of such incentives as a main obstacle to revealing consumer preferences for public goods has been part of conventional wisdom since Paul Samuelson's well-known articles on the subject in the mid-fifties (1954). However, a presentation of the problem had already been made by Wicksell (1896).

In this article an attempt is made to find out, from a more practical viewpoint, where the intensive discussion of demand-revealing methods for public goods during the last ten years has taken us. A main problem seems to be that the perspective of the economists participating in this discussion has been influenced too little by political scientists or observers of practical policy for useful instruments to emerge from this research work. A set of requirements for demand-revealing mechanisms in order for such mechanisms to be adopted in practice are suggested here. A particular example of how these requirements could be met is also presented.

Prior to a discussion about *how* to estimate consumer demand—or willingness to pay—for public goods we shall say something about *why* such estimates are desirable. One reason for doing so is that the relevance of this kind of research has recently been questioned. Another is that—as will be argued below—the "how" issue is in practice closely linked to why this kind of estimation techniques are worth looking for.

II. Why?

Johansen (1977) has recently argued that the emphasis on the problem of misrepresentation of preferences in public good theory is misplaced. His main argument for this view is that he does not "know of many historical records or other empirical evidence which show convincingly that the problem of correct revelation of preferences has been of any practical significance" (p. 147) in governmental decision-making. "What matters for the actual decision is the revelation of preferences by the politicians in the actual decision-making process" (p. 149). Politicians, Johansen goes on to say, try to persuade others; thus, they inevitably reveal the preferences embodied in their argumentation. And to succeed and survive as politicians, they must show their constituents by the stands they take that they work hard in the interest, i.e. for the preferences, of their constituents. Thus, politicians have to act in a way that tends to reveal these preferences. In fact, "the two-tier system of electors and representatives tends to diminish the significance and relevance of the theoretical problem of unwillingness to reveal preferences for public goods" (p. 151).

Aside from Johansen's conclusion stated in the first sentence of the preceding paragraph, few economists would disagree, I think, with the general implication of these views. The revelation issue has no particular interest *given* the present institutions of the two-tier democratic system. But that, as I see it, is beside the point. Why economists have been busy trying to find an approach to estimating individual preferences for public goods is because they want to explore ways of implementing a process of "direct democracy" for certain isses, i.e. have consumers telling their government exactly what their views are about specific public goods instead of letting output decisions rely on the blunt interpretations of these views by politicians. And if consumers were given the opportunity to state their willingness to pay for a specific public good—to be produced or not depending on the information provided by these direct statements—then the possibility that people might misrepresent their willingness to pay would constitute a real problem. The reason is to be found of course in the presence of economic incentives to understate preferences when individual payments are related to the response (the "free-rider" incentive emphasized by Samuelson and others) and to overstate preferences when individual payments are not related to the response.

In passing, we may question whether in fact present institutions are all that free from misrepresentation problems. Johansen admits that joint undertakings by more than one municipality may run into problems of the "free-rider" type (p. 151). We may add similar misrepresentation problems—but of the opposite sign—concerning municipalities in particular in cases where the national government offers large subsidies to public-good type investments in roads, etc. This latter situation is, moreover, just one of many examples where the allocation of a given budget among projects (for road construction or other more or less specific kinds of expenditure) is separated from the question of determining the size of the budget or of a specific kind of earmarked government revenue, thus creating incentives for misrepresentation of preferences. That is to say, politicians will vote for high public expenditure to the benefit of their constituents in one context and for a low fiscal burden on the same group in another context. Whenever such a separation and such "sub-optimization" behavior are made possible in the democratic two-tier process, it will produce instances of revelation problems.

Integrating the financing and the output decisions in the present political process may or may not reduce the risk for the emergence of such revelation problems. If the voters want more of their favorite kind of public expenditure and want to pay less to the government, it is hard to know exactly what set of preferences their representatives will reveal. So, in order to know what trade-offs people actually do want to make, the present two-tier system may not always offer an ideal solution. Other solutions need to be analyzed.

Now, for general or local institutional changes towards more direct consumer influence to take place in a non-revolutionary manner, approval from the present system of government is required. In this perspective, it may be questioned whether recent emphasis in public good theory has been adequate. A considerable part of the contributions to this theory has dealt with what must appear to non-economists as highly complex, technical solutions to the misrepresentation problem. Such devices will hardly convince laymen in government in many countries about the superiority of alternatives to the present system for public decision-making. If I am correct in this view and to the extent that these theoretical contributions cannot be seen as work in progress with a promise of quite another—and more intuitive—end-product in the future, there seems to be a risk for misplaced emphasis here.

There is another possible reason, though, a more cynical one perhaps, why it may be argued that the revelation problem has been overemphasized. It may simply be difficult to convince politicians that *any* method of direct consumer "power", however obvious its superiority to outsiders, could or should replace the present decision-makers. In other words, politicians may hesitate to abstain from their present influence even in those few and specific public good issues for which a "referendum" approach would be applicable at all. Although politics in democracies is probably competitive enough to prevent a situation where the introduction of new instruments for public decision-making (if "people" want them) were permanently and effectively blocked, this hesitation or direct opposition from a possibly large number of politicians would reduce the chances of governments adopting or even experimenting with new instruments of this type. And this seems to reinforce the requirement that a proposed alternative procedure must contain a realistic and compelling promise to the general public of being "obviously better" than the procedure it is supposed to replace and must for that purpose be quite easy to grasp (pass what we shall call an "intelligibility" requirement) to stand a chance of ever being used in practice.

Improvement in the quality of information about demand for public goods is one reason why it is worthwhile to explore demand revelation procedures. Another is that estimation of option values and consumer's surplus for decreasing-cost industries, cf. Bohm (1977), would require similar mechanisms. Still other reasons exist and may in fact turn out to carry more weight from the politician's point of view. To be able to pursue an effective distribution policy, we need to know how preferences vary among individuals or social groups. If individual demand could be estimated, the distributional impact of the production of specific public goods and of the financial decisions involved would be better known. Even more important for today's politicians may be that information about willingness to pay for specific activities in the public sector could expand the financial capacity for this sector in a way that would not be possible by using general taxes. The basis for this belief is of course that the payments implied here would to a large extent appear as fees for specific services rather than taxes which may be regarded primarily as losses of private purchasing power.

It is against this background of the ability of demand-revealing methods to influence the basis for financial, distributional and allocational decisions in large parts of the public sector that we now turn to some central aspects of the question of how to estimate individual willingness to pay (WTP) for public goods. Before doing so we should emphasize, however, that we do not under any circumstances envisage use of such methods in everyday political decision-making. They should rather be relevant to use now and then when politicians find themselves (or are found to be, in some constitutionally specified way) incapable of reaching a "well-founded" decision, i.e. in highly controversial cases and/or in cases which involve important matters of principle.

III. How?

Most of the discussion about estimating WTP for public goods in the literature has focused on finding a mechanism where revelation of true preferences would be a dominant strategy given a rather narrow pay-off definition. In this section we use another perspective and discuss what amounts to a necessary condition for demand-revealing mechanisms to be politically acceptable. A concrete example of how this condition can be met is given in the next section.

A relevant point of departure is to ask whether actual misrepresentation of individual preferences (say, in a local referendum, perhaps on a sample basis) is a fact or a myth. That certain incentives to conceal true preferences may be present in a particular approach to investigating such preferences does not *prove* that preferences will actually be misrepresented. There may be other— counteracting or dominating—kinds of incentives present as well which would produce a net result of revealed preferences. For example, it has been observed for a long time that the fact that a majority of people participate in general elections violates the "free-rider" hypothesis. Applying this hypothesis to voting behavior indicates that the voter would abstain from voting as he has, practically speaking, no influence on the outcome whereas he has to bear all the costs of voting, i.e. the trouble of getting to the ballot box despite travel expenses, bad weather, etc. That many people actually do vote in general elections—from some 50 % in the US to some 80 % in Nothern Europe, for example—indicates that other aspects, i.e. aspects outside the free-rider argument, influence behavior.

It is not clear how actual voting behavior should be explained. One possibility is of course that the presence of important moral issues, democratic obligations, etc. "force" people to behave as they do. On the other hand, it is possible to point to instances where "moral pressure" has not been able to produce similar results. Sweden—where a conscience of international solidarity is assumed to exist among a relatively large part of the population—may provide a case in point. In a poll in Malmö some years ago, people were asked (1) whether they would like to increase Swedish government aid to less-developed countries and, as a separate question, (2) whether they would like this to take place even if taxes would be raised in proportion. In spite of the fact that question no. 2 was asked right after the answer had been given to question no. 1 and that this was just another opinion poll, *half* of the supporters of increased aid in the first round vanished in the second round—40 % said "yes" to question no. 1, whereas only 20 % said "yes" to question no. 2. Here, economic incentives obviously affected people's reported preferences for a public good (in the form of "solidarity" or income transfer to the poor).

Given, as these observations indicate, that economic incentives *may or may not* influence responses with respect to issues of so to speak high moral content (concerning representation in a democracy, international solidarity, etc.), it can also be observed that economic incentives need not *dominate* the responses on issues of "lesser dignity". In the non-hypothetical experiment with collective decision-making in Bohm (1972) where people reported a WTP for, and—if relevant—paid for, a closed-circuit TV broadcasting of a show, the stated average WTP did not differ significantly among groups whose payment consequences varied a great deal.[1] In other words, incentives to overstate and understate demand, with actual requirements to pay when relevant, did not result in significant differences in behavior (average WTP stated) by representative samples of the population (in Stockholm, 1969) concerning a "trivial" public-good type of service.

Already on the basis of these observations it seems fair to draw the conclusion that in a particular case we cannot foresee whether the existence of economic incentives will dominate or be dominated by other incentives that may be present. The odds may change one way or the other due to the issue involved, the investigation design, etc. but the uncertainty will basically remain. Even if we could prove time and again that a given set of economic incentives exists but does not dominate in a particular demand estimating mechanism, we cannot be sure what will happen the next time (and) when the mechanism is used for actual public choice decisions. In fact, once the results of such a mechanism are relied upon, it will be particularly profitable for individuals or groups to "bluff" and try to take "free rides".

For these reasons and given that direct demand information is asked for, it will continue to be important to look for demand-revealing mechanisms with no incentives for misrepresentation of preferences. But would the invention of such a mechanism meet all needs and guarantee satisfaction to politicians and voters? Probably not. It seems unlikely that satisfaction can ever be guaranteed in a situation like this. A mechanism that convinces economists (as experts) that incentives for misrepresentation are absent in the sense that it does not pay to be dishonest, or that it pays to be honest, may still fail to convince (enough) politicians. And, to put the two groups on a more equal footing, it might not have convinced enough economists either, if they had to stake a substantial part of their future income or professional status on this belief. In practice, things may go wrong as politicians, administrators or voters could misunderstand the rules of the referendum or just because something has been overlooked. And somewhere along the line up to the decision to press the "go" button, someone may have to rely on someone else—say, politicians may have to rely on research carried out by economists—and such confidence may simply not materialize or, once there, it may quickly dissipate.

The point here is not to raise doubts about the feasibility of demand revela-

---

[1] More specifically, in some groups individual payment consequences were related to actual responses; thus, there were incentives to understate preferences. In other groups, e.g. where no individual payments were required, there were incentives to overstate preferences. And in still others, there were no clearcut incentives in any direction.

tion in practice. The point is instead to suggest that actual application of methods of direct decision-making for public goods will require that the method can be checked for systematic misrepresentation. That is to say, it must be possible to judge whether in fact a bias is absent in a particular application, not only in principle or in a laboratory setting. Otherwise, I submit, it will be hard to convince voters, politicians and governments to use the method as a public choice instrument on a more permanent basis and/or to make them abide by a counter-intuitive outcome in a particular case.

To satisfy this second requirement—counting the "intelligibility" requirement mentioned in the preceding section as a first requirement—may turn out to be quite difficult. So far the discussion in the literature has focused on finding a single demand-revealing approach capable of avoiding most or all incentives to misrepresentation, without being subjected to a test against another approach to the estimation problem.[1]

To indicate how the second "acceptability" requirement—let us call it the "control" requirement—may be met, we shall discuss two possible alternatives here. One is the interval method suggested in Bohm (1972) and (1977) which will be dealt with in some detail in the next section. The other is simply that of using two different methods, each of which is *a priori* believed to avoid incentives to misrepresent preferences. The idea here is that the "control" requirement would be satisfied by one *a priori* unbiased method checking another, each used on a separate representative sample of the population. Thus, if both methods produced the same average WTP, in general as well as in relevant strata (income groups or other), there would be enough assurance— by assumption—that correct revelation of preferences has occurred.

As this approach to meeting the "control" requirement calls for not one but two different methods for correct revelation of demand, it does not look all that simple to achieve, at least not at the present time. So far, all existing proposals have been subject to criticism:

(1) Several proposals are based on the same general idea, first developed for use with respect to public goods by Clarke (1971), but discussed also in papers by Groves, Loeb, Ledyard, Green, Laffont and others.[2] The main point here is that a person i whose reported WTP_i influences the outcome—i.e. whether an indivisible project should be accepted ($\Sigma\ WTP_i >$ costs) or when the optimal volume of a divisible public good is changed—should pay whatever net costs this influence imposes on others. Although it can be shown that people would not have any incentives to misrepresent their preferences under fairly general conditions, there are a number of situations in which misrepresentation may still occur. For example, problems arise (*a*) when income elasticities for public goods differ from zero or (*b*) when the payments just mentioned reach non-

---

[1] See e.g. the mechanisms proposed by Clarke (1971), Groves–Ledyard (1977*a*) and others with similar basic ideas.
[2] An example of this proposal is used by Vernon Smith in his article in this issue.

trivial aggregate amounts or (c) when these payments are likely to affect very few people, possibly giving rise to careless information gathering and hence poor decisions. Moreover, voters may gain by forming coalitions.[1] Although some of these problems are reduced by using random samples instead of participation by the population as a whole,[2] others remain and new problems can arise. In addition, it seems unlikely that this approach will pass the "intelligibility" requirement. According to the method, each individual may pay a specific amount (in addition to his general or specific contribution to financing the production of the good) which is derived in a complex fashion and based on a rather subtle argument. The appendix to Vernon Smith's article in this issue presents a case in point where it seems unlikely that economists are able to convince ordinary people—and their political representatives—why and how the method works.

(2) Aside from this main group of proposals, others have been suggested, most of which have not been able to survive for any substantial period of time. Thus, the methods suggested, e.g., by Drèze & de la Vallée Poussin (1971) and Malinvaud (1971), require that people follow a minimax strategy although it is far from certain that they would actually do so. Other methods such as the one proposed by Kurz (1973), simply shift the "bluffing" incentives from one stage of the procedure to another, achieving only an increase in complexity.[3]

Thus, to sum up, there does not seem to exist any fool-proof method assuring incentives to reveal true preferences, let alone any method that can be understood by ordinary people and by "hostile" politicians. Thus, at the present time at least, it can hardly be possible to have two different demand-revealing methods check one another in order to fulfill the control requirement which we have assumed to be essential for adoption of such methods. Let us therefore turn to another possible solution to this problem.

IV. An Example

Given that we do not seem to be able to use a set of methods which meet even the requirements traditionally made by economists—i.e. the presence of incentives to reveal true preferences—we may try to set out from another angle. Assume that we had two methods both of which were simple to understand, and in both of which there were economic incentives to misrepresent preferences. If, moreover, we knew that the direction of these incentives differed between the two and that, in addition, there were other factors acting as incentives to *reveal* preferences, a fulfillment of the "control" requirement is conceivable and would be all we needed for the system to be operational.

---

[1] For a summary of most of these problems, see Groves & Ledyard (1977b) p. 139.
[2] See e.g. Green & Laffont (1976).
[3] See comments in Newbery (1974) and Bohm (1977).

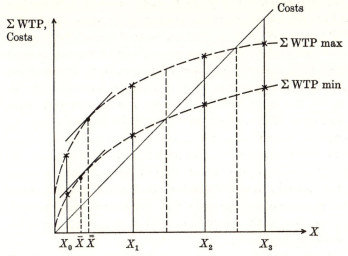

Fig. 1

An example of this approach is discussed in some detail in Bohm (1972, p. 123) and (1977). Here it is assumed that each of two large samples of the population is confronted with the task of revealing their true WTP_i ($\geqslant 0$) for a given public good project (or a limited set of alternative volumes of a divisible good). If the project were to be carried out, people in the first sample would pay an amount equal to or at least related to their stated WTP, whereas people in the second sample would pay a given, symbolic amount only or nothing at all. As the relevant information is given to each sample in advance, there would exist economic incentives, in the first sample, to understate WTP and in the second sample, to overstate WTP (at least for all with a true WTP > the given small fee $\geqslant 0$). That these incentives would exist is assumed here to be possible to make obvious to everybody.[1] If the average WTP reported by the two samples coincided, we would have to assume that incentives to misrepresent WTP have been dominated by incentives to reveal true preferences and thus that this average WTP value would be the true one.

The reason why this approach is at all conceivable for producing the desired result is based on the following. There are some indications, cf. Bohm (1972), that the existence of incentives to misrepresent preferences may not be sufficient for preferences actually to be distorted when at the same time, there are motives for giving truthful answers ("help guide public decisions by actual preferences" and other moral arguments). Moreover, such motives may be reinforced, e.g., by making responses non-anonymous.

If reported WTP would differ between the two samples, there is still the possibility that useful information about true preferences could be obtained

---

[1] In the experiment in Bohm (1972) this was explained to participants in each sample before they made their binding WTP statements.

in this way. As the first sample would reveal *at most* a value equal to the true average WTP and the second sample would reveal *at least* a value equal to the true average WTP, we would end up with an interval containing the true WTP. Thus, with an *indivisible* public good, we could still determine in some cases that aggregate WTP exceeds (falls short of) project costs. This is shown by volume $X_1(X_3)$ in Fig. 1, assuming that this volume illustrates the indivisible good. If, on the other hand, $X = X_2$, we remain uncertain about whether or not aggregate WTP exceeds costs. But if the interval of the aggregate WTP is narrow, we may interpret this as a case of indifference. With a *divisible* good for which there are WTP estimates given for $X = X_0$, X_1, X_2 and X_3 and where intermediate values are derived by interpolation, we would have to assume that optimal X is somewhere between $\bar{X}$ and $\bar{\bar{X}}$ in Fig. 1 (where minimum and maximum marginal aggregate WTP, respectively, equals marginal costs). Thus, depending on the interval obtained, an approximation of the optimal volume could be determined.[1]

To sum up, the important things to note about the "interval method" suggested here are

(*a*) that even if the control requirement is not met, the results of the two tests may be useful by providing a sufficiently narrow interval for average

---

[1] To be more specific, the mechanism suggested here could work as follows. For simplicity, let us assume a discrete public good the production of which will be carried out if average WTP exceeds total costs per capita (or part thereof for a good with considerable durability). Production will be financed by the beneficiaries in some approximative fashion, determined by responses from people in the two samples and related to characteristics such as income, family size, location, etc. The payments from the total population of beneficiaries may be adjusted to reduce collection costs and to reach given distribution policy goals at minimum costs; cf. Bohm (1971). Two sufficiently large stratified samples are drawn from the local (or national) population affected by the project. Information about the project as well as about the "referendum"—including information about possible incentives for and against misrepresentation—is provided to everybody and in particular to people in the two samples. An open discussion can be expected in the mass media up to the date of the "representative referendum". Those who have been sampled to participate are required to do so on the same grounds as people who are subpoenaed as witnesses in ordinary court proceedings. Even the compensation for expenses, etc. could be the same as that relevant for court witnesses.

At the "referendum", the participants are again informed about the project in a way that has been determined by the legislative government. If the average WTP coincides for the two samples and exceeds per capita project cost, the project will be accepted and people in the samples will have to pay according to the rules stated in each case (in relation to WTP stated in sample I and the given fee, if any, in sample II). The legislative government will determine payments for the rest of the population or the population as a whole as suggested above (e.g. through changes in taxes—with restitution to people in the samples).

If average WTP cannot be determined by one figure (when estimates from the two samples coincide) or narrowed down to a small interval, such that the minimum (from sample I) and the maximum (from sample II) are far apart and appear on different sides of the given cost figure, we know that (*a*) the control requirement has not been met, i.e. truthful answers have not been given in one or both of the samples, and (*b*) the difference between the two is so large that the project cannot be accepted, rejected or regarded as indifferent on the basis of these results. In this case—or formally: as soon as a certain maximum divergence stated *ex ante* by the government has been surpassed by the actual difference between the two WTP estimates—the government will have to make a decision about the project in the traditional way.

WTP; this is not possible for mechanisms which—in contrast to this method—simply try to achieve *non-distorted* responses from each of the two separate tests involved and for which deviations between the two cannot be interpreted as an interval containing the true WTP (as, for example, both may produce understatements);

(*b*) that the existence of the control requirement—the comparison between the two tests—will act as an (additional) incentive not to distort responses, as that would contribute to making the tests less valuable as a decision instrument, at worst even useless; at first sight, it may look like this incentive would be present for any pair of tests, i.e. that is would be a result of the introduction of the control requirement *per se*; but it will hardly be convincing (i) to suggest that two *non-distorting* methods are used and (ii) to emphasize at the same time that distortions will be checked, revealed and make the whole process useless by the force of the control requirement; and

(*c*) that the "intelligibility" requirement is met in perhaps the most direct and simplest way possible, i.e. with no attempts to "manipulate" the information problem in order to make telling the truth the dominant strategy at the expense of the simplicity of the question to be posed.

As we have already pointed out, the method suggested here is not to be interpreted as a proposed "final" solution to the problem of revealing demand for public goods in practice and in cases where the traditional political process does not seem to be sufficient or satisfactory. But it has been proposed as a method that can be used as a starting-point for experimental applications in the real world, say for local public good decisions (environmental quality, availability of public transportation facilities, etc.). Without such real-world experiments little can be accomplished by way of real progress in the field of public choice mechanisms. However, for such experiments and other applications of direct decision-making in society to be acceptable to government, the methods proposed must meet certain minimum standards of "intelligibility" and "quality control", as has been emphasized here. If not, it will be difficult to convince politicians and ordinary people that public choice by direct "demand-revealing" methods will represent an improvement. And regardless of how well a particular method performs in laboratories and with non-representative samples, the laboratory tests—however indispensable they are initially—can never substitute for practical, real-world experiments. Thus, failure to meet requirements of practical politics—some of which I hope we have touched upon here—may keep public choice mechanisms in the laboratories forever.

12 *P. Bohm*

References

Bohm, P.: An approach to the problem of estimating demand for public goods. *Swedish Journal of Economics*, pp. 55–56, March, 1971.

Bohm, P.: Estimating demand for public goods: An experiment. *European Economic Review 3*, 111–130, 1972.

Bohm, P.: Estimating access values. In *Public economics and the quality of life* (ed. L. Wingo & A. Evans). Baltimore, 1977.

Clarke, E.: Multipart pricing of public goods. *Public Choice 8*, 19–33, 1971.

Drèze, J. & de la Vallée Poussin, D.: A tatonnement process for public goods. *RES*, pp. 133–150, April 1971.

Green, J. & Laffont, J. J.: Revelation des preferences pour les bien publics: Première partie. École Polytechnique (mimeo), 1976.

Groves, T. & Ledyard, J.: Optimal allocation of public goods. *Econometrica*, May 1977 a.

Groves, T. & Ledyard, J.: Some limitations of demand-revealing process. *Public Choice XXIX-2*, 107–124 and 139–143, Spring 1977 a.

Groves, T. & Loeb, M.: Incentives and public inputs. *J. Publ. Econ. 4*, 211–226, 1975.

Johansen, L.: The theory of public goods: Misplaced emphasis? *J. Publ. Econ. 7*, 147–152, 1977.

Kurz, M.: An experimental approach to the determination of the demand for public goods. *J. Publ. Econ. 3*, 329–348, 1974.

Malinvaud, E.: A planning approach to the public good problem. *Swedish Journal of Economics*, pp. 96–117, March 1971.

Newbery, D.: Comment on Kurz, op. cit., in *J. Publ. Econ.*, November 1974.

Samuelson, P.: The pure theory of public expenditures. *Rev. Econ. Stat. 36*, 387–389, 1974.

Smith, V.: An experimental comparison of three public good decision mechanisms. *Scand. J. Econ.* (this issue).

Wicksell, K.: *Finanztheoretische Untersuchungen und das Steuerwesen Schwedens.* Jena, 1896.

HEDONIC PRICES, PROPERTY VALUES AND MEASURING ENVIRONMENTAL BENEFITS: A SURVEY OF THE ISSUES

*A. Myrick Freeman III**

Bowdoin College, Brunswick, Maine, USA and Resources for the Future, Washington, D.C., USA

Abstract

This paper provides a review of the theoretical basis and the assumptions required in order to use hedonic price equations derived from property value data to obtain measures of the prices and the inverse demand functions for environmental amenities such as air quality. It also includes a review and assessment of existing empirical applications of the technique to problems of air and water quality and urban noise.

I. Introduction

Since Ridker & Henning's (1967) pioneering study, there has been growing interest in using property value data as a source of information on the benefits to be expected from controlling environmental disamenities such as air pollution, water pollution, and noise. Along with this interest there has been continuing controversy and debate over the proper theoretical framework for the analysis of property values and the interpretation of regression coefficients.[1] Although other consistent theoretical models are possible,[2] most attention has focused on the theory of hedonic prices. Rosen (1974) presented a general theoretical framework for using hedonic prices to analyze the demand for and supply of attributes for differentiated products. And Freeman (1974) showed how this framework could be used to interpret existing studies of the property value–air pollution relationship. More recently, at least two major empirical efforts, Harrison & Rubinfeld (1978 a) and Nelson (1978 b) have been based explicitly on the hedonic price framework.

At the same time that the hedonic technique has been proposed and utilized by some, it has been criticized by others on various grounds.[3] The criticisms

---

* I am indebted to V. Kerry Smith for helpful comments. All responsibility for errors is my own.
[1] See, for example, Freeman (1971) and Anderson & Crocker (1972).
[2] See Polinsky & Shavell (1976), Polinsky & Rubinfeld (1977), and Lind (1973).
[3] See, for example, Lave (1972) and (1978), Smith (1976), Mäler (1977), Harris (1978), and Pearce (forthcoming).

include skepticism that observed associations between air pollution and property values reflect a true relationship rather than spurious correlation, claims that the assumptions such as equilibrium in the housing market are so unrealistic as to render the empirical technique invalid, and attacks on the underlying theory as requiring unnecessarily restrictive assumptions about such things as the nature of utility functions.

In this paper I attempt to assess the validity of some of these criticisms. It must be acknowledged at the outset that the hedonic technique is not capable of capturing benefits that people experience away from their place of residence, for example, air quality at the work place, water quality at recreational sites, and so forth. Also, if other techniques are used to estimate other "categories" of benefits such as health or household soiling, they cannot simply be added to property value benefits since they may involve double counting. But these comments are not directed at the logic and validity of the hedonic price technique, *per se*, but rather at the way in which property value benefit information is combined with other information in assessing the total benefits of pollution control.

In sections that follow I will first briefly review the hedonic technique. The technique involves two separate and conceptually distinct steps: using the hedonic price equation to estimate marginal implicit prices of characteristics, and using these implicit prices to estimate inverse demand functions or marginal willingness to pay functions for groups of households. Subsequent sections will consider each of these steps in more detail, paying particular attention to the assumptions and type of data necessary to implement the technique. Then, since one of the issues is the validity of the observed relationship between property values and environmental amenities, I will review the results of existing studies. Of particular interest will be the consistency of empirical results and the degree to which other variables possibly affecting property values have been controlled for.

To preview my conclusions, one's assessment of the hedonic technique seems to depend upon which end of the telescope one looks through in examining the theory, the assumptions, and the data. The theory is logical and consistent, but it involves a substantial simplification and abstraction from a complex reality. The assumptions are never completely realized in practice. But this is a dubious test of the validity of an empirical model. It is the nature of models in economics that their assumptions are to some extent unrealistic. The data are inadequate; variables are measured with error; and the definitions of empirical variables seldom correspond precisely to the theoretical constructs. But all of these criticisms can be raised against virtually any empirical work in economics. The hedonic technique for estimating benefits seems to pass the appropriate tests about as well, or as poorly, as any empirical technique for estimating such things as demand functions, production functions, consumption functions, and so forth.

II. The Theory and Overview

Estimating the demand for a characteristic of a housing unit, for example its air quality, involves a two step procedure in which first the implicit price of the characteristic is estimated by the application of the hedonic price technique, and then the implicit price is regressed against observed quantities and other variables such as income to estimate the demand function itself. Houses constitute a product class differentiated by characteristics such as number of rooms and size of lot. The price of a house can be taken to be a function of its structural, neighborhood, and environmental characteristics. More formally, let H represent the product or commodity class—housing. Any unit of H, say h_i, can be completely described by a vector of its characteristics, including locational, neighborhood and environmental characteristics. If S_j, N_k and Q_m indicate the vectors of site, neighborhood, and environmental variables respectively, then the price of h_i is a function of the levels of those characteristics:

$$P_{hi} = P_h(S_{i1}, ..., S_{ij}, N_{i1}, ..., N_{ik}, Q_{i1}, ..., Q_{im}). \tag{1}$$

The function P_h is the hedonic or implicit price function for H. If P_h can be estimated from the observations of the prices and characteristics of different models, the price of any possible model can be calculated from knowledge of its characteristics.

The marginal implicit price of a characteristic can be found by differentiating the implicit price function with respect to that characteristic. For an environmental characteristic:

$$\partial P_h / \partial Q_m = P_{Q_m}(Q_m) \tag{2}$$

gives the increase in expenditure on H that is required to obtain a house with one more unit of Q_m, *ceteris paribus*.

If (1) is linear in the characteristics, then the implicit prices are constants for households. But if (1) is nonlinear, then the implicit price of an additional unit of a characteristic depends on the quantity of the characteristic being purchased and, depending on the functional form of (1), perhaps on the quantities of other characteristics as well. Equation (1) need not be linear. Linearity will occur only if consumers can "arbitrage" attributes by untying and repackaging bundles of attributes (Rosen, 1974, pp. 37–38).

Assume that equation (1) has been estimated for housing in an urban area. If the household is assumed to be a price taker in the housing market, it can be viewed as facing an array of implicit marginal price schedules for various characteristics. A household maximizes its utility by simultaneously moving along each marginal price schedule until it reaches a point where its marginal willingness to pay for an additional unit of each characteristic just equals the marginal implicit price of that characteristic. If a household is in equilibrium, the marginal implicit prices associated with the housing bundle actually chosen

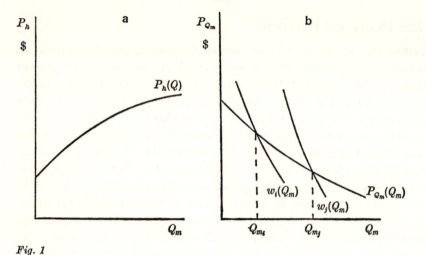

Fig. 1

must be equal to the corresponding marginal willingnesses to pay for those characteristics.

Now let us consider only the implicit price of Q_m. Fig. 1a shows the partial relationship between P_h and Q_m as estimated from (1), that is, holding all other characteristics constant. Fig. 1b shows the marginal implicit price of Q_m, $P_{Q_m}(Q_m)$. It also shows the inverse demand or marginal willingness to pay curves for two households $w_i(Q_m)$ and $w_j(Q_m)$ and the equilibrium positions for these two households. Each household chooses a location where its marginal willingness to pay for Q_m, is equated with the marginal implicit price of Q_m. Thus the implicit price function is a locus of household equilibrium marginal willingnesses to pay.

The first stage just described develops a measure of the price of Q_m but does not directly reveal or identify the inverse demand function for Q_m. The second stage of the hedonic technique is to combine the quantity and implicit price information in an effort to identify this inverse demand function. It is hypothesized that the household's demand price or willingness to pay for Q_m is a function of its level, income, and other household variables which influence tastes and preferences. In other words:

$$w_i = w(Q_{mi}, M_i, ...). \tag{3}$$

Each household's observed $P_{Q_m}(Q_{mi})$ is taken to be a measure of w_i. Can this demand function be identified with the information at hand?

There are two special cases. First, if the hedonic price function is linear in Q_m, identification of the inverse demand function is not possible. This is because the marginal implicit price is constant. The second special case arises when all households have identical incomes and utility functions. In this case, equation (2) is itself the inverse demand function. Recall that the marginal implicit price curve is a locus of points on households' marginal willingness to pay curves. With identical incomes and utility functions, these points all fall on the same marginal willingness to pay curve.

If neither special case applies then the supply side of the implicit market for the characteristic must be examined. There are three possibilities. First, if the supply of houses with given bundles of characteristics is perfectly elastic at the observed prices, then the implicit price function of a characteristic can be taken as exogenous to households. A regression of observed levels of the characteristic against the observed implicit prices as defined by (2), incomes, and other socio-economic characteristics of households should identify the demand function. Second, if the available quantity of each model is fixed, households can be viewed as bidding for fixed quantities of models with desired bundles of characteristics. A regression of each household's marginal willingness to pay as measured by its implicit price against the quantity of the characteristic actually taken, incomes and other variables should identify an inverse demand function. Finally, if both the quantities demanded and quantities supplied of characteristics are functions of prices, a simultaneous equation approach can be used.[1]

A major reason for estimating hedonic prices and inverse demand functions is to be able to measure the benefits of changes in the level of environmental amenities. Briefly, a household's marginal benefit for a small improvement in amenities is its marginal willingness to pay—as estimated by the marginal implicit price it faces. For a non-marginal change the benefit is approximated by the area under the inverse demand curve for the change in question.[2] And aggregate benefits for an urban area are found by summing the relevant household measures across all households.

III. Measuring Marginal Implicit Prices and Willingness to Pay

In this section I examine several issues relating to the use of the hedonic price equation as a basis for measuring the marginal implicit prices actually paid by households for housing characteristics such as environmental quality.

Perceptions. One criticism which is sometimes leveled against the application of the property value approach to air pollution is that households really do not perceive differences in air quality or the effects of air pollution. This criticism is not directed at the underlying theoretical model, and it would not seem to be applicable to the use of the model for other types of amenities such as noise. But even in the case of air pollution, this is basically an empirical question. It is hypothesized that air pollution enters utility functions nega-

---

[1] For further discussion of this case, see Rosen (1974), pp. 48–51.
[2] This assumes income effects are small. This and other aspects of benefit measurement are discussed in more detail in Freeman (1979).

tively; and the model of household behavior predicts that utility differences will be reflected in price differences among housing units. The hypothesis can be rejected if the usual statistical procedures do not find an association between air pollution and property values. To be sure, observed associations do not prove causation. They may be due to chance or due to correlation between a third variable not included in the regressions and property values. But when such associations are found in repeated statistical experiments with different data sets and different cities, they tend to support the hypothesis. We will review the empirical evidence concerning the possible association in a later section.

Equilibrium. Interpreting the marginal implicit prices as measures of households' marginal willingnesses to pay requires the assumption that each household is in equilibrium with respect to a given vector of housing prices and that the vector of housing prices is the one that just clears the market for a given stock of housing and attributes including environmental amenities. In other words it is the price vector which makes all participants in the market in aggregate just willing to hold the existing stock of housing. For these two aspects of equilibrium to be fully achieved, we require first that households have full information on all housing prices and attributes and that their transactions and moving costs be zero, and second that the price vector adjust instantaneously to changes in either demand or supply. The market for housing can be viewed as a stock-flow model where the flow (change in stock) is a function of prices, but the prices at any point in time are determined only by the stock at that point in time.

Now this idealized model is clearly not an accurate representation of real world housing markets. But in evaluating the strength of this criticism of the hedonic price model, one must focus on several distinct issues. The first concerns the accuracy of the price data itself. Where the data are based on assessments, appraisals, or self-reporting, they may not correspond to actual market prices. The errors in measuring the dependent variable will tend to obscure any underlying relationship between true property value measures and environmental amenities. But estimates of the relationship will not be biased unless the errors themselves are correlated with other variables in the model. The best evidence on this question comes from comparisons of owners' self-reported values and expert appraisals. In general, the errors appear to be small on the average and random.[1] Also, some studies have been able to use actual sales data. Results are broadly consistent between those based on self-reported values and those based on actual transactions.

---

[1] Kain & Quigley (1972) report no significant correlations between the errors and various descriptive characteristics of the housing bundles being valued. See also Nelson (1978*a*). Although the comparison is with expert appraisals, not market transactions, appraisors use analyses of the sale prices of comparable properties as a major basis for establishing appraised values. Hence, appraisals should be closely correlated with market values with only a small and random error component.

A second set of issues concerns the speed of adjustment of the market to changing conditions of supply and demand. If adjustment is not complete, observed marginal implicit prices will not accurately measure household marginal willingnesses to pay. The major question is whether imperfect adjustment will lead to systematic biases in estimates of willingness to pay.

Consider first households' imperfect adjustment to changing prices. Even though housing prices change, households will not move unless the potential utility gain to returning to full equilibrium exceeds the information costs, transactions costs, and moving costs associated with the change. These costs help to define a band within which observed marginal implicit prices can diverge from household marginal willingnesses to pay for housing attributes. An increase in housing prices need not affect the marginal implicit prices of attributes. But if housing prices change so that the marginal implicit price schedule for an attribute moves consistently in one direction, households will consistently lag in their adjustment to that change. And the marginal willingnesses to pay will be overstated or understated according to whether the marginal implicit price is rising or falling. I am not aware of any analyses of time trends of marginal implicit prices that could shed light on the empirical importance of this source of bias.

This discussion has presumed that the changes in marginal implicit prices were exogenous to households. But these changes will only occur in response to changes in households' demands or changes in the supplies of attributes. A similar line of reasoning applies here. If either supply or demand is changing continuously in one direction, this can bias estimates of marginal willingness to pay. For example, if the demand for an attribute is increasing, marginal implicit prices will underestimate true marginal willingnesses to pay. This is because marginal willingnesses to pay will not be translated into market transactions which affect marginal implicit prices until the potential utility gains pass the threshold of transactions and moving costs.

A third issue concerns expectations about future environmental amenity levels. Market prices for long-lived assets such as housing reflect the discounted present value of the stream of *expected* future services from that asset. A change in expectations about future environmental amenity levels can affect housing prices and marginal implicit prices independently of the present level of these amenities. For example, if there are widespread expectations of an improvement in air quality, and the market adjusts reasonably quickly to these expectations, the price differential between presently dirty and clean houses should decrease. Correlating these prices with existing levels of air pollution would lead to an underestimate of the marginal implicit price of air quality.[1]

To summarize, divergences from full equilibrium of the housing market in

---

[1] See, for example, Mäler (1977), p. 360.

many circumstances will only introduce random errors into the estimates of marginal willingnesses to pay. However, where market forces are moving continuously in one direction, or are expected to move in one direction, incomplete market adjustment and/or full adjustment to changing expectations can introduce biases in both directions. One should be much more cautious about utilizing the hedonic price approach in those cities and at points in time during which market forces and environmental quality levels are changing rapidly. (Granted that "rapidly" is an imprecise term.) However, it is also possible in these circumstances to determine the direction of bias. Thus, estimates of marginal willingness to pay or benefits derived from such studies can be labeled as upper bound or lower bound on the basis of that analysis.

Limited Range of Alternative Models. In order to interpret observed marginal implicit prices as equilibrium marginal willingnesses to pay, it is necessary to assume that there is a sufficiently wide variety of housing models available such that every household is in equilibrium. The implicit price function defines an opportunity locus across attribute space. A household chooses a housing model such that its indifference surface is tangent to the given opportunity locus, provided that a model with that precise set of attributes is available. If not, the household must pick the nearby housing model which gives the highest utility level. But then the first order conditions for utility maximization are not satisfied as equalities.[1]

The model is based on an assumption that the implicit price function is smooth or differentiable, and continuous. But this is an artifact of the statistical and mathematical technique. There are two sorts of problems. First, the statistically fitted implicit price function is a better approximation the larger the number of units and the more continuous the variation in characteristics among units. A small number of distinctly different types of housing units might be better represented by an opportunity surface consisting of a series of linear segments, but where households could only locate at the corners. The fewer the number of types of units, the greater is the error introduced by treating computed marginal implicit prices as representing equilibrium marginal willingnesses to pay. However, this in itself should not introduce *bias* into the estimates derived from the technique. And in any event, for large urban housing markets there seems to be wide variation in the types of units available. The smooth continuous implicit price function should be a reasonable approximation of reality.

The second type of problem arises if there are no units available with particular combinations of attributes. If there are substantial gaps in the opportunity locus, some households will not be able to satisfy the first order conditions as equalities. This could be a problem for certain subsets of the urban population. Harrison & Rubinfeld (1978 b) have uncovered an anomaly which

---

[1] Mäler (1977) discusses this set of issues on pp. 361–362.

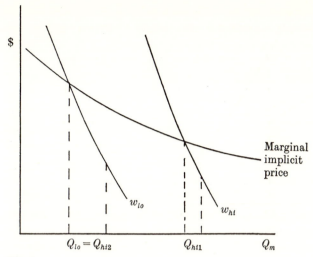

Fig. 2

might be explained by this phenomenon. They estimated both an implicit price function for housing in the Boston SMSA and marginal willingness to pay as a function of nitrogen oxides levels and incomes. Fig. 2 shows the marginal implicit price function for nitrogen oxides (Q_m) and the estimated marginal willingness to pay functions for high income and low income households. In examining the distributional implications of a change in nitrogen oxides levels, Harrison & Rubinfeld found that some high income households experienced a large benefit due to their initial location in a high nitrogen oxide area. This is contrary to the implications of the simple model for two reasons. First, high income households should locate in low pollution areas and thus have low willingnesses to pay *at the margin* for air quality improvements. Also, the postulated policy generated lower improvements in air quality in those areas with higher initial air quality levels.

One possible explanation for the anomaly is that some high income households wish to consume bundles of housing with low nitrogen oxides *and* high levels of some other attribute, say the cultural amenities of the urban environment, but that there are no housing units available which supply these two attributes jointly in the appropriate combination. If that is the case, the marginal implicit price function would not exist to the right of Q^* in Fig. 3. The high income household would settle at Q^* because that is the best it can do. But the observed marginal implicit price (P_q) can no longer be taken as representing the equilibrium marginal willingness to pay for the high income household.

How important is this problem in practice? As the example indicates, one cannot rule it out on *a priori* grounds. In fact, the problem is almost certain to exist for some sub-groups in some urban areas. But one need not conclude

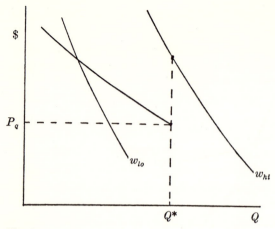

Fig. 3

that aggregate estimates are so unreliable as to be of no use because the aggregate model does not perfectly replicate the situation of every component of the aggregate. This is a problem to which empirical researchers must be sensitive. Examination of the disaggregated behavior of the model such as that carried out by Harrison & Rubinfeld could be helpful in identifying the existence of such problems and judging their seriousness.

Market Segmentation. Mahlon Straszheim (1974) was the first to raise the question of market segmentation in the context of estimating hedonic price functions for housing. He argued that the urban housing market really consisted of a series of separate, compartmentalized markets with different hedonic price functions in each. As evidence in support of the segmentation hypothesis, Straszheim showed that estimating separate hedonic price functions for different geographic areas around San Francisco Bay reduced the sum of squared errors for the sample as a whole.

For different hedonic price functions to exist in an urban area two conditions must be met. First, purchasers in one market stratum must not participate significantly in other market strata. In other words, there must be some barrier to mobility of buyers among market strata. These barriers could be due to geography, discrimination, lack of information, or a desire for ethnically homogeneous neighborhoods. The second condition is that either the structure of demand, the structure of supply, or both must be different across regions. Either buyers in separate sub-markets must have different structures of demands, or the structure of characteristics of the housing stocks must be different. Even with buyer immobility, if demand and supply structures are the same, they will produce similar structures of hedonic prices. And perfect mobility and information on the part of buyers will eliminate differences in the implicit prices for any characteristic across market strata.

If market segmentation does exist, the hedonic price function estimated for the urban area as a whole will provide faulty estimates of the implicit prices facing subsets of buyers in different market segments. If market segmentation does exist, separate hedonic price functions must be estimated for each segment.

It is not clear how significant the problem of market segmentation is at the empirical level for air pollution-property value studies. Only two studies have tested their data for market segmentation. Harrison & Rubinfeld (1978a) stratified their Boston data on the basis of income, accessability to employment, and household social status. They did not report the effect of stratification on the implicit price function. But they did report that estimates of benefits calculated from the implicit price function were reduced by up to 41 % depending upon the basis for market stratification. Thus there apparently was a significant effect on the implicit price function. On the other hand, Nelson (1978a) stratified his Washington, D.C. sample according to urban vs. suburban Census tracts. A Chow (F) test could not reject the hypothesis that the hedonic price functions were the same in the two submarkets. In a study which did not include air pollution, Schnare & Struyk (1976) stratified their sample of individual sales transactions from the Boston SMSA on the basis of: median income of the Census tract in which the housing unit was located; number of rooms in the housing unit; a measure of the accessability of the housing unit; and by political jurisdiction. Their tests indicated different hedonic price functions for sub-markets stratified by these characteristics.

It should be noted that the existence of market segmentation does not render the hedonic price technique invalid. Rather, it makes its application more difficult. If the appropriate basis for segmentation can be identified, it is conceptually possible to estimate separate implicit price functions for each sub-market. Although these functions would be different across markets, they each would accurately reflect the outcome of the market process in each sub-market. Thus, they could be used to estimate equilibrium marginal willingnesses to pay.

The Utility Function. Does the estimation of hedonic price equations impose any restrictions on the structure or arguments of households' utility functions? Recall that the implicit price function is a reduced form equation reflecting the interaction of supply and demand in a housing market. It is based on the hypothesis that the price of a unit of housing is a function only of its characteristics. Buyer characteristics should not enter the equation since the characteristics of potential buyers are the same for all housing units.[1]

There are two aspects of households' utility functions which do have a role in the specification of the implicit price function. First, the only housing characteristics which can affect housing prices are those which matter to

[1] If there is market segmentation, buyer characteristics may be one basis for stratifying the market. But within sub-markets, buyer characteristics are the same.

households. So the housing characteristics used to explain housing prices should be the same as those which are arguments in households' utility functions. If a characteristic matters but is omitted from the hedonic price equation, the coefficients of other characteristics could be biased.

Second, the way in which a particular characteristic enters a utility function can, in conjunction with the structure of supply of characteristics, affect the shape of the hedonic price function. For example, unless the utility function is strongly separable in a particular characteristic, a household's marginal willingness to pay for that characteristic will depend upon the levels of other characteristics as well. This means that the functional form of the implicit price function should allow for the possibility that the marginal implicit price of a particular characteristic might not be independent of the levels of other characteristics as well. The functional form should also allow for the possibility that the marginal implicit price function of a characteristic may be either upward sloping or downward sloping. The slope of the marginal implicit price function cannot be deduced from examining the utility function. Rather it depends on the interaction of demand and supply forces.

IV. Inverse Demand Functions

Estimation of inverse demand functions for housing attributes such as environmental quality involves a second stage of analysis in which observations of households' quantities actually taken are combined with estimates of implicit prices generated from the hedonic price function. For each household in a housing market we have one observation of a price and quantity combination. The question is whether the cross-section data for all households operating in the same market can be used to estimate household demand or inverse demand functions. In this section, I deal with two issues: the identification problem, and the necessary restrictions on utility functions.

The Identification Problem. The steps necessary to identify properly the demand function for a characteristic depend on what assumptions are made about the supply side of the implicit market. One approach is to assume that the supply of air quality is perfectly inelastic with respect to price or willingness to pay at each residential location; see Harrison & Rubinfeld (1978*a*). In other words, at a given location, air quality is independent of households' willingness to pay. Thus a fully identified inverse demand curve could be estimated by regressing equilibrium marginal prices on quantities, incomes, and other variables.

Nelson (1978*b*) took a different approach based on a model of the supply of land to residential uses. With the total urban land area fixed, the supply for residential uses is inversely related to the demand for urban land for alternative uses. If the price for residential land increases, land will be shifted away from other uses toward housing. The difficulty with this approach is that there is no economic or behavioral mechanism linking the supply of land to the air quality over that land or the willingness to pay for air quality. An increase in the willingness to pay for air quality does not necessarily mean an increase in the demand for land; and if the demand for residential land increases, it could be met with land of either high or low air quality.[1]

The supply mechanism affecting the implicit price of air quality is the number of houses with a given air quality. For example, the larger the number of clean air houses, the lower their price relative to other types of houses, *ceteris paribus*, and the lower the marginal implicit price of clean air derived from the hedonic price equation. The number of houses of high air quality can be increased either by an improvement in air quality over the urban area, or by increasing the number of houses available in the clean air region. With present institutional arrangements, the former can be assumed to be unresponsive to price; but the latter may be somewhat price elastic.

The question of which assumption, exogenous or endogenous supply, is more appropriate boils down to the speed of the supply side adjustment to price changes relative to the speed at which housing prices adjust to changes in supply. In order to use the hedonic price approach at all, it is necessary to assume that the observed housing prices approximate equilibrium prices. The assumption of rapid price adjustment is basic to the technique. On the other hand, since supply adjustments typically require changes in land use patterns including replacing old structures and adding to overhead capital, they are likely to proceed slowly—at speeds measured in years. This is an argument for treating the supply side as exogenous. But it is recognized that the question is an empirical one. And there may be instances, for example in rapidly growing regions, where the short run assumption would be inappropriate.

The Utility Function. One question is whether it is necessary to assume identical utility functions or underlying structures of preferences for all households. The answer is yes.[2] Whenever observations of households' prices and quantities are pooled to estimate demand functions, it is necessary to assume that all households in the pool have structures of demand which are the same except for those variables which are controlled for in the regression equation. The control variables normally include income, but also could be extended to include other socio-economic characteristics postulated to affect demand. Examples might include age, family size, or education.

Some form of this assumption is necessary for all empirical demand estimation. The question is not whether the assumption is reasonable, but whether

[1] Nelson specified the offer price of land as a function of its quantity. But in the context of his model, quantity of residential land should be a function of price and the determinants of non-residential land use.
[2] For a strong defense of the proposition that tastes are not only stable over time but similar among people, see Stigler & Becker (1977).

all of the appropriate "taste" variables affecting demand have been included in the model specification. In the case of air pollution, there have been only two studies utilizing the hedonic price technique which have gone beyond the stage of measuring marginal implicit prices and have attempted to estimate inverse demand functions; see Nelson (1978 b) and Harrison & Rubinfeld (1978 a). In both cases, their inverse demand functions included no taste variables other than income. The lack of other control variables might be an alternative explanation for the anomaly in the Harrison & Rubinfeld results mentioned earlier. Some high income individuals without children might have a different marginal rate of substitution between urban amenities and air quality than other individuals with similar incomes but different family situations. If the estimated demand function had included variables to reflect differences in demographic characteristics, this anomaly might not have appeared.

A second question concerns possible restrictions on the assumed form of the underlying utility function. Some form of restriction may be useful in simplifying the demand or inverse demand functions to be estimated. Separability is perhaps the most helpful form of restriction in that it makes the demand for a good a function only of the prices of those goods in the same utility branch. Other prices and quantities can be omitted from the demand function being estimated without biasing the price coefficients. The simplest case is if the utility function is separable in the environmental amenity. Then the inverse demand function makes marginal willingness to pay a function only of the amenity, income and other taste parameters. This is the implicit assumption underlying the studies by Harrison & Rubinfeld (1978 a) and Nelson (1978 b). Harrison & Rubinfeld reported that they did investigate the results of including levels of other housing attributes in their marginal willingness to pay functions. They said that in general these variables had little effect on estimates of total willingness to pay for non-marginal changes in air quality. However, some of these additional variables were significant in their willingness to pay equations.[1]

If the utility function is not in fact separable, then the omission of other price or quantity variables will bias the estimate of the effect of the environmental amenity on marginal willingness to pay. A less restrictive assumption would be that the utility function is separable in the attributes of housing including the amenity. Even this form of separability may be too restrictive in principle. There could be non-housing goods or services which are either complements to or substitutes for various attributes of housing, including environmental quality. However, even where no separability conditions can be reasonably invoked, one can still reasonably argue that many cross-price effects are close enough to zero to ignored. Also, individuals in a single urban area constituting a unified market face identical prices for most undifferentiated

---

[1] See Harrison & Rubinfeld (1978 a), p. 90.

goods and services. Therefore, the prices of those goods which are the same across all individuals can be omitted from the demand function specification. Finally, there may be cases where one would expect the marginal willingness to pay for an amenity to depend upon the quantity of some non-housing good or service consumed. An example might be the ownership of musical instruments and the marginal willingness to pay to avoid noise. Then variables reflecting these consumption patterns should be included in the marginal willingness to pay function. But the justification is that they are proxies for differences in the underlying preference structure.

In summary, whether some form of separability assumption should be invoked seems not to be an important question in itself. What is important is the list of variables to be included in the model specification. And here, judgment and experience with the data will probably turn out to be the best guide.

V. Empirical Studies of Amenities and Property Values

The purpose of this section is to review those studies of housing prices which have been based on the hedonic price technique and which have included some type of environmental amenity as an explanatory variable. I am aware of fifteen different studies which have included some measure of air quality. These cover eleven different cities in the U.S. and Canada. Other studies have used measures of noise, water quality, and proximity to shoreline.

Most of the air pollution studies have used data from the U.S. Census of Housing and Population, both for property value and rental measures and for explanatory variables. For each Census tract the Census reports the median of owner estimates of the property for owner occupied housing. As an alternative to the aggregate Census data, Crocker (1970), B. Smith (1978) and Sonstelie & Portney (1977) were able to use data on transactions in individual properties in their studies of Chicago and San Mateo County. The Census also reports rents paid for renter occupied housing. Goodwin (1976) studied the rental market only. Anderson–Crocker (1971) and Spore (1972) estimated separate relationships for both property values and rentals. In these two studies the effect of air pollution on rentals does not appear to be as strong as on property values.

As for air pollution measures, the earlier studies focused primarily on the major stationary source air pollutants, i.e., sulfur dioxide and suspended particulates. One problem with the air pollution data is that they are often not contemporary with data on property values and other explanatory variables. For example, all four of the St. Louis studies used 1963 pollution variables to explain 1960 property values. The most extreme case is Peckham's study of Philadelphia (1970) which uses 1969 pollution data to explain 1960 property values. Those studies using property values from the 1970 Census have been able to use essentially contemporary air pollution data.

Four studies, Nelson (1978*b*), Harrison–MacDonald (1974), Harrison–Rubinfeld (1978*a*), and Sonstelie & Portney (1977), have focused attention on mobile-source pollutants, i.e., oxidants and nitrogen oxides. The Harrison–MacDonald and Harrison–Rubinfeld studies were innovative in their reliance on air pollution values calculated from a dispersion model rather than from actual readings. The question here is whether the state-of-the-art in dispersion modeling is adequate to support this use of the output of such models.

Of major interest is the extent to which these studies have controlled for other variables hypothesized to effect property values, that is, have they reduced the likelihood that the observed correlation between air pollution and property values is spurious. It is not practical in the space allowed to present a detailed review of the data and model specification for each of these studies. The studies have used explanatory variables which fall into two groups: characteristics of the property, including location, lot size and structural characteristics; and characteristics of the neighborhood. The latter category includes socio-economic characteristics of the neighborhood population, and public services such as schools, police, and accessibility to parks. Some studies controlled for as few as two and as high as ten property characteristics and as few as two and as high as twenty-three neighborhood characteristics. Two studies controlled only for neighborhood, omitting any property characteristic variables.

It is important to control for accessibility to the central business district (CBD) and the value of reduced travel time by including some accessability variable in the property value equation. The effects of accessability could be confounded with the effects of air pollution (which is often worse closer to the CBD). All but one of the studies used distance to CBD or some other locational measures to control for accessability. The exception is the Harrison–MacDonald (1974) study of Los Angeles where it is difficult to identify a single center to use as a point of reference. Instead Harrison & MacDonald used a variable which reflected accessability to major freeways.

Overall, the selection of explanatory variables seems to be almost haphazard. Convenience and data availability appear to be the major determinants of this part of model specification. Virtually all of the studies reviewed can be criticized on one or another aspect of their model specification. The variety of model specifications raises some questions about the extent to which results are sensitive to the choice of explanatory variables.

One of the purposes of the Harrison–Rubinfeld (1978*a*) study was to examine the sensitivity of the air pollution–property value relationship (and benefit estimates derived therefrom) to the specification of the hedonic housing price functions. They experimented with various functional forms, and they re-estimated the relationship after deleting or adding other pollution measures and measures of property and neighborhood characteristics. They concluded that the estimates of the implicit price function for air quality are quite sensitive to the specification of the housing value equation. However, given the implicit price function, estimates of the inverse demand function and benefits are relatively stable across alternative specifications.

It is difficult to summarize the results of the studies reported here, since they cover a number of cities, different time periods, use different data bases, empirical techniques, and model specifications. However, two things stand out. First, the hypothesis that property values within an urban area are affected by air pollution is generally supported by the evidence. Only two studies, Wieand (1973) and Steele (1972) report negative results. They were both based on alternatives to the standard property value dependent variable. Second, the numerical values reported are generally plausible and broadly consistent both within cities as derived from different studies and between cities. However, precise comparisons are not warranted because of differences in the approaches taken.

Nelson's study (1978*a*) of Washington was unique in that he included two different types of environmental amenities—air quality and reduced noise from traffic. He found that the significant coefficients for both sets of variables were statistically significant and within the range of results from other studies.[1]

The hedonic technique has also been applied to water quality. David (1968) investigated property values surrounding sixty artificial lakes in Wisconsin. Lakes were classified as having poor, moderate, or good water quality by officials at State agencies. Water quality was a significant variable in explaining property values around the sixty lakes.

Brown & Pollakowski (1977) estimated the values of access to the shoreline and "set back" or open space between the residential area and the shoreline. They regressed prices of properties around lakes in Seattle on distance from shoreline and distance of set back along with other structural and locational characteristics. They assumed identical utility functions and income so that they could interpret the marginal implicit price function as a marginal willingness to pay curve. Coefficients were of the expected sign and statistically significant.

VI. Conclusions

In this paper I have attempted to examine in some detail a number of criticisms of the hedonic price technique as applied to measuring the demand for environmental amenities in order to determine whether they represent fundamental problems or whether they can be classified as normal discrepancies between

---

[1] Nelson also reviewed the results of other hedonic studies of the effect of both aircraft and traffic noise on property values. See Chapter 6.

the theoretical ideal and the practical realities of the sort empirical research always confronts. It must be acknowledged that there are many respects in which the actual data diverge from the theoretical ideal and in which the assumptions about the nature of the housing market and preferences are oversimplifications. But the question is not whether the model is perfect, but rather does it provide a usable vehicle for increasing our knowledge?

The results from over a dozen studies indicate the model has substantial explanatory power with respect to housing prices. The major questions concern the possibility of market segmentation and limits on the range of available models which may force some households into corner solutions. Also the Harrison–Rubinfeld work indicates that hedonic price functions are sensitive to model specification. There is substantially less experience with using marginal implicit prices to estimate inverse demand functions for amenities such as air quality. But here, the empirical problems seem less severe, provided that the first stage analysis yields accurate estimates of marginal implicit prices.

Finally, while I believe that the hedonic price technique does offer promise as a means of estimating demands, few of the studies so far published are fully satisfactory in terms of their use of data, empirical technique and interpretation. There is much to be learned by studying new cities, and reworking existing data sets to take advantage of our greater understanding of the hedonic price technique. These studies should also attempt to investigate more carefully some of the issues identified in this paper (for example, market segmentation and the identification problem) in an effort to determine the extent and seriousness of the problems they pose.

References

Anderson, Robert J. & Crocker, Thomas: Air pollution and property values: A reply. *Review of Economics and Statistics*, November 1972.

Anderson, Robert J. & Crocker, Thomas: Air pollution and residential property values. *Urban Studies*, 1971.

Brown, Gardner M. & Pollakowski, Henry O.: Economic valuation of shoreline. *Review of Economics and Statistics*, August 1977.

Crocker, Thomas: *Urban air pollution damage functions. Theory and measurement.* Riverside, University of California, 1970 (available through NTIS: PB 197-668).

David, Elizabeth L.: Lake shore property values: A guide to public investment in recreation. *Water Resources Research*, August 1968.

Freeman, A. Myrick, III: Air pollution and property values: A methodological comment. *Review of Economics and Statistics*, November 1971.

Freeman, A. Myrick, III: On estimating air pollution control benefits from land value studies. *Journal of Environmental Economics and Management*, 1974.

Freeman, A. Myrick, III: *The benefits of environmental improvement: Theory and practice.* Johns Hopkins University Press, 1979.

Goodwin, Susan A.: Measuring the value of housing quality: A note. *Journal of Regional Science*, April 1977.

Harris, A. H.: Valuing environmental amenity: A critique of the house price approach. *University of Aberdeen, Depart-*

ment of Political Economy, Discussion Paper 78-01, 1978.

Harrison, David, Jr & MacDonald, Robert: Willingness to pay in Boston and Los Angeles for a reduction in automobile-related pollutants. In National Academy of Sciences, *Air quality and automobile emission control, Vol. IV: The cost and benefits of automobile control*. Washington, D.C., 1974.

Harrison, David, Jr & Rubinfeld, Daniel L.: Hedonic housing prices and the demand for clean air. *Journal of Environmental Economics and Management*, 1978 a.

Harrison, David, Jr & Rubinfeld, Daniel L.: The distribution of benefits from improvements in urban air quality. *Journal of Environmental Economics and Management*, 1978 b.

Kain, John F. & Quigley, John M.: Note on owner's estimate of housing value. *Journal of the American Statistical Association* 67, no. 340, December, pp. 803–06.

Lave, Lester: Air pollution damage: Some difficulties in estimating the value of abatement. In *Environmental quality analysis* (ed. Allen V. Kneese and Blair T. Bower). Johns Hopkins University Press for Resources for the Future, 1972.

Lave, Lester: Comment. In *Approaches to controlling air pollution* (ed. Ann Friedlaender). MIT Press, 1978.

Lind, Robert C: Spatial equilibrium, the theory of rents, and the management of benefits from public programs. *Quarterly Journal of Economics*, May 1973.

Mäler, Karl-Goran: A note on the use of property values in estimating marginal willingness to pay for environmental quality. *Journal of Environmental Economics and Management*, October 1977.

Nelson, J. P.: *Economic analysis of transportation noise abatement*, Cambridge, 1978 a.

Nelson, J. P.: Residential choice, hedonic prices, and the demand for urban air quality. *Journal of Urban Economics*, 1978 b.

Peacre, D. W.: The valuation of pollution damage: Noise nuisances. In *Readings in environmental economics* (ed. J. Butlin). London, forthcoming.

Peckham, Brian: Air pollution and residential property values in Philadelphia. Process, 1970.

Polinsky, A. Mitchell & Rubinfeld, Daniel L.: Property values and the benefits of environmental improvements: Theory and measurement. In *Public economics and the quality of life* (ed. Lowdon Wingo and Alan Evans). Johns Hopkins University Press, 1977.

Polinsky, A. Mitchell & Shavell, Steven: Amenities and property values in a model of an urban area. *Journal of Public Economics*, January–February 1976.

Ridker, Ronald & Henning, John A.: The determinants of residential property values with special reference to air pollution. *Review of Economics and Statistics*, 1967.

Rosen, Sherwin: Hedonic prices and implicit markets: Product differentiation in pure competition. *Journal of Political Economy*, January–February 1974.

Schnare, Ann B.: Racial and ethnic price differentials in an urban housing market. *Urban Studies*, 1976.

Schnare, Ann B. & Struyk, Raymond J.: Segmentation in urban housing markets. *Journal of Urban Economics*, April 1976.

Smith, Barton A.: Measuring the value of urban amenities. *Journal of Urban Economics*, 1978.

Smith, V. Kerry: *The economic consequences of air pollution*. Ballinger, 1976.

Sonstelie, Jon C. & Portney, Paul R.: Gross rent and a reinterpretation of the Tiebout hypothesis, 1977.

Spore, Robert: *Property value differentials as a measure of the economic costs' of air pollution*. Pennsylvania State University, Center for Air Environment Studies, 1972.

Steele, William: The effect of air pollution on the value of single-family owner-occupied residential property in Charleston, South Carolina. Masters Thesis, Clemson University, 1972.

Stigler, G. J. & Becker, G. S.: De gustibus non est disputandum. *American Economic Review*, March 1977.

Straszheim, Mahlon: Hedonic estimation of

housing market prices: A further comment. *Review of Economics and Statistics*, August 1974.

Wieand, Kenneth F.: Air pollution and property values: A study of the St. Louis area. *Journal of Regional Science*, April 1973.

Zerbe, Robert, Jr: *The economics of air pollution: A cost benefit approach*. Ontario Department of Public Health, 1969.

ESTIMATES OF HOUSEHOLDS' PREFERENCES FOR ENVIRONMENTAL QUALITY AND OTHER HOUSING CHARACTERISTICS FROM A SYSTEM OF DEMAND EQUATIONS*

Melville L. McMillan

University of Alberta, Edmonton, Canada

Abstract

Attempts to measure the willingness to pay for public goods, such as environmental quality, have relied largely on estimates derived directly from hedonic functions explaining property values despite recognized limitations. Here, hedonic prices are used to create a system of budget share (demand) equations for housing characteristics so that the demand for the environmental public commodity can be estimated within the housing budget constraint. Estimated expenditure, price and substitution elasticities are derived for both direct and indirect specifications. The assumptions of homotheticity and additivity of the underlying preferences are tested for and rejected.

I. Introduction

Developments in the measurement of the demand for public goods have often emerged from efforts to determine the demand for environmental quality. In particular, witness the popular use of the hedonic regression technique, since the work of Ridker & Henning (1967) and Anderson & Crocker (1971), to explain property values and establish implicit prices for the associated attributes. These results are often used to estimate demand for environmental quality and other public commodities despite the criticism of Freeman (1971) and Polinsky & Shavell (1975 and 1976), that it is usually inappropriate to use the marginal prices derived from hedonic regressions to estimate the willingness to pay for a non-marginal change. This approach can be further criticized because it focuses upon the demand for a particular attribute in isolation of other attributes and commodities. To recognize the interdependencies among demands, it is necessary to examine demands using a system of equations in which the budget constraint implies that greater expenditures on one good reduces expenditures on others. The purpose of this study is to

---

* This research was supported in part by a grant from the Humanities and Social Sciences Research Fund, University of Alberta. D. Gillen offered valuable comments. J. Chenier and A. Sharpe provided programming assistance.

examine the demand for environmental quality in conjunction with other housing characteristics by employing hedonic prices in a system of demand equations framework.

Complete demand systems, as they are often called, have usually been used to study consumer demand for private goods, typically at a highly aggregated level.[1] Until recently, the functional forms employed implied additive and/or homothetic preferences (particularly if the systems were to be consistent with utility maximization) which placed severe restrictions on the estimated expenditure and price elasticities. Homotheticity implies constant expenditure proportions while additivity constrains the values which the elasticities of substitution and, in turn, the price elasticities may take. Since the introduction of flexible functional forms, e.g., the translog utility function of Christensen, Jorgenson & Lau (1975) and the generalized Leontief function of Diewert (1974), it is possible to derive estimates without these restrictions from a functional form consistent with utility maximization.

In this study the translog utility function is utilized to establish a system of demand equations for four housing characteristics—structural features, interior space, site characteristics and quiet (i.e., freedom from aircraft noise).[2] Both direct and indirect versions of the model are estimated. Expenditure, price and substitution elasticities are estimated and the additivity and homotheticity of preferences assumptions tested. The paper proceeds by first reviewing the translog utility function.

II. The Translog Model

A direct utility function U expressed as

$$\ln U = \ln U(X_1, X_2, ..., X_n)$$

can be written in the translog form

$$\ln U = \sum_{i=1}^{n} \alpha_i \ln X_i + \frac{1}{2} \sum_{i=1}^{n} \sum_{j=1}^{n} \beta_{ij} \ln X_i \ln X_j \tag{1}$$

where, for symmetry, $\beta_{ij} = \beta_{ji}$ and the quantities of good consumed, X_i, are greater than zero. Maximizing the translog function subject to the budget constraint $\sum_{i=1}^{n} p_i X_i = M$ (where p_i is the price of X_i and M is total expenditure) yields the budget share equations

$$s_i = \frac{p_i X_i}{M} = \frac{\alpha_i + \sum_{j=1}^{n} \beta_{ij} \ln X_j}{\sum_{j=1}^{n} \alpha_j + \sum_{j=1}^{n} \sum_{i=1}^{n} \beta_{ij} \ln X_j} \qquad (i = 1, ..., n). \tag{2}$$

---

[1] Barten (1977) and Brown & Deaton (1972) review these studies.
[2] The translog model was selected because it is believed to perform better than the generalized Leontief when there exists a high degree of substitutability among commodities.

An indirect utility function V expressed as

$$\ln V = \ln V\left(\frac{p_1}{M}, \frac{p_2}{M}, \dots, \frac{p_n}{M}\right)$$

can be written in the translog form

$$-\ln V = \sum_{i=1}^{n} \alpha_i \ln \frac{p_i}{M} + \frac{1}{2} \sum_{i=1}^{n} \sum_{j=1}^{n} \beta_{ij} \ln \frac{p_i}{M} \ln \frac{p_j}{M} \tag{3}$$

where $\beta_{ij} = \beta_{ji}$. Using Roy's identity,

$$\frac{p_i X_i}{M} = -\frac{\partial \ln V}{\partial \ln p_i} \bigg/ \frac{\partial \ln V}{\partial \ln M} \quad (i = 1, \dots, n),$$

the following budget share equations can be derived.

$$s_i = \frac{p_i X_i}{M} = \frac{\alpha_i + \sum_{j=1}^{n} \beta_{ij} \ln \frac{p_i}{M}}{\sum_{j=1}^{n} \alpha_j + \sum_{j=1}^{n} \sum_{i=1}^{n} \beta_{ij} \ln \frac{p_i}{M}} \quad (i = 1, \dots, n) \tag{4}$$

Consumer preferences characterized by either the direct or indirect budget share equations need neither be additive nor homothetic. Preferences will be additive if $\beta_{ij} = 0$ $(i \neq j, i, j = 1, \dots, n)$ and homothetic if $\sum_{j=1}^{n} \beta_{ij} = 0$ $(i = 1, \dots, n)$. Only if the utility function is additive and homothetic (i.e., linear logarithmic) will the direct and indirect translog functions represent the same preferences. Otherwise, with the presence of second order terms, the direct and indirect translog specifications, either as utility functions themselves or as second-order approximations of some other utility functions, represent different utility functions which are not self-dual.

An error term is added to each budget share equation to provide the stochastic specification. The share equations are estimated using price, expenditure and consumption data. As the budget shares must sum to one, the disturbances of any $n-1$ equations determine the disturbance of the remaining equation. Consequently, the full model can be deduced from estimates of $n-1$ equations. Finally, since the share equations are homogeneous of degree zero in the parameters, a normalization of the parameters is required for estimation. The normalization $\sum_{i=1}^{n} \alpha_i = 1$ is adopted.

Ideally, a system of demand equations should encompass all commodities, but such a specification is impossible here. It is permissible, however, to examine the demands for housing characteristics themselves if housing is a weakly separable branch of the utility function; that is, if the marginal rates of substitution between housing characteristics are independent of the quantities of goods in other branches. This implies that the demand for housing characteristics is determined by the budget allocation to the housing branch and the prices of housing characteristics—i.e., that households first decide on how much of their budget they will allocate to housing and then, given this housing budget, they decide on the combination of housing characteristics to acquire with it. Since this decision procedure for the housing purchase seems reasonable, separability of the housing branch is assumed thereby reducing the information and computation required.

III. Data

Houses are composed of or associated with a large number of attributes (e.g., floor area, number of bedrooms, fireplace, lot size, proximity to schools, political jurisdiction, environmental amenities, etc.) occurring in a wide variety of combinations. While the demand for each such attribute might be definable, it is impractical to do so for the many individual features which are commonly recognized as influencing house values. While one wishes to restrict the size of the system to be estimated, one does not want to discard any relevant information. A means of resolving this problem is to combine the numerous observed features of a house into a few basic characteristics representing the major factors homebuyers seek and consider in their search. The aggregation of attributes into fewer fundamental characteristics of the housing bundle is of necessity arbitrary but four characteristics have been chosen for analysis here—structural features of the house, interior space, site or location, and freedom from aircraft noise or quiet. The specific attributes are assigned to each basic characteristic in the following way:

(*a*) structure includes age of the house, presence of a fireplace, garage with property, brick exterior, and style of home (if a duplex or a bungalow);

(*b*) space includes floor area, number of four piece bathrooms, number of bedrooms, and developed basement;

(*c*) site includes lot size, distance to the central business district and local zoning (if single family or apartment);

(*d*) quiet, a measure of freedom from local aircraft noise.[1]

This assignment tends to parallel that made by King (1976) in his analysis of the demand for housing characteristics in that structure features, interior space and site are identified as basic characteristics in both, but differ in that a public good, environmental quality (i.e. quiet), is included while a measure of structural quality is deleted due to the lack of data.

Data on the price and quantities (other than the quantity of quiet) of the basic housing characteristics necessary for estimation of the budget share equations are not explicitly available in the housing market which reports

[1] The term attributes refers to specific features of a house while characteristics refers to their various aggregations.

only house attributes and house price. However, the value of a house is determined by the bundle of attributes associated with it. Different houses have different bundles and the market process in balancing supply and demand establishes a price function or hedonic relationship in which market value is a function of the attributes tied to the unit. In hedonic analysis, home market values are regressed against house attributes such as floor area, lot size, quiet, etc. in an attempt to determine the price function and its parameters. From the estimated equation the implicit prices of each housing attribute can be derived. This information on the specific attributes can then be combined to define prices and quantities for the aggregated housing characteristics—structure, space and site.

House attributes and prices are analyzed for the residential area surrounding the Edmonton Industrial Airport which the Ministry of Transport's Noise Exposure Forecast (NEF) studies indicate is affected by aircraft noise.[1,2] Aircraft noise, or alternatively the freedom from aircraft noise, is an environmental public good characteristic of housing in that area. The primary data came from 352 house sales in the affected area in the period September 1975 through September 1976. Realtors' multiple listings data provided information specific to the house and sale. This information was supplemented by data on distance to the central business district, zoning and freedom from aircraft noise which was defined as quiet, where quiet equals 38 minus the NEF value.

Hedonic equations of both the linear and the double logarithmic forms were estimated on the 352 observations using 17 housing attributes.[3,4] The estimated parameters from the linear form provide an approximation of the unit price of each attribute. These estimated prices are used to establish the share of housing expenditures on each attribute and subsequently to determine the share spent on each of the aggregated characteristics. The uniform unit prices from the linear estimation result in a lack of variation among the normalized price variables, p_j/M, in the indirect utility function budget share equations

---

[1] The Canadian Air Transportation Administration uses a Noise Exposure Forecast (NEF) index to measure and assess noise due to aircraft about Canadian airports. This index is a composite of a measure of effective perceived noise levels (by aircraft type and runway) and the frequency and timing of flights; see Muskin & Sorrentino (1977). NEF values are not reported below 25, the point beyond which few complaints arise. Aircraft noise, however, may still influence property values beyond that point and for that reason the study area was extended by extrapolating NEF contours to a level of 20. No homes in the sample were associated with an NEF value in excess of 37.

[2] The estimation of willingness to pay for freedom from aircraft noise from variations in property values is believed suitable as the area experiencing NEF values in excess of 25 is small (including about 8 % of the City of Edmonton homes) and open implying that differences in the environmental amenity among houses will be reflected fully in property values. See Polinsky & Shavell (1976).

[3] Both the linear and double logarithmic forms give parallel results with respect to fit and the significance of coefficients. A version of the double log form is presented in McMillan, Reid & Gillen (1978).

[4] In addition to those attributes mentioned above, the effective tax rate and a time variable were also included which did not relate to specific characteristics. The share equations seek to explain the expenditure on housing for the remaining 15 attributes, i.e., standardized for effective tax rate, date of sale and other factors (the constant term).

and prevent estimation in that form with that data. However, if, as expected, willingness to pay for an extra unit of an attribute diminishes as the quantity increases, the value of a marginal (and average) unit depend upon the quantity available. Marginal valuations or marginal prices can be derived from the parameter estimates of the double log form of the hedonic equation. Taking the derivative of the double log equation with respect to the i attribute results in $p_i = \partial S/\partial X_i = \hat{\gamma}(S/X_i)$ where p_i is the change in value of the house due to the incremental unit, $\hat{\gamma}$ is the estimated coefficient of $\ln X_i$ in the hedonic regression, S is the market value or sale price of the home, and X_i is the quantity. Variation in the quantities of each attribute (e.g., floor area, number of bedrooms, distance to downtown) among houses implies variation of the marginal valuations or prices placed on the attribute in contrast to the uniform prices imputed from the linear form. It is these marginal prices of the attributes which are used to derive the normalized prices, p_j/M, of the aggregated characteristics used in the estimation of the budget share equations for the indirect form of the translog model.

The Divisia index, a frequently used mechanism for aggregation in production studies, e.g. Berndt & Wood (1975), provides a relatively unrestrictive method of constructing an index of prices or quantities of the aggregated characteristics from the component attributes. The discrete cross-sectional Divisia index for the quantity of aggregated good r composed of s components is

$$\ln q_r - \ln q_r^0 = \sum_s w_s \left(\ln q_s - \ln q_s^0 \right) \tag{5}$$

where the 0 superscript indicates the base value and the weight $w_s = \frac{1}{2}[(p_s q_s/\sum p_s q_s) + (p_s^0 q_s^0/\sum p_s^0 q_s^0)]$ is an average of the observation's expenditure share on that component and the base share.[1] For the corresponding price index, p's replace the q's. Divisia quantity indexes were created for structure, space and site using average quantities for the base values and prices derived from the linear hedonic estimation for calculation of the weights. The same weights were used in constructing the price index, but in order to achieve the variation in prices required for estimation, differences in the natural logs of the marginal prices (derived from the double log form of the hedonic equation) were used.[2] Consequently, the price index used to obtain the normalized

---

[1] The time-series index is normalized with respect to the value in the previous period rather than a constant base and in the discrete form is known as the Tornqvist chain-link index. The Divisia index corresponds closely to the index implied by the homothetic translog function which further implies the ability to optimize among the components of the aggregated commodity; see Christensen & Maser (1975) and Fuss (1977). Fuss (1977) uses this feature to examine energy demand in a four factor, two-stage model with optimization first within the energy sector among its components and second optimization among energy and other factors. Murray (1978) discusses the problems and implications of utilizing hedonic prices to establish composite commodity indexes in housing.

[2] King (1976) used price indexes representing the cost of a standard bundle of each characteristic in seven different towns in the New Haven metropolitan area based upon the results of hedonic price equations for each.

prices in the indirect translog model is not a true Divisia index but one calculated in a similar manner.

IV. Estimation

In estimating the translog model, the direct and indirect specifications will, in the presence of second-order terms, imply different consumer preferences. Which specification is to be preferred is not obvious. Since prices, not quantities, are usually assumed exogenous in demand theory, the indirect model may be preferred in most cases as it estimates budget shares or demand as a function of normalized prices. However, the interaction between prices and quantities must be recognized, particularly in certain markets like that for agricultural products, when current quantities influence prices more so that current prices influence quantities. Christensen & Maser (1977) have estimated the demand for meat using both the direct and indirect translog models and, while the elasticities derived from each differ, there was no basis for preferring one set of estimates over the other. In this study it seems reasonable to expect the direct specification to perform better. The reason for this is twofold. First, current housing prices, and the implicit prices of housing characteristics, are determined by current quantities while the quantities of housing characteristics will be slow to respond to prices in a built-up area as additional units cannot be added readily nor are the characteristics of old units easily modified. Second, because the prices assigned to the characteristics are obtained from hedonic estimates based on the quantities available, the characteristic prices utilized are endogenously determined. Thus, because of the relatively long lag in supply response and the use of imputed prices, it is believed that the direct specification with its indirect demand function is to be preferred and is expected to out-perform the indirect translog specification.

Because of the relationship among the error terms due to the budget constraint, the parameters are obtained from the estimate of a system of three rather than the full set of four demand equations. In order that the parameter estimates not depend upon the equation omitted, an iterative estimation procedure is used which produces invariant estimates asymptotically equivalent to the maximum likelihood estimates for linear systems. This technique has been used by Christensen & Maser (1975, 1977) in their studies of consumer demand and by Humphrey & Moroney (1975) and others in factor demand studies.

V. Results

Parameter estimates of the translog models are presented in Table 1 where, as throughout the remainder of the paper, the housing characteristics are denoted by the subscripts T for structure, P for space, I for site and Q for quiet. Homothetic, additive and unrestricted versions of both the direct and indirect specifications of the model were attempted but the indirect additive and indirect unrestricted versions failed to converge so no results are available for those two cases. In the four cases remaining, all coefficients are significant at the one percent level of confidence except for β_{TP} in the direct unrestricted version.[1]

The parameter estimates are themselves of limited interest as they do not reflect in an obvious way the characteristics of households' preferences. In addition, the values of the coefficients depend upon the index of prices or quantities which can vary with the indexing procedure adopted and in this instance also with the measures of the component attributes. Christensen & Maser (1977) show, however, that such rescaling of the indexes does not effect the derived elasticities and test results.

The fit of the share equations for each housing characteristic is indicated by the R^2 values presented in Table 2. The two homothetic versions of the model offer parallel results, explaining the expenditure shares of space and site better than those of structure and quiet. The direct unrestricted and direct additive forms explain more of the variation of each equation with the greatest improvement being in the fits of the equations for structure and quiet. Of those two, the unrestricted form has marginally greater explanatory power in each equation.

Since the homothetic form offers the only parallel comparison of the direct and indirect models, note that on the grounds of goodness of fit there is no reason for preferring one specification over the other. It is possible to evaluate the alternative versions of the direct translog model to determine whether there are significant differences in their explanatory power. Specifically, tests are conducted to establish whether or not the homotheticity and additively restrictions can be rejected. Homotheticity requires that $\sum_j \beta_{ij} = 0$. There are four such restrictions. Additivity requires that $\beta_{ij} = 0$ for $i \neq j$. There are five such restrictions. F-tests are conducted to establish whether the overall decline in fit resulting from the imposition of these restrictions is statistically significant. The F-statistics and critical values appear in Table 3.[2] Both hypotheses are rejected. Unfortunately, however, inspection of their bordered Hessians reveals that both the unrestricted and additive cases of the direct translog model fail to satisfy the convexity conditions, a fact that helps to explain

---

[1] The "unrestricted" version is actually constrained by the condition that $\sum\sum \beta_{ij} = 0$ $(i \neq j)$ in addition to the symmetry and normalization restrictions previously noted. Adding this restriction somewhat improves the t-values without otherwise affecting the results implied by the parameters. The restriction is not necessary when the translog function is interpreted as a utility function in itself but is required if, when viewing the translog function as a second-order approximation of some arbitrary utility function, the approximation of an additive function be itself additive.

[2] F-tests have been used by Christensen, Jorgenson & Lau (1973) and Christensen & Maser (1975). An alternative, likelihood ratio, test described in Christensen, Jorgenson & Lau (1975) gives the same result.

Table 1. *Parameter estimates of translog functions*

t-values in parentheses. Subscripts indicate structure (T), space (P), site (I) and quiet (Q).

Parameter	Indirect homothetic	Direct homothetic	Direct additive	Direct unrestricted
α_T	.2258	.2503	.2420	.2431
	(124.6)	(116.1)	(151.4)	(152.9)
α_P	.4298	.4327	.4389	.4383
	(328.1)	(313.9)	(385.1)	(371.4)
α_I	.2080	.2069	.2068	.2064
	(286.5)	(274.4)	(339.6)	(340.6)
α_Q	.1064	.1100	.1123	.1122
	(183.1)	(180.5)	(359.9)	(368.5)
β_{TT}	−.1731	.1728	.3908	.4026
	(−28.51)	(27.79)	(37.42)	(38.32)
β_{TP}	.1117	−.1119	0	.0042
	(29.44)	(−28.63)		(1.129)
β_{TI}	.0539	−.0535	0	.0102
	(24.12)	(−23.79)		(3.974)
β_{TQ}	.0074	−.0074	0	.0053
	(4.373)	(−4.330)		(4.513)
β_{PP}	−.2123	.2126	.3837	.3587
	(−67.32)	(65.99)	(77.13)	(45.75)
β_{PI}	.0834	−.0835	0	−.0083
	(40.73)	(−40.74)		(−2.598)
β_{PQ}	.0172	−.0172	0	−.0059
	(12.62)	(−12.49)		(−3.468)
β_{II}	−.1444	.1441	.2041	.1957
	(−60.34)	(61.08)	(65.30)	(52.81)
β_{IQ}	.0070	−.0071	0	−.0055
	(6.193)	(−6.302)		(−2.205)
β_{QQ}	−.0317	.0317	.0310	.0291
	(−27.34)	(27.25)	(56.04)	(43.35)

some later results. Convex indifference curves do exist for the two homothetic versions of the model. Monotonicity conditions are satisfied in all cases.

The nature of householders' preferences implied by these models is indicated by the estimated elasticities which are reported here as calculated at the mean values of the characteristics. Elasticity formulas for the direct and indirect models are outlined in Christensen & Maser (1975, 1977). Since the three elasticities of interest (expenditure, price and the Allen partial elasticities of substitution) are related by the Slutsky equation

$$\eta_{ij} = s_j \sigma_{ij} - s_j \eta_{im}$$

the third elasticity (the elasticity of substitution, σ_{ij}, in the indirect specification, and the uncompensated price elasticity, η_{ij}, in the direct case with η_{im} the expenditure elasticity) can be determined from the other two.

Table 2. *R² for share equations*

Share equation	Indirect homothetic	Direct homothetic	Direct additive	Direct unrestricted
Structure	.7045	.6936	.8390	.8451
Space	.8722	.8668	.9096	.9098
Site	.8508	.8504	.9043	.9073
Quite	.6186	.6172	.8993	.9086

Expenditure elasticities for housing characteristics are displayed in Table 4. The assumptions of a homothetic utility function implies that the expenditure elasticities equal one, hence there is no information concerning actual expenditure elasticities to be obtained from either the direct or indirect version with the homothetic restrictions. That the assumption that all expenditure elasticities equal one is unsuitable is indicated in the elasticities obtained from the better fitting less restrictive versions. These indicate that both space and site characteristics are quite expenditure elastic while quiet is expenditure inelastic. The value for structure is surprising. Both cases indicate that it is an inferior characteristic. As the structure characteristic continues to display unusual results, further comment on the possible reasons for this are deferred until all the elasticities are presented.

Estimated price elasticities are presented in Table 5. Own price elasticities are all negative and elastic in the two homothetic cases although the direct case indicates much greater elasticities for all characteristics but quiet. Somewhat smaller but still high price elasticities for space and site are obtained from the direct additive and unrestricted versions. Those two direct models also have slightly larger price elasticities for quiet but over all four cases the estimated price elasticities for quiet are quite consistent. The elasticities for structure in the additive and unrestricted forms however, are not negative but positive, contrary to expectations. This perverse pattern continues in the cross-price elasticities where almost every term envolving structure (T) has a negative sign. All cross-price elastics are positive in the two homothetic cases but again the values are substantially larger for the direct alternative. Generally speaking, the price elasticities estimated for the direct models indicate a much

Table 3. *F-tests of homotheticity and additivity restrictions on the direct translog model*

Hypotheses	Number of restrictions	Calculated F-statistic	Critical value (0.01 level)
Homotheticity	4	214.78	3.34
Additivity	5	11.49	3.04

Table 4. *Expenditure elasticities* (η_{im})

Housing component	Indirect homothetic	Direct homothetic	Direct additive	Direct unrestricted
Structure	1.0	1.0	-0.31	-1.96
Space	1.0	1.0	1.20	2.03
Site	1.0	1.0	2.62	3.10
Quiet	1.0	1.0	0.29	0.23

higher degree of response than the indirect model. Also, as might be expected, the responses to changes in the price of the structure, space and site character- istics are larger than those to changes in the price of quiet. In summary, the only estimated price elasticity which is consistent across all equations is the own-price elasticity of quiet but while less uniform, other price elasticities estimated from the direct models exceed those from the indirect specification.

The estimated Allen partial elasticities of substitution (Table 6) are diverse. The two homothetic forms indicate that all characteristics can be substituted for one-another but the degree of substitutability implied by the direct version is much greater. Without the homotheticity restriction, structure appears complementary with other characteristics. The only overall consistencies among the substitution elasticities from the alternative cases are the relatively low values estimated to exist between quiet and the other characteristics, the

Table 5. *Estimated price elasticities* (η_{ij})

	Indirect homothetic	Direct homothetic	Direct additive	Direct unrestricted
η_{TT}	-1.65	-15.15	3.89	5.57
η_{PP}	-1.50	-7.57	-3.47	-2.15
η_{II}	-1.70	-8.24	-6.56	-6.23
η_{QQ}	-1.30	-1.29	-1.42	-1.44
η_{PT}	0.27	6.45	-1.47	-2.81
η_{IT}	0.26	6.20	-3.42	-2.96
η_{QT}	0.07	0.33	-0.33	-0.20
η_{TP}	0.42	10.24	-1.70	-2.79
η_{IP}	0.40	1.68	7.20	6.12
η_{QP}	0.16	0.72	0.63	0.51
η_{TI}	0.20	4.85	-2.07	-1.36
η_{PI}	0.20	0.83	3.84	3.23
η_{QI}	0.07	0.24	0.82	0.88
η_{TQ}	0.03	0.13	-0.07	0.16
η_{PQ}	0.04	0.18	0.06	-0.06
η_{IQ}	0.03	0.13	0.17	0.15

Table 6. *Estimated Allen partial elasticities of substitution* (σ_{ij})

	Indirect homothetic	Direct homothetic	Direct additive	Direct unrestricted
σ_{TP}	0.97	24.33	-4.36	-9.22
σ_{TI}	0.98	23.40	-10.28	-9.12
σ_{TQ}	0.26	1.25	-0.93	-0.52
σ_{PI}	0.96	4.00	19.74	18.89
σ_{PQ}	0.38	1.71	1.79	1.55
σ_{IQ}	0.32	1.18	4.23	4.80

relatively high (absolute) values among structure, space and site, and the greater (absolute) values associated with the direct relative to the indirect specification.

A troublesome point with these results is that for the two better fitting cases, the structural characteristic appears as an inferior good complementary to other characteristics. While this might have simply reflected a failure of the direct additive and unrestricted versions to satisfy convexity conditions in a locale about the mean values, it did not as convexity conditions were also not met (and estimated elasticities hardly changed) at a lower value of quiet.[1] Rather, the reason for the unexpected behaviour of the structural characteristic relates to its definition. Unlike the other characteristics the component attributes of structure are, with one exception (age), measured with binary rather than by a more continuous form of variable. Although the actual quantities (and qualities) of attributes such as garages, fireplaces and type of exterior finish, and the expenditures made upon them, do vary in a rather continuous fashion and in relation to overall house value, the present measure fails to capture that continuity. Instead, the index is lumpy and so erroneously implies that once such a feature (e.g. a garage) is acquired, no further consumption or expenditure on such services is made regardless of the increment in the consumption and expenditure on other housing characteristics. Because of this imperfection, the structural characteristic appears inferior and complementary. Better data on the quality of structural attributes and a more continuous specification would probably alleviate the difficulty.[2]

Although this problem with the structural index detracts from the results, they are still useful. Indeed, given the nature of the characteristic as measured, the results of the less restrictive forms seem more valuable as they allow the inconsistency between the data and the assumptions to appear. This explains

[1] The average level of quiet was rather high (an NEF value slightly below the minimum NEF = 25 usually reported). Calculations were also made using the average level of quiet of homes within the area having NEF values of 25 or greater.

[2] King (1976) obtains results indicating complementarity between structure and space (somewhat differently defined than here) but structure is a normal, not an inferior, commodity in his analysis.

the close parallel between the estimates of the additive and unrestricted cases. An improved structural index should, however, reveal structure to be a normal good, modify the structure related elasticities and increase the consistency of the estimates among all three direct cases.

VI. Summary and Conclusions

In this paper hedonic prices were used in conjunction with a system of budget share equations as an alternative approach towards examining and extending our knowledge of the demand for an environmental amenity and other housing characteristics. The results of the translog model used here are more general than those of King's (1976) study of (private) housing demand in that both the direct and indirect specifications are tested. While the direct specification was believed superior, a good comparison was not possible as results were only available for the homothetic version of the indirect specification and neither homothetic version performed as well as the direct additive and direct unrestricted versions. Despite the relatively good performance of the additive version, additivity assumptions (like the homotheticity assumptions) were rejected.

Although a complete comparison of the direct and indirect models cannot be made, the results of the direct version were relatively similar and contrasted with those of the indirect case. Elasticity estimates were flawed by a deficiency in the structural index which resulted in the structural characteristic appearing as an inferior and complementary commodity. Otherwise, the results seemed reasonable. In the nonhomothetic versions where expenditure elasticities are not constrained to one, the estimated value for quiet was low while those for space and site were high. King's estimates indicated that the demand for both space and site were expenditure inelastic but his definitions differed somewhat from those used here and these results are derived from the direct as opposed to his indirect specification. King also found own-price elasticities to be inelastic while here the estimated values from both the direct and indirect versions are elastic with those from the direct specifications (with the exception of that for quiet) being notably greater. In comparison to the usual estimates of the price and income elasticities for housing, -0.75 to -1.5 and 0.75, respectively according to Polinsky (1977) and Rosen (1978), the higher elasticities appear reasonable given the greater substitutability expected among housing components than between housing and other goods. Indeed, the estimated Allen partial elasticities of substitution are high among all the characteristics but quiet. Here also, the direct estimates exceed the indirect. The difference in the magnitude between the directly and indirectly estimated elasticities (although somewhat more modest for the nonhomothetic direct cases) is important but, unfortunately, it cannot be established from this evidence which is the preferred specification. What has been successfully demonstrated, however, is that households' preferences for public type commodities can be revealed through systems of equations models.

References

Anderson, R. J. & Crocker, T. D.: Air pollution and residential property values. *Urban Studies 8*, 171–180, 1971.

Barton, A. P.: The systems of consumer demand functions approach: a review. *In Frontiers of quantitative economics*, vol. IIIA (ed. M. D. Intriligator). North-Holland, 1977.

Brendt, E. R. & Wood, D. O.: Technology, prices and the derived demand for energy. *Review of Economics and Statistics 57*, 259–268, 1975.

Brown, A. & Deaton, A.: Models of consumer behavior. *Economic Journal 82*, 1145–1236, 1972.

Christensen, L. R., Jorgenson, D. W. & Lau, L. J.: Transcendental logarithmic production frontiers. *Review of Economics and Statistics 55*, 28–45, 1973.

Christensen, L. R., Jorgenson, D. W. & Lau, L. J.: Transcedental logarithmic utility functions. *American Economic Review 65*, 367–384, 1975.

Christensen, L. R. & Maser, M. E.: Cost of living indexes and price indexes for U.S. meat and produce, 1947–1971. In *Household production and consumption* (ed. N. E. Terleckyj). National Bureau of Economic Research, 1975.

Christensen, L. R. & Maser, M. E.: Estimating U.S. consumer preferences for meat with a flexible utility function. *Journal of Econometrics 5*, 37–53, 1977.

Diewert, W. E.: Applications of duality theory. In *Frontiers of econometrics*, vol. II (ed. M. D. Intriligator and D. A. Kendrick). North-Holland, 1974.

Freeman, A. M. III: Air pollution and property values: a methodological comment. *Review of Economics and Statistics 53*, 415–416, 1971.

Fuss, M. A.: The demand for energy in Canadian manufacturing. *Journal of econometrics 5*, 89–116, 1977.

Humphrey, D. B. & Moroney, J. R.: Substitution among labor, capital and natural resource products in American manufacturing. *Journal of Political Economy 83*, 57–82, 1975.

King, A. T.: The demand for housing: a Lancasterian approach. *Southern Economic Journal 43*, 1077–1087, 1976.

McMillan, M. L., Reid, B. G. & Gillen, D. W.: An approach towards improved estimates of willingness to pay for public 'goods' from hedonic price functions: a case of aircraft noise. Research paper 78-4. University of Alberta, 1978.

Murray, M. P.: Hedonic prices and composite commodities. *Journal of Urban Economics 5*, 188–197, 1978.

Muskin, J. B. & Sorrentino, J. A.: Externalities in a regulated industry. *American Economic Review 67*, 770–774, 1977.

Polinsky, A. M.: The demand for housing: a study in specification and grouping. *Econometrica 45*, 447–462, 1977.

Polinsky, A. M. & Shavell, S.: Amenities and property values in a model of an urban area. *Journal of Public Economics 5*, 119–130, 1976.

Ridker, R. G. & Henning, J. A.: The determinants of residential property values with special reference to air pollution. *Review of Economics and Statistics 49*, 246–256, 1967.

Rosen, H. S.: Housing decisions and the U.S. income tax: An econometric analysis. Econometric Research Program Research Memorandum No. 218. Princeton University, 1977.

OBSERVING PREFERENCES FOR EDUCATIONAL QUALITY: THE WEAK COMPLEMENTARITY APPROACH*

Gregory G. Hildebrandt

United States Air Force Academy, Colorado Springs, Colorado, USA

Timothy D. Tregarthen

University of Colorado, Colorado Springs, Colorado, USA

Abstract

This paper applies the weak complementarity approach to the problem of estimating the demand for school quality and other local public goods. Using the same data used by Oates (1969) in his classic study, a demand function for housing is estimated, from which the efficient relative levels of public goods provision are computed. The statistical problems involved in estimating a housing demand function from cross-section data are discussed.

I. Introduction

Paul Samuelson's scepticism about the prospects for obtaining information about the demand for public goods has helped to stimulate a considerable amount of research aimed at overcoming the difficulties he identified; Samuelson (1954, 1969). Indeed, this special issue of the *Journal* is illustrative of this development. In this paper, we exploit the interdependence of the demands for a local public good, educational quality, and a private good, housing, in order to calculate a relative level of educational quality consistent with Samuelsonian efficiency conditions. Using this interdependency, which Mäler (1974) has referred to as "weak complementarity", we thus are able to derive normative conclusions concerning the efficient level of educational quality for a community. We also consider the efficient provision of other local public goods.

In an important paper exploring implications of the Tiebout hypothesis,

---

* We are grateful to Wallace Oates for his generosity in making available the data used in this paper.

Oates (1969) estimated a hedonic price relationship between housing prices and a variety of private and public characteristics for 53 residential communities in New Jersey, all of which are in metropolitan New York. In an informal discussion, he suggested the possibility of using this relationship to determine whether public services were being provided at efficient levels by local governments (1969, pp. 966–967). We use the Oates data here to explore this issue more formally, and to illustrate the efficacy of the weak complementarity approach.

The use of the weak complementarity method requires, in this analysis, an interdependence in the demands for housing and local public goods, the existence of a price for housing at which the marginal rate of substitution of income for each local public good is zero, and the constancy of the marginal utility of income with respect to housing prices and the provision of local public goods. While the weak complementarity approach normally assumes that consumers regard levels of public goods as parameters, it can also be used with the assumption that these levels may be choice variables. This generalization requires only that we assume that individuals select the optimal level of a private characteristic, which is in this case housing. By allowing the possibility that local public goods are either choice variables or parameters, we avoid the problem of specifying the nature of market equilibrium. A general theoretical treatment of the weak complementarity approach is provided in Bradford & Hildebrandt (1977).

In Section II of this paper we develop the weak complementarity approach in a spatial context, and show that the marginal valuation of a consumer for public goods such as school quality can be computed by taking the derivative of the integral of the demand function for housing over prices ranging from the existing price to the price at which public goods are valueless at the margin. We present the empirical analysis in Section III. In that section, we deal with several important statistical issues, including whether the demand relationship for housing can be identified, see Epple, Zelenitz & Visscher (1978), the possible heteroscedasticity of the demand function, and the separability of the hedonic price function for housing so that price per room can be computed. After claiming the successful resolution of these questions, we present normative implications for the levels of public goods provision. Brief concluding remarks are presented in Section IV.

II. Weak Complementarity in a Spatial Context

We assume that characteristics $(R, \mathbf{X}, \mathbf{Q})$ are embodied in each consumer's residence, where R is the number of rooms in the dwelling, $\mathbf{X}$ is a vector of other private characteristics such as the age of the dwelling and its distance from a central business district, and $\mathbf{Q}$ contains public characteristics including educational quality and the provision of other local public goods.[1] The value of each residence will depend on these embodied characteristics as given by a hedonic price function $H(R, \mathbf{X}, \mathbf{Q})$.[2]

Each consumer maximizes the value of a preference indicator subject to a budget constraint, and may be viewed as being in either a long run or a short run optimization position. In the long run, the consumer selects all components of the vector $(R, \mathbf{X}, \mathbf{Q})$ and the consumption level of all other goods, denoted here by W, a numeraire with a price of unity. If, however, the consumer is in a short run optimization position, then certain of the characteristics will be parameters rather than choice variables. In either optimization position, the consumer faces the following budget constraint:

$$\frac{H(R, \mathbf{X}, \mathbf{Q})}{d} + TH(R, \mathbf{X}, \mathbf{Q}) + W = M, \tag{1}$$

where d is a discount factor which converts the value of a dwelling to a periodic cost, T is the effective property tax rate (T thus reflects the property tax rate and the assessment ratio used in assessing the value of the residence for tax purposes), and M is money income.

We assume that the hedonic price function is separable and of the form:

$$H(R, \mathbf{X}, \mathbf{Q}) = RJ(\mathbf{X}, \mathbf{Q}), \tag{2}$$

where J is the value per room of a residence. This separability assumption cannot be justified *a priori*; the validity of this assumption is, however, supported if the hedonic price function is a multiple of the number of rooms as in (2). We show below that this is the case in the problem at hand.

The gross price per room for a time period is thus given by:

$$P(\mathbf{X}, \mathbf{Q}) = \frac{J(\mathbf{X}, \mathbf{Q})}{d} + TJ(\mathbf{X}, \mathbf{Q}). \tag{3}$$

The gross price per room as given in (3) thus incorporates the discount factor and periodic tax payments. Given (3), the budget constraint (1) can be rewritten as:

$$RP(\mathbf{X}, \mathbf{Q}) + W = M. \tag{4}$$

We now define an indirect utility function V which is conditional upon the public characteristics $\mathbf{Q}$; the private characteristics R, $\mathbf{X}$, and the numeraire W are assumed to have been selected optimally by the consumer. Our assumption that the marginal utility of income is constant with respect to the price

---

[1] Boldface is utilized to designate vector valued variables.
[2] For a discussion of the properties of hedonic price functions, see Rosen (1974).

per room P and the public characteristics $\mathbf{Q}$ suggests that we can write this indirect utility function in the following form:[1]

$$V = \frac{M^{(1-\delta)}}{(1-\delta)} + f(P(\mathbf{X}, \mathbf{Q}), \mathbf{Q}). \tag{5}$$

Note that (5) is applicable for any $\mathbf{Q}$, whether or not these characteristics have been selected optimally. Further, it applies to $(P, \mathbf{Q})$ combinations that might not be consistent with $P(\mathbf{X}, \mathbf{Q})$. To emphasize this point, we will delete the arguments of P in the remainder of the analysis.

We seek to obtain the consumer's marginal evaluation of one member of $\mathbf{Q}$, educational quality, which we designate as Q_1. For any P, the marginal rate of substitution of money income for Q_1 is given by:[2]

$$\frac{V_{Q_1}}{V_M} = M^\delta f_{Q_1}(P, \mathbf{Q}), \tag{6}$$

which can be rewritten as:

$$\frac{V_{Q_1}}{V_M} = M^\delta f_{Q_1}(\bar{P}, \mathbf{Q}) + \int_{\bar{P}}^{P} [\partial(V_{Q_1}/V_M)/\partial\xi]\, d\xi, \tag{7}$$

where $\bar{P}$ is an arbitrary price per room. Note that the functional form of the utility function (5) implies $\partial(V_{Q_1}/V_M)/\partial P = \partial(V_P/V_M)/\partial Q_1$. This is true because:

$$\frac{V_p}{V_M} = M^\delta f_p(P, \mathbf{Q}), \tag{8}$$

and $f_{PQ_1} = f_{Q_1P}$ by Young's Theorem.

We now assume that there exists a price for housing so high that Q_1 is valueless at the margin. This price might, for example, exhaust such a high fraction of money income that a consumer will not exchange M for Q_1. Let this price be $\bar{P}$, so that (7) becomes:

$$\frac{V_{Q_1}}{V_M} = \int_{\bar{P}}^{P} [\partial(V_P/V_M)/\partial Q_1]\, d\xi. \tag{9}$$

Using Roy's Identity, the demand for rooms, R^*, can be written:

$$R^* = -V_P/V_M = -M^\delta f_p(P, \mathbf{Q}) \equiv M^\delta g(P, \mathbf{Q}).[3] \tag{10}$$

---

[1] Starting with a direct utility function of the general form $U(W, R, \mathbf{X}, \mathbf{Q})$, we utilize the assumption that W, R, and $\mathbf{X}$ are selected optimally to write the indirect utility function as $U(M - P(\mathbf{X}, \mathbf{Q})R, R(P(\mathbf{X}, \mathbf{Q}), M), \mathbf{X}(P(\mathbf{X}, \mathbf{Q}), M)\mathbf{Q})$. The assumption that the marginal utility of income is constant with respect to P and $\mathbf{Q}$ implies that this indirect utility function must be of the form $V = g(M) + f(P(\mathbf{X}, \mathbf{Q}), \mathbf{Q})$. We utilize a special case of this separable function, in which $g(M) = M^{(1-\delta)}/(1-\delta)$.

[2] The symbol $f_{Q_1}(P, \mathbf{Q})$ is the partial derivative of f with respect to the public characteristic Q_1. Although P is a function of X and $\mathbf{Q}$, the indirect utility function (5) applies for any $(P, \mathbf{Q})$ combination; it is mathematically permissable to hold P constant while varying Q_1.

[3] Note that for the demand function (10), the income elasticity of demand is constant, $(dR^*/dM) \cdot (M/R^*) = \delta$.

The marginal rule of substitution of money income for Q_1, evaluated at $(M, P, \mathbf{Q})$, can be written:

$$\frac{V_{Q_1}}{V_M} = M^\delta \int_P^{\bar{P}} g_{Q_1}(\xi, \mathbf{Q}) \, d\xi. \tag{11}$$

The marginal valuation of Q_1 can thus be obtained by computing the derivative of the integral of the demand function for number of rooms, R. The possibility that Q_1 and P might enter the demand functions of other goods need not concern us; we require only that the assumptions above be met. A further difficulty, of course, is presented by our inability to observe $\bar{P}$. Happily, this turns out to be no problem in the computation of the optimum level of Q_1 in terms of other public characteristics.

III. Empirical Application

The indirect utility functions of individual consumers who reside in a particular area will be parameterized by the variable $\theta_i = \beta \varepsilon_i$, where β is the average value of the parameters, and ε_i accounts for deviations of the ith consumer. The parameter θ_i is assumed to be multiplicative with the function f of the indirect utility function specified in (5). Thus, under the specified parameterization, the demand function of the ith consumer for rooms can be written:

$$R_i^* = M_i^\delta g(P, \mathbf{Q}) \beta \varepsilon_i. \tag{12}$$

Note that we are continuing to suppress the arguments for P.

Taking the log of this demand function (12), and utilizing a first order approximation in the logs of g, we have:[1]

$$\ln R_i^* = \ln \beta + \delta \ln M_i + \alpha_0 \ln P + \alpha_1 \ln Q_1 + \dots + \alpha_k \ln Q_k + \ln \varepsilon_i, \tag{13}$$

assuming k characteristics in Q. We assume that the distribution of ε_i is lognormal, so that $\ln \varepsilon_i$ is normally distributed with $E(\ln \varepsilon_i) = 0$.

The data used by Oates (1969) were employed in this study. These data are taken primarily from 1960 observations in New Jersey.[2] The data include observations for what might be regarded as the "median" household in each community: median number of rooms (R), median family income (M), and the median value of owner-occupied dwellings.[3] Observed public characteristics include school quality (S, measured as expenditure per pupil), other local public goods (N, measured as public non-school spending per capita),

---

[1] Taking the log of both sides of (12), we get $\ln R_i^* = \delta \ln M_i + \ln g + \ln \beta + \ln \varepsilon_i$. Now, $\ln g(P, \mathbf{Q})$ can be rewritten as $\ln g (\exp \ln P, \exp \ln \mathbf{Q})$. Utilizing a first-order approximation about $\ln P$ and $\ln \mathbf{Q}$ equal zero, and entering the remaining terms, we get (13).

[2] See Oates (1969) for a discussion of the data base.

[3] The household with the median number of rooms in a community may not, of course, be the household with the median family income. It is, however, a reasonable approximation to think of "the" median household for each community.

and an environmental variable (C, measured as the value of commercial/ industrial property per capita).[1]

An ordinary least squares regression yielded the following result, with t-statistics given below in parentheses:

$$\ln \hat{R} = -1.178 + 0.470 \ln M - 0.404 \ln P + 0.175 \ln S + 0.144 \ln N - 0.027 \ln C$$
$$(-3.34)\ (10.91)\qquad (-5.84)\qquad (3.14)\qquad (5.75)\qquad (-2.36)$$
$$R^2 = 0.851. \qquad (14)$$

Note that other private characteristics, including age of dwelling and distance from a central business district, are determined in their own demand relationships; neither these nor other private characteristics were significant when included in the regression.

While the relationship estimated has properties that are remarkable for cross section data, there are several statistical issues that must be addressed. These include the use of ordinary least squares, whether the demand function can be identified, heteroscedasticity, and separability. We discuss these in turn.

In our theoretical model, we set aside the problem of distinguishing between short run and long run equilibria by allowing the public characteristics (S, N, and C in this case) to be *either* choice variables or parameters. If they are choice variables, however, then they would be correlated with the error term $\ln \varepsilon_i$ in (13). Rather than making the choice variable assumption and using two-stage least squares, we prefer to allow both possibilities. In addition to the defense of greater generality for this procedure, we feel that the ordinary least squares approach can be justified for its minimum variance property; see Goldberger (1963, pp. 359–360).

The second, and perhaps most worrisome, issue is identifiability. However, it is likely that the hedonic price function $H(R, \mathbf{X}, \mathbf{Q})$ depends on variables which do not enter the utility functions or budget constraints of consumers. These might include population density, population, and population change. Even if consumers regard these variables as important indicators of, say, quality of life, the demand relationship may still be identifiable. Suppose, for example, that individuals are concerned about community population size. It seems reasonable to assume that individuals will differ in their assessments of this variable; a change in population may increase the demands of some consumers for number of rooms and decrease it for others. Thus, even if population size (or change in population size) does enter the utility functions of some consumers, it may cancel out of the aggregate demand function or, in the case here, the demand function of the "average" median consumer.

---

[1] One would, of course, like better measures than these. It is unlikely, for example, that "expenditures per pupil" is a good measure of school quality. It is not, however, obvious that other possible measures (e.g., test scores, income levels of graduates) would be better, particularly in light of the wide range of roles that schools play in society.

Further, because a change in a variable like population size will tend to create a long run disequilibrium condition, and is not directly part of the consumer's choice problem in the short run, it will contribute to the identification of (13).

The third statistical problem in our analysis is heteroscedasticity. One can assume that Var $(\ln \varepsilon_i) = \sigma^2$, and is thus invariant across individuals. A random sample of observations would then generate a homoscedastic error term. However, only observations of the "median" household in each community were used in estimating (13). This creates a problem, because if $\ln \varepsilon_i$ is distributed normally, then the variance of the median is $\sigma_{md}^2 = \pi\sigma^2/2A_j$, where A_j is the number of residences in the community from which the median was drawn. The appropriate transformation to deal with this heteroscedasticity would be to multiply each term in (13) by $\sqrt{A_j}$ and then to estimate the transformed model using ordinary least squares. However, such a model would be difficult to interpret. It is our view that an estimated relationship should lend itself to economic interpretation. Further, an examination of the residuals in (14) did not suggest the presence of a heteroscedasticity problem.

Finally, there is the problem discussed above of the separability of the hedonic price function, i.e., whether $H(R, \mathbf{X}, \mathbf{Q})$ can be written as $RJ(\mathbf{X}, \mathbf{Q})$. Our estimate of the hedonic price function yielded:

$$\ln \hat{H} = -1.391 + 1.012 \ln R + 0.347 \ln S + 0.158 \ln N - 0.106 \ln D$$
$$\quad (-2.78) \quad (5.99) \qquad (3.38) \qquad (2.50) \qquad (-4.28)$$

$$\quad + 0.116 \ln A - 0.196 \ln T - 0.017 \ln K - 0.015 \ln C,$$
$$\quad (5.20) \qquad (-2.71) \qquad (-0.77) \qquad (-0.66)$$

$$R^2 = 0.855, \qquad (15)$$

where H is the median value of owner-occupied dwellings, D is distance from mid-town Manhattan, A is the percentage of dwellings built since 1950, T is the effective tax rate, and K is the population density. R, S, N, and C are the same variables used in (14). The coefficient for $\ln R$ is 1.052 $(t = 6.70)$ when one deletes K and C and estimates (15). The assumption of separability thus seems to be a reasonable approximation.

It is our view that the use of ordinary least squares to estimate (14) is appropriate for the economic issue we are addressing. The statistical properties of (14) permit the derivation of normative conclusions concerning the levels of public goods provision in the Oates sample of communities. We utilize (14) in (11) to solve for the marginal rates of substitution of money income M for school quality (S), non-school public goods provision (N), and environmental quality (C). We obtain:

$$V_S/V_M = 0.0902 M^{0.470} S^{-0.825} N^{0.144} C^{-0.027} [\bar{P}^{0.596} - P^{0.596}] \qquad (16\text{a})$$

$$V_N/V_M = 0.0742 M^{0.470} S^{0.175} N^{-0.866} C^{-0.027} [\bar{P}^{0.596} - P^{0.596}] \qquad (16\text{b})$$

$$V_C/V_M = -0.0139 M^{0.470} S^{0.175} N^{0.144} C^{-1.027} [\bar{P}^{0.596} - P^{0.596}]. \qquad (16\text{c})$$

Because $\bar{P}$, the price of rooms at which the public good is valueless, is almost certainly outside the range of observations available, its presence in (16) poses a difficulty. It is not, however, an intractable one.

We assume that the median household's marginal rate of substitution is equal to the average. Then the sum of marginal rates of substitution is found by multiplying the median household's rate times the number of residences in the community; the efficient provision of the good requires that this sum be equal to the marginal cost of providing the public good. We can use this relationship for any two of the public goods to eliminate $\bar{P}$ and solve for the level of one of the public goods in terms of the other. Note that the marginal cost of S is equal to the number of pupils in public schools in the community, B_j; and the marginal cost of N is equal to the community's population, G_j. Using (16a) and (16b), when the Samuelsonian efficiency conditions are satisfied:[1]

$$N_j^* = 0.8226 \frac{B_j}{G_j} S_j^*. \tag{17}$$

For a specified community in which B and G are known, we can thus calculate the optimal relationship between N and S. Then the optimal levels of S and N, consistent with total community expenditures E, can be computed. Expenditures are given by:

$$B_j S_j + G_j N_j = E_j.[2] \tag{18}$$

Using (17) with (18) we get:

$$S_j^* = \frac{0.5486\, E_j}{B_j} \tag{19a}$$

$$N_j^* = \frac{0.4514\, E_j}{G_j}. \tag{19b}$$

To illustrate the use of these relationships, we consider the community of Glen Rock, New Jersey, in which 94 % of the dwellings were owner occupied in 1960. The following data are applicable to this community:[3]

Expenditures (E) in Glen Rock in 1960 were \$2 094 516. Given this E, our estimate of the efficient level of expenditures per pupil is \$408; the efficient level of non-school public spending per capita is \$73 (the actual expenditures

---

[1] Our estimate of the demand relationship is for homeowners only, and thus does not apply to communities with renters. Applying the analysis to communities with renters would require either that information about renters be included in the estimate of the demand function, or the not unreasonable assumption that the demand functions for homeowners are identical to those of renters.

[2] If a change in E were achieved by changing the property tax, then the effective property tax rate and, in turn, the gross price per room might vary. Such a price effect, however, would not influence our results.

[3] See Oates (1969, pp. 969–970) for sources of this data.

Table 1. *Glen Rock, New Jersey*

Median value of owner-occupied dwellings (H)	$22 600
Effective property tax rate (T)	0.02669
Annual gross price per room (P)	$300.00
Median number of rooms (R)	6.4
Median family income (M)	$11 260
Expenditure per pupil (S)	$543
Non-school public spending per capita (N)	$44
Value of commercial/industrial property per capita (C)	$799
Number of owner-occupied dwellings (A)	3 331
Population (G)	12 900
Number of students enrolled in public schools (B)	2 812

were $543 and $44 respectively). Because we do not have an estimate of the marginal cost of changing the amount of commercial and industrial property, we have not attempted to estimate the efficient relationship between C and S or N.

IV. Conclusion

The weak complementarity approach appears to be an extremely promising one for estimating the efficient levels of public goods provision. Even in the case of housing demand and local public goods, in which we are not able to estimate the price, $\overline{P}$, at which public goods are valueless, we can estimate the correct fractions of a given level of total expenditures that should be devoted to each public good. Further theoretical and empirical work may yield methods of estimating $\overline{P}$, thus greatly increasing the power of the analysis.

The problem of identification is also one which we feel deserves continuing attention. We *think* that our demand function (13) is identifiable, but more empirical work is needed on the respective roles of variables in the hedonic price function and the demand function. It should be noted that the issue we have confronted is one facing all cross section analyses of demand.

The notion that consumers will, all other things equal, increase their demand for housing in response to an increase in the provision of local public goods is a compelling one. The ability to exploit this relationship in order to obtain reasonably precise estimates of the efficient levels of provision of these goods should prove to be an important policy tool.

References

Bradford, D. & Hildebrandt, G.: Observ-able public good preferences. *Journal of Public Economics 8*, 111–131, 1977.

Epple, D., Zelenitz, A. & Visscher, M.: A search for testable implications of the Tiebout hypothesis. *Journal of Political Economy 86*, 405–426, 1978.

Goldberger, A.: *Econometric theory*. Wiley, New York, 1964.

Mäler, K.: *Environmental economics*. Johns

Hopkins University Press, Baltimore, 1974.

Oates, W.: The effects of property taxes and local public spending on property values: An empirical study of tax capitalization and the Tiebout hypothesis. *Journal of Political Economy 77*, 957–971, 1969.

Rosen, S.: Hedonic prices and implicit markets. *Journal of Political Economy 82*, 34–55, 1974.

Samuelson, P.: The pure theory of local expenditure. *Review of Economics and Statistics 36*, 387–389, 1954.

Samuelson, P.: Pure theory of public expenditure and taxation. In *Public economics* (ed. J. Margolis & H. Guitton), pp. 98–123, 1969.

AN EXPERIMENTAL COMPARISON OF THREE PUBLIC GOOD DECISION MECHANISMS

*Vernon L. Smith**

University of Arizona, Tucson, Arizona, USA

Abstract

Three public good mechanisms, all sharing the characteristics of collective excludability, unanimity and budget balance, are compared: The mechanisms differ in ways that are hypothesized to effect free-riding behavior with the Auction mechanism expected to show the least, and the Free-Rider and Quasi Free-Rider mechanisms showing the greatest such behavior. All three mechanisms yield mean quantities of a public good that are significantly greater than the free-rider quantity. However, the Auction mechanism provides a mean quantity of the public good which is significantly larger than that of the other two procedures, and closer to the Lindahl optimal quantity.

I. Introduction

Coinciding with the recent theoretical contributions of incentive compatible mechanisms for the provision of public goods, e.g. Clarke (1971), Groves (1973), Groves & Ledyard (1977), several experimental studies have tested various propositions in public goods theory; see Bohm (1972), Sweeny (1973), Marwell & Ames (1977), Ferejohn, Forsythe & Noll (1979), and Smith (1979 a, b). All of these widely differing studies tend to support the proposition that decentralized mechanisms exist that allow a collective to choose and finance optimal or near-optimal quantities of a public good. Three of these studies, Ferejohn, Forsythe & Noll (1979), and Smith (1979 a, b), have assumed implicitly, if not explicitly, that collectives cannot be expected to provide optimal quantities of a public good unless a decision mechanism is used that provides explicit individual incentives that favor the optimal provision of the public good. In other words, it is assumed that free-riding will occur in the absence of incentives designed to prevent free-rider behavior. One study, Bohm (1972), tested several alternative cost imputation rules for the provision of a discrete

* I am grateful to the National Science Foundation for providing research support, and to Michael Vannoni for writing the PLATO programs for all three public good mechanisms.

public good. The mean contributions to the public good under the alternative methods did not differ significantly from each other or from a "free-rider" control method; these results led to the conclusion that the free-rider problem may have been exaggerated. However, as noted in Smith (1979a), it is possible to interpret Bohm's alternative methods as representing versions of the Auction Mechanism in Smith (1979a), which excludes members of a collective from enjoying the surplus from a public good if the cost of the good is not covered. This exclusion characteristic may provide a disincentive to free-ride. Two experimental papers, Sweeny (1973) and Marwell & Ames (1977), provide evidence for only a very weak version of the free-rider hypothesis in the context of experimental paradigms that appear to provide strong free-riding incentives. Consequently, if a particular incentive compatible mechanism is found to produce no significant free-rider behavior, it is uncertain as to how much of these "good results" are attributable to the mechanism and how much to a residual core of non free-rider behavior.

Smith (1979a) compared three public good mechanisms under the condition of no income effects: (1) The Groves–Ledyard quadratic cost allocation Mechanism, (2) The Auction Mechanism (which are both incentive compatible in the sense that Pareto optimal allocations are among the set of Nash equilibria), and (3) The incentive incompatible Lindahl Mechanism. Under the experimental conditions studied the Groves–Ledyard and Auction Mechanisms produced comparable, and approximately optimal, quantities of the public good, whereas the Lindahl Mechanism seriously underprovided the public good. However, there are other, and simpler, "free-rider" mechanisms than the Lindahl mechanism studied in Smith (1979a). In the analysis to follow we compare the Auction Mechanism and a Free-Rider Mechanism of similar structure with the objective of isolating the incremental effect of the alleged incentive properties of the Auction Mechanism. We also provide the results of several experiments with a Quasi Free-Rider Mechanism which combines features from both the Auction and Free-Rider mechanisms in an attempt to further delineate the forces at work in these different institutions.

The three public good mechanisms studied here all share the following characteristics: Collective excludability, unanimity,[1] and budget balance. All three exploit the fact that prior to the actual provision of a pure public good a collective, and thus each member, can be excluded from the benefits of the good by not providing it. If the unanimity–excludability feature is a prominent element in discouraging free-rider behavior, then with none of these procedures should we observe strong free-riding, i.e. sample public good quantities should be significantly greater than the theoretical free-rider quantity of the public good. Also common to all three public good mechanisms is the following experimental context: The economy consists of one private and one public good.

---

[1] This unanimity feature is reminiscent of Wicksell's (1896) views on the possibility of the voluntary provision of public goods.

Each consumer agent i $(i=1, 2, ..., I)$ has an endowment ω_i of the private good, and a payoff function (known privately) $V^i(y_i, X)$, increasing and quasi-concave in (y_i, X), yielding V^i dollars if i retains $y_i(0 \leqslant y_i \leqslant \omega_i)$ units of the private good and the collective of I members chooses to produce X units of the public good. A unit of the public good can be produced with q units (a constant) of the private good.

The three mechanisms differ only in terms of the bid-proposal decisions of the members, and the public and private information reported to each member of the collective after each decision trial. We describe these differences in the three sections to follow.

II. The Auction Mechanism

In the Auction Mechanism each individual chooses a 2-tuple (B_i, X_i), where $B_i = \omega_i - y_i$ is the bid in private good units that i contributes to the production of the public good and X_i is the quantity of the public good proposed by i. We define:

(a) The collective's proposed quantity of the public good is the mean proposal $\bar{X} = \sum_{\forall k} X_k / I$.

(b) The partial mean proposal (excluding i) is $\bar{X}_i = \sum_{\forall j \neq i} X_j / (I-1)$.

(c) The partial sum of bids (excluding i) is $\hat{B}_i = \sum_{\forall j \neq i} B_j$.

(d) The residual unit cost of the public good to i is $q - \hat{B}_i / \bar{X}_i$, and his share of the cost of the collective's proposal is $(q - B_i / \bar{X}_i) \bar{X}$.

(e) Collective agreement requires each i to accept his share of cost by bidding that amount and to accept the collective's proposed quantity of the public good as his personal proposal, i.e. agreement occurs when there is unanimity in the sense that $B_i = (q - \hat{B}_i / \bar{X}_i) \bar{X}$ and $X_i = \bar{X} \forall i$. The process by which these conditions can be met will be discussed below.

The payoff to i is then

$$v_i = \begin{cases} V^i[\omega_i - (q - \hat{B}_i / \bar{X}_i) \bar{X}, \bar{X}], & \text{if } B_i = (q - \hat{B}_i / \bar{X}_i) \bar{X}, \quad X_i = \bar{X}, \forall i. \\ V^i[\omega_i, 0], & \text{if } B_i \neq (q - \hat{B}_i / \bar{X}_i) \bar{X} \quad \text{or } X_i \neq \bar{X}, \quad \text{for any } i, \end{cases} \tag{1}$$

where we assume $V^i[\omega_i, 0] < V^i(y_i, X) \forall y_i < \omega_i, X > 0$.

If each i chooses (B_i, X_i) to maximize v_i, the resulting conditions correspond to those of a Lindahl equilibrium, which is also a Nash equilibrium. However, (1) defines a great many Nash equilibria that are not Lindahl equilibria. A maximum of v_i requires agreement as defined above and

$$-(q - \hat{B}_i / \bar{X}_i)(1/I) V_1^i + (1/I) V_2^i = 0$$

or

$$B_i = (q - \hat{B}_i / \bar{X}_i) \bar{X}, \quad \forall i \tag{2}$$

$$X_i = \bar{X}, \quad \forall i \tag{3}$$

$$\frac{V_2^i}{V_1^i} = q - \hat{B}_i/\bar{X}_i, \quad \forall i \tag{4}$$

Since (3) implies $\bar{X}_i = \bar{X}$, from (2)

$$B_i + \hat{B}_i = q\bar{X} \tag{5}$$

and from (4), (2) and (5)

$$\sum_{\forall k} \frac{V_2^k}{V_1^k} = \sum_{\forall k} (q - \hat{B}_k/\bar{X}_k) = \frac{\sum\limits_{\forall k} B_k}{\bar{X}} = \frac{B_i + \hat{B}_i}{\bar{X}} = q. \tag{6}$$

Equations (4) and (6) define an interior Lindahl equilibrium $(y_1^0, ..., y_I^0, X^0)$. This is also a Nash equilibrium since if all $j \neq i$ bid $B_j^0 = \omega_j - y_j^0$, and propose $X_j = X^0$, agent i's best choice is $B_i^0 = \omega_i - y_i^0$ and $X_i = X^0$; otherwise he prevents agreement and receives payoff $V^i(\omega_i, 0) < V^i(y_i^0, X^0)$.

That there are numerous Nash equilibria that do not satisfy (4) and (6) is seen by considering any $(y_1^*, ..., y_I^*, X^*)$ such that $V^i(y_i^*, X^*) > V^i(\omega_i, 0) \; \forall i$ and $\sum_{\forall i} \omega_i = \sum_{\forall i} y_i^* + qX^*$. Then if $\forall j \neq i$ $B_j = \omega_j - y_j^*$, $X_j = X^*$, agent i's best choice is to agree to the arrangement by setting $B_i = \omega_i - y_i^* = -\sum_{j \neq i} \omega_j + \sum_{i \neq j} y_j^* + qX^*$, and $X_i = X^*$.

All the experiments to be reported below used the PLATO computer system with visual display consoles to program subjects through an iterative decision process. Such a system is particularly effective in standardizing procedures, eliminating possible discretionary experimenter effects, recording subject choices, performing routine calculations, and displaying the appropriate private or public information to the subjects. The appendix records a summary of the instructions for the Auction Mechanism as they were presented to each subject by PLATO.

In the Auction Mechanism process each trial begins with each subject entering the choice (B_i, X_i) into his or her terminal. PLATO then computes $(\sum_{\forall i} B_i, \bar{X})$, and transmits this message to each subject. If $\sum_{\forall i} B_i < q\bar{X}$ PLATO computes each individual's share of cost $(q - B_i/\bar{X}_i)\bar{X}$ which is received as a private message by each i, and then PLATO proceeds to the next trial. If $\sum_{\forall i} B_i = q\bar{X}$, each agent's share of cost is set equal to his bid $q\bar{X} - \sum_{j \neq i} B_j = B_i$, this fact is reported to each i, and PLATO goes into a voting mode in which each agent is asked to type "yes" or "no" indicating whether he wishes to accept or not accept as final the arrangement resulting from that trial. If $\sum_{\forall i} B_i > q\bar{X}$, before the voting mode is entered, PLATO modifies the collective decision $(\sum_{\forall i} B_i, \bar{X})$ so that the "center" retains none of the bid surplus. This is achieved by giving each individual a "rebate" as follows: The outcome $(\sum_{\forall i} B_i, \bar{X})$ is adjusted to give $(\sum_{\forall i} B_i', \bar{X}')$ where the vector from $(\sum_{\forall i} (\omega_i - B_i), \bar{X})$

to $\sum_{\forall i} (\omega_i - B_i')$, $\bar{X}'$) is orthogonal to the production possibility frontier and the point $(\sum_{\forall i} (\omega_i - B_i')$, $\bar{X}'$) lies on the frontier. Consequently, the adjusted quantity of the public good, and the adjusted bid of i are

$$\bar{X}' = \frac{\bar{X} + q \sum_{\forall k} B_k}{1 + q^2},$$

$$B_i' = \frac{B_i q \bar{X}'}{\sum_{\forall k} B_k}.$$

(7)

The process stops on trial $t^* \leqslant T$ if the arrangement resulting from trial t^* is brought to a vote, and all i vote "yes". Otherwise the process stops on trial T. In the unanimity case subject i receives $V^i[\omega_i - B_i'(t^*)$, $\bar{X}']$ dollars in cash. Otherwise he receives $V^i[\omega_i, 0]$.

The above description of the Auction Mechanism has two conditions that will be varied in the alternative experimental "control" mechanisms to be discussed below:

(1) Each i chooses on each trial a desired or proposed quantity of the public good, and the collective's proposal is defined as the mean of these individual proposals.

(2) After each trial for which the aggregate of the bids are insufficient to cover the cost of the mean proposal, each individual receives an imputation or share of the cost $(q - \hat{B}_i/\bar{X}_i)\bar{X}$ where the "price" $(q - \hat{B}_i/\bar{X}_i)$ to each i depends only on the choices of all $j \neq i$. It is hypothesized that this imputation gives each i an incentive to "meet the market" by adjusting his responses as if in an ordinary private goods market in which each agent faces a competitive price determined by the actions of other agents; see Smith (1979a).

A Free-Rider Mechanism, described in the next section eliminates both of these conditions, while a Quasi Free-Rider Mechanism, described in Section IV, retains condition (1) but alters (2).

III. A Free-Rider Mechanism

In the Free-Rider Mechanism each i chooses a bid only, $B_i = \omega_i - y_i$. The collective's proposed quantity of the public good is $X' = \sum_{\forall k} B_k/q$, and the payoff to i is simply

$$V_i = V^i[\omega_i - B_i, (B_i + \hat{B}_i)/q].$$

(8)

If each i chooses B_i to maximize v_i, this results in the free-rider equilibrium $(y_1', y_2', ..., y_I'; X')$ defined by the conditions

$$\frac{V_2^i}{V_1^i} \leqslant \frac{\sum_{\forall i} (\omega_i - y_i')}{X'} = q,$$

(9)

where $y_i' = \omega_i$ if $<$ holds for any i. Conditions (9) allow for boundary solutions $y_i' = \omega_i$ since they occur in the experimental design reported in Section V.

In the PLATO experimental process using the Free-Rider Mechanism, on each trial each i chooses B_i. PLATO then computes the group's proposal $X = \sum_{\forall k} B_k/q$, reports the result to each subject, and proceeds directly into the voting mode described in the previous section. If the arrangement is unanimous "yes", the process stops and each i is paid $V^i(\omega_i - B_i, \sum_{\forall k} B_k/q)$ dollars in cash. Otherwise, the process proceeds to another trial, with a maximum of T trials. If by trial T no group proposal has received unanimous approval, the process stops and each i receives $V^i(\omega_i, 0)$.

IV. A Quasi Free-Rider Mechanism

This mechanism retains condition (1) in Section II, requiring each i to state a desired quantity of the public good, but alters the cost imputation procedure in condition (2). In the Quasi Free-Rider Mechanism each i chooses a 2-tuple (B_i, X_i) on each trial. If $\sum_{\forall i} B_i \geqslant q\bar{X}$ each member votes on whether to accept the allocation as final after receiving a rebate of any overbid of cost.[1] If $\sum_{\forall i} B_i < q\bar{X}$ PLATO computes each individual's share of cost as simply $q\bar{X} = \hat{B}_i = q\bar{X} - \sum_{\forall j \neq i} B_j$.

Hence, the payoff to i is

$$v_i = \begin{cases} V^i[\omega_i - (q\bar{X} - \hat{B}_i), \bar{X}], & \text{if } B_i = q\bar{X} - \hat{B}_i, \ \bar{X}_i = \bar{X}, \ \forall_i. \\ V^i[\omega_i, 0], & \text{if } B_i \neq q\bar{X} - \hat{B} \quad \text{or } X_i \neq \bar{X}, \quad \text{for any } i. \end{cases} \tag{10}$$

If v_i is at a maximum with respect to (B_i, X_i) then we must have $B_i = q\hat{B} - \hat{B}_i$, $X_i = \bar{X}$ and $-q(1/I)_1^{y^i} + (1/I)_2^{y^i} \leqslant 0$, and therefore the free-rider condition (9) above must be satisfied.

V. Experimental Design and Results

The instructions for the Free-Rider and Quasi Free-Rider PLATO experiments are the same as those reported in the appendix for the Auction Mechanism with appropriate changes to allow for the different cost imputation and rebate rules in the Quasi Free-Rider experiments and for the fact that each i chooses only a bid on each trial in a Free-Rider experiment.

If the cost imputation information and procedure in the Auction Mechanism is effective in reducing Free-Rider behavior, then experimental outcomes with

---

[1] In this rebate procedure PLATO first rounds $\bar{X}$ to the nearest integer, then determines if the overbid is sufficient to allow an integer increase in the size of the public good, i.e. the largest $n = 0, 1, 2, \ldots$ such that $\sum_{\forall i} B_i \geqslant q(\bar{X} + n)$ was computed. Any remaining bid surplus is then rebated to each i in proportion to i's bid. Hence, if agent i's bid was B_i the adjusted bid becomes $B_i' = B_i q(\bar{X} + n)/\sum_{\forall k} B_k$ where $\bar{X} + n$ is the adjusted proposed size (an integer) of the public good. Results reported in Smith (1979b) find no significant difference between this rebate procedure and that described in Section II.

Table 1. *Experimental design*

$I = 6, q = 2, X^0 = 9, X' = 3.33$

Parameter	Parameter class		
	I	II	III
α_i	0.24	0.96	0.8
β_i	0.96	0.24	0.8
a_i	1.5	1.5	1.5
ω_i	5	10	6
y_i^0, LE			
Private quantity	1	8	3
y_i', Free-Rider			
Private quantity	1.67	10	6

this mechanism should provide larger quantities of the public good than the Free-Rider Mechanism. The Quasi Free-Rider Mechanism retains the Auction Mechanism condition (1) but alters the cost imputation condition (2) so as to encourage Free-Rider behavior. If condition (1) is an important feature tending to discourage free-riding even though the cost imputation rule does not, then the Quasi Free-Rider Mechanism should yield public good quantities somewhere between those yielded by the other two mechanisms. If condition (1) is not an important feature inhibiting free-riding then public good quantities provided by the Free-Rider and Quasi Free-Rider Mechanisms should not be distinguishable from each other, but should be significantly less than public good quantities provided by the Auction Mechanism. All three mechanisms use the exclusionary unanimity stopping rule. If this Wicksellian unanimity condition is of importance in inhibiting free-rider behavior, then all three mechanisms should yield public good quantities that are greater than the free-rider quantity.

These hypotheses will be tested using data from three series of PLATO experiments, each series corresponding to one of the three mechanisms described above. Prior to the commencement of each PLATO experiment it is initialized by specifying numerical values for $(I, T, q, \omega_i, a_i, \alpha_i, \beta_i)$ where I is the number of subjects in an experimental collective, T is the maximum number of trials, q is the unit cost of the public good, ω_i is the endowment of subject i, and the payoff function in dollars for i is $V^i \equiv a_i y_i^{\alpha_i} X^{\beta_i}$. For all the experiments reported here, $q = 2$ and $I = 6$, with two subjects in each of three payoff-endowment parameter classes. Table 1 lists the payoff and endowment parameters, the Lindahl equilibrium private quantities, y_i^0, and the free-rider private quantities, y_i', corresponding to each of the three parameter classes used in the experiments. With these parameters the Lindahl equilibrium quantity of the public good from (4) and (6) is $X^0 = 9$; the free-rider equilibrium quantity from (9) is $X' = 3.33$. In order that the effect of endowment not be

Table 2. *Bid-quantity outcomes, PLATO. Auction Mechanism experiments*

$I = 6$, $q = 2$, $X^0 = 9$, $X' = 3.33$, $T = 10$. Figures within parentheses denote final trial choices in experiments failing to reach agreement

Subject ...	1	2	3	4	5	6		
Parameter class ...	I $\omega_1 = 5$	II $\omega_2 = 10$	III $\omega_3 = 6$	I $\omega_1 = 5$	II $\omega_2 = 10$	III $\omega_3 = 6$	X^*, Final quantity	t^*, Final trial
Lindahl Equilibrium bids, $\omega_i - y_i'$ ...	4	2	3	4	2	3		
Final bids, B_i^*								
A1	3	3	3	2	1	3	7.5	9
A1'	2.98	4.96	2.98	2.98	0.99	0.99	7.93	10
A2	(1.5)	(4)	(4)	(0)	(6)	(1)	(8.83)	(10)
A3	3.92	3.92	2.94	3.92	2.94	0.98	9.3	7
A3'	1.97	1.97	1.97	1.97	4.93	1.97	7.4	9
A4	3.61	4.51	3.61	0.90	4.51	4.51	10.83	1
A4'	3.81	4.76	4.76	1.90	0	4.76	10	8
A5	(0.99)	(9.88)	(3.95)	(3.95)	(1.98)	(1.98)	(11.37)	(10)
A5'	3	1	1	4	10	3	11	10
A6	3.73	7.47	0.93	2.8	0	2	8.87	9

confounded with preference for the public good, the parameters in Table 1 were chosen so that the low endowment condition ($\omega_1 = 5$) is associated with a relatively large Lindahl equilibrium bid ($\omega_1 - y_1^0 = 4$), while the high endowment condition ($\omega_2 = 10$) is associated with a relatively small Lindahl equilibrium bid ($\omega_2 - y_2^0 = 2$). That is "rich" subjects have a weak preference, while "poor" subjects have a strong preference for the public good relative to the private good.

A total of 102 subjects, enrolled in undergraduate and graduate courses in economics or business, participated in 27 experiments (10 Auction, 8 Free-Rider and 9 Quasi Free-Rider Mechanism experiments). The subjects were invited to participate in a decision making experiment, for which they would receive $2 when they arrived and would be paid whatever they earned in the experiment when they finished. The total amount earned under these conditions was approximately $2 400. Whenever there was sufficient time a 6-member experimental group participated in a series of two sequential experiments in which the second was considered an "experience" session. At the beginning of each experiment the subjects were randomly assigned to each parameter-endowment class, and to each computer terminal.

Tables 2, 3 and 4 list the final-trial bids for each subject (B_i^*), the final-trial quantity of the public good (X^*), and the number of the final trial (t^*) for each of the 27 experiments. Each experiment is identified by a letter indicating the institutional treatment and a number indicating the sequential order in which an experimental session in the series occurred. A prime by the number indicates

Table 3. *Bid-quantity outcomes PLATO. "Free-Rider" Mechanism experiments*

$I = 6$, $q = 2$, $X^0 = 9$, $X' = 3.33$, $T = 10$

Subject ... Parameter class ... Free-Rider bids, $\omega_i - y_i'$ ...	1 I $\omega_1 = 5$ 3.33	2 II $\omega_2 = 10$ 0	3 III $\omega_3 = 6$ 0	4 I $\omega_4 = 5$ 3.33	5 II $\omega_5 = 10$ 0	6 III $\omega_6 = 6$ 0	X^*, Final quantity	t^*, Final trial
Final bids, B_i^*								
F1	2	1	1	2	0	1	3.5	8
F2	3	3	2	3	5	2	9	1
F3	3	7	1	3	1	2	8.5	8
F3'	1	7	1	2	7	1	9.5	1
F4	4	2	1	2	4	1	7	10
F5	3	7	1	1	3	2	8.5	1
F5'	3	7	3	3	0	0	8	7
F6'	0	4	0	2	0	3	4.5	10

an experiment with experienced subjects, i.e. the second experiment in a session with the same subjects. Thus A4 is the first experiment in the fourth Auction Mechanism session; F5' is the second experiment in the fifth Free-Rider Mechanism session. The only exception to this pattern is F6' which followed A6 using the same 6 subjects.

Two of the Auction Mechanism experiments, A2 and A5, failed to reach agreement. Based on the results of thirty-eight Auction Mechanism experiments reported in Smith (1979*b*), it appears that approximately 10 per cent

Table 4. *Bid-quantity outcomes. Quasi Free-Rider Mechanism experiments*

$I = 6$, $q = 2$, $X^0 = 9$, $X' = 3.33$, $T = 15$

Subject ... Parameter class ... Free-Rider bids, $\omega_i - y_i'$ ...	1 I $\omega_1 = 5$ 3.33	2 II $\omega_2 = 10$ 0	3 III $\omega_3 = 6$ 0	4 I $\omega_4 = 5$ 3.33	5 II $\omega_5 = 10$ 0	6 III $\omega_6 = 6$ 0	X^*, Final quantity	t^*, Final trial
Final bids, B_i								
Q1	1	3	3	1	4	2	7	1
Q1'	2.8	5.6	1.867	1.867	0.933	0.933	7	2
Q2	1.882	1.882	1.882	0.941	6.588	2.824	8	11
Q3	3	2	2	2	1	2	6	15
Q3'	1	4	3	3	1	4	8	2
Q4	1	6	3	5	0	4	9	9
Q4'	3.76	2.82	2.82	2.82	0	3.76	8	3
Q5	4	0	2	3	1	2	6	15
Q5'	0.93	6.53	0	0	0.93	5.6	7	12

Table 5. *Mean provision of the public good*

Mechanism	Inexperienced subjects	Experienced subjects	Pooled
Free-Rider	7.3	7.3	7.3
Quasi Free-Rider	7.2	7.5	7.3
Auction	9.12	9.08	9.10[a]

[a] This mean is 7.9 if the two disagreement experiments are counted at the free-rider quantity (3.33).

fail to reach agreement under this institution. None of the experiments using the alternative mechanisms failed to reach agreement.

The mean quantity of the public good provided by each of the three institutions in inexperienced and experienced collectives is shown in Table 5. Experience is clearly not an effective treatment variable for any of the institutions. This result is also reported in Smith (1979b) for the Auction Mechanism using different payoff-endowment parameters, and collectives of size 3, 6 and 9. The pooled (across experience) means in Table 5 show that the Auction Mechanism provides larger quantities of the public good in those experiments reaching agreement than is provided by the alternative institutions.

Table 6 records the α (Type I error) and $1-\beta$ (power) probabilities, where the null hypothesis, H_0, is that the sample means for each mechanism came from a population with mean equal to the theoretical free-rider quantity (3.33), and the alternative hypothesis, H_1, is that the sample means came from a population with mean equal to the Lindahl equilibrium quantity (9). The first row of selected α probabilities is used to calculate the critical values, X_c (for each mechanism), above which we reject H_0 (accept H_1) if the sample mean exceeds X_c. The calculations are based on the t-distribution with sample sizes shown in Table 6 and sample variances computed from the X^* observations in Tables 2, 3 and 4. These critical values are then used to compute the $1-\beta$

Table 6. *Error and power probabilities for Free-Rider (H_0) and Lindahl Equilibrium (H_1) hypotheses*

Institution	Free-Rider mechanism $N_f = 8$	Quasi Free-Rider mechanism $N_q = 9$	Auction mechanism $N_a = 8$
α = probability of rejecting H_0 (accepting H_1) when H_0 is true	0.001	0.001	0.001
$1-\beta$ = probability of accepting H_1 (rejecting H_0) when H_1 is true	0.93	0.91	0.93
Critical value, X_c	6.8	4.8	5.6

Table 7. *Mean bids by parameter class and mechanism*

Mechanism	Parameter class		
	I $\omega_1 = 5$	II $\omega_2 = 10$	III $\omega_3 = 6$
Free-Rider	2.31	3.62	1.38
Quasi Free-Rider	2.17	2.63	2.59
Auction	2.91	3.50	2.65
Lindahl equilibrium bids	4	2	3

probabilities or the so-called "power" of the test. For example, for the free-rider mechanism (Column 2, Table 6), $X_c = 3.33 + t_\alpha \sqrt{V_f/N_f} = -1.69$ corresponding to a Type II error $\beta < 0.07$, and hence $1 - \beta > 0.93$. For each mechanism the sample mean (Column 4, Table 5) exceeds the critical value shown in Table 6 and we reject H_0 in favor of H_1. However, the outcomes in the Auction Mechanism provide significantly stronger support for H_1 then either of the other mechanisms. This is indicated by a t-test comparison of the Auction Mechanism mean with the pooled mean of the other two mechanisms, giving a t-value of 2.14 with $\alpha < 0.05$, i.e., we reject the hypothesis of no difference between the Auction and the alternative mechanisms. However, the "better" results in the Auction Mechanism seem to be achieved at the cost of a somewhat higher failure to reach unanimity than in the alternative institutions.

Table 7 shows the mean bids of subjects in each parameter class for each institution. These results are generally consistent with those reported in Smith (1979b) for the Auction Mechanism. In all three institutions the mean bids differ from the corresponding Lindahl equilibrium bids. Consequently, although the Auction Mechanism provides public good quantities that approximate the Lindahl equilibrium quantity the private good allocations do not approximate the Lindahl equilibrium quantities. As is seen in Table 7 this is because subjects with low endowment (5 or 6) tend to contribute less, while subjects with high endowment (10) contribute more, than is required for a Lindahl allocation.[1]

VI. Summary

The Auction Mechanism is compared with two mechanisms in which conventional analysis implies that free-riding will occur in the provision of a pure public good. However, all three mechanisms employ a unanimity stopping rule so that the condition of group excludability is present in each institution. The principal conclusions are:

---

[1] See Smith (1979b) for a regression model test of the hypothesis that these deviations from the Lindahl allocation are within the Pareto optimal set for collectives of size 3.

1. The Auction Mechanism yields public good quantities that are significantly greater than the theoretical free-rider quantity, but that are not significantly different from the theoretical Lindahl equilibrium quantity of the public good.

2. In the Auction Mechanism there appears to be a somewhat greater tendency of groups to fail to reach unanimity on a final allocation. If these "no agreement" sessions are included in the calculations the Auction Mechanism does not produce significantly larger quantities of a public good than the alternative mechanisms.

3. Both of the free-rider mechanisms yield public good quantities significantly larger than the theoretical free-rider quantity. Hence, under unanimity, it appears that empirical support for the free-rider hypothesis is very weak. This result is consistent with that reported by Bohm (1972) Sweeny (1973) and Marwell–Ames (1977) using quite diverse experimental paradigms.

4. The bidding pattern in all three institutions reveals a central tendency of subjects with small endowments to contribute less, and subjects with large endowments to contribute more, to the provision of a public good, than is predicted by the theoretical Lindahl equilibrium allocation.

An unresolved question is whether the absence of strong free-rider behavior in all three mechanisms is due to the exclusionary unanimity stopping rule employed. It is proposed that an aswer to this question be attempted by replication of the Free-Rider experiments without the voting mode, i.e., the group decision is defined as whatever outcome prevails on trial T following $T-1$ practice trials.

References

Bohm, P.: Estimating demand for public goods: An experiment. *European Economic Review 3*, 111–130, 1972.

Clarke, E.: Multipart pricing of public goods. *Public Choice 2*, 17–33, Fall 1971.

Ferejohn, J., Forsythe, R. & Noll, R.: An experimental analysis of decision making procedures for discrete public goods: A case study of a problem in institutional design. In *Research in experimental Economics* (ed. V. Smith). JAI Press, Greenwich, 1979, in press.

Groves, T.: Incentives and teams. *Econometrica 41*, 617–33, July 1973.

Groves, T. & Ledyard, J.: Optimal allocation of public goods: A solution to the free-rider problem. *Econometrica 45*, 783–809, May 1977.

Marwell, G. & Ames, R.: Experiments on the provision of public goods. I. Resources, interest, group size, and the free-

rider problem. Social Behavior Research Center, Working Paper 77-1, 1977.

Smith, V.: Incentive compatible experimental processes for the provision of public goods. In *Research in experimental economics* (ed. V. Smith). JAI Press, Greenwich, 1979 *a*, in press.

Smith, V.: Experiments with a decentralized mechanism for public good decision. Forthcoming in *American Economic Review*, 1979 *b*.

Sweeny, J.: An experimental investigation of the free-rider problem. *Social Science Research 2*, 277–292, 1973.

Wicksell, K.: Ein neues Prinzip der gerechten Besteuerung. In *Finanztheoretische Untersuchungen*, Jena 1896. Translated by J. M. Buchanan, "A new principle of just taxation", in *Classics in the theory of public finance*, 72. Musgrave and Peacock Rd., 1958.

Appendix

INSTRUCTIONS

This is an experiment in the economics of group decision
making.   The instructions are simple, and if you follow
them carefully and make good decisions you may earn a
CONSIDERABLE AMOUNT OF MONEY which will be paid to you in
cash at the end of the experiment.   Various research
foundations have provided funds for this research.

You are a member of a group that must decide upon, and
bear the cost of, a jointly shared facility (like, for
example, a neighborhood swimming pool.) The group must
decide on the size, X, of the commonly shared facility.
Each member has a specified number of work days available
to divide between private use and a contribution to
building the joint facility.   The value to you if the
group decides on a facility of size X, and if you use "y"
days for your own use is given in your personal pay- off
table.

Each unit of the joint facility requires 2 mandays of
work.   Hence the total workdays required is 2X if the
group agrees on a facility of size X. Your share of total
facility work requirements is determined from a series of
trial bids.

The following will be an example based on your personal
payoff table. However, your available workdays MAY NOT
apply to you in the experiment. Take as much time with
the instructions as you feel you need.
                    PRESS NEXT TO CONTINUE

Number of days available=9   EXAMPLE!

X \ Y	1	2	3	4	5	6	7	8	⑨	10	11	12
1	1.00	3.38	4.93	6.11	7.08	7.90	8.61	9.25	9.83	10.36	10.85	11.30
2	3.38	6.11	7.90	9.25	10.36	11.30	12.12	12.86	13.52	14.13	14.69	15.21
3	4.93	7.90	9.83	11.30	12.50	13.52	14.41	15.21	15.93	16.59	17.20	17.76
4	6.11	9.25	11.30	12.86	14.13	15.21	16.16	17.00	17.76	18.46	19.10	19.70
5	7.08	10.36	12.50	14.13	15.46	16.59	17.58	18.46	19.26	19.99	20.66	21.29
6	7.90	11.30	13.52	15.21	16.59	17.76	18.79	19.70	20.53	21.29	21.99	22.63
7	8.61	12.12	14.41	16.16	17.58	18.79	19.85	20.79	21.64	22.42	23.14	23.81
8	9.25	12.86	15.21	17.00	18.46	19.70	20.79	21.76	22.63	23.44	24.18	24.86
9	9.83	13.52	15.93	17.76	19.26	20.53	21.64	22.63	23.53	24.35	25.11	25.81
10	10.36	14.13	16.59	18.46	19.99	21.29	22.42	23.44	24.35	25.19	25.96	26.68
11	10.85	14.69	17.20	19.10	20.66	21.99	23.14	24.18	25.11	25.96	26.75	27.48
12	11.30	15.21	17.76	19.70	21.29	22.63	23.81	24.86	25.81	26.68	27.48	28.23

At the beginning of each trial you independently select a
bid representing your contribution of work days for the
joint facility, and a proposed facility size x. (The facility
size YOU propose will be referred to with a small-case x.
The average proposal size of the group will be referred to
with a capital X. Your number of workdays available is the
circled number on the y-column of your chart. Your bid is
a deduction from your workdays available; this determines
your desired workdays for your own use (y).) Your bid and
facility size choices are to be typed in after the arrow
when requested. If you make a mistake or change your mind,
press the ERASE key to erase one digit at a time. When you
are finished typing your decision in a trial, press the NEXT
key.   PRESS NEXT TO CONTINUE

Now let's see how the process works. Suppose you are
member number 1. Further suppose you choose to bid 3
days of work and propose a facility size of 5. PLATO
will record the bids and proposals of all members.
PLATO will then compute the sum of all work bids, your
share of the facility cost, and the average proposal
size. Press NEXT to see the mechanics of this process
or BACK to review what you have covered.

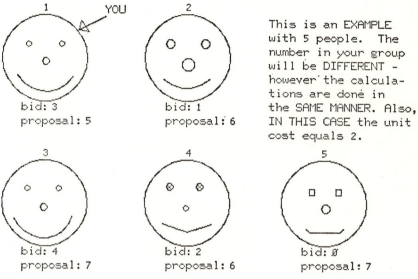

This is an EXAMPLE
with 5 people. The
number in your group
will be DIFFERENT -
however the calcula-
tions are done in
the SAME MANNER. Also,
IN THIS CASE the unit
cost equals 2.

1 YOU	2
bid: 3	bid: 1
proposal: 5	proposal: 6
3	4	5
bid: 4	bid: 2	bid: Ø
proposal: 7	proposal: 6	proposal: 7

These are the five members. Remember in this example
you are number 1. Press NEXT to enter their bids and
proposals.

The sum of the bids is 1Ø. The average proposed size is 6.2.

The sum of the bids of all other members is 7. (1Ø-3)

Your share of facility cost is: (unit cost - sum of bids of
     all others/average proposal of others) × (the average
     group proposal). In this case,
     (2 - 7/6.5) × 6.2 = 5.72

The value to you of the trial decision is obtained from your personal payoff table by finding the row for X (average proposal size) and the column for y (the number of workdays left for your own use). The resulting dollar value can be found at their intersection. Press NEXT to see how this would look in the example.

EXAMPLE!

y X	1	2	3	4	5	6	7	8	(9)	1Ø	11	12
1	1.ØØ	3.38	4.93	6.11	7.Ø8	7.9Ø	8.61	9.25	9.83	1Ø.36	1Ø.85	11.3Ø
2	3.38	6.11	7.9Ø	9.25	1Ø.36	11.3Ø	12.12	12.86	13.52	14.13	14.69	15.21
3	4.93	7.9Ø	9.83	11.3Ø	12.5Ø	13.52	14.41	15.21	15.93	16.59	17.2Ø	17.76
4	6.11	9.25	11.3Ø	12.86	14.13	15.21	16.16	17.ØØ	17.76	18.46	19.1Ø	19.7Ø
5	7.Ø8	1Ø.36	12.5Ø	14.13	15.46	16.59	17.58	18.46	19.26	19.99	2Ø.66	21.29
6	7.9Ø	11.3Ø	13.52	15.21	16.59	17.76	18.79	19.7Ø	2Ø.53	21.29	21.99	22.63
7	8.61	12.12	14.41	16.16	17.58	18.79	19.85	2Ø.79	21.64	22.42	23.14	23.81
8	9.25	12.86	15.21	17.ØØ	18.46	19.7Ø	2Ø.79	21.76	22.63	23.44	24.18	24.86
9	9.83	13.52	15.93	17.76	19.26	2Ø.53	21.64	22.63	23.53	24.35	25.11	25.81
1Ø	1Ø.36	14.13	16.59	18.46	19.99	21.29	22.42	23.44	24.35	25.19	25.96	26.68
11	1Ø.85	14.69	17.2Ø	19.1Ø	2Ø.66	21.99	23.14	24.18	25.11	25.96	26.75	27.48
12	11.3Ø	15.21	17.76	19.7Ø	21.29	22.63	23.81	24.86	25.81	26.68	27.48	28.23

Your bid = 3   Your share of cost = 5.72

Your proposal = 5   Average proposal size = 6.2

                               Work days for
                               personal use = 3.28

NOTICE: PLATO will adjust
for fractional values!!

                               Value of decision
                               to you = $14.23

                               Total bid = 1Ø

This process will be repeated for at most 10 trials.
In order that the process stop, TWO events must occur.

1. On any single trial each member's bid must be equal
   to his share of cost. If the sum of all bids exceed
   the cost of the average facility size, all members
   get a rebate such that the bid of each is equal to
   his share of cost. Note in the previous example
   that the total bid (10) was less than the cost of
   the average facility size (2×6.2 = 12.4).

2. Each member must vote to accept his share of cost
   and accept the group's average proposal. Hence,
   the vote must be unanimous for the decision to be
   finalized. If not, the group will go to the next
   trial and will have to meet condition (1) over again.

   You will be given additional instructions about the
   voting procedure on any trial that satisfies (1).

       PRESS -NEXT- TO CONTINUE OR -BACK- TO REVIEW

If the process stops by these rules, then you will
receive a cash payment equal to the value of your
final decision. Otherwise you will receive nothing

The personal payoff table and number of days available
are NOT the same for all members. It is your own
private information. Do not speak to any other parti-
cipant. Feel free to earn as much cash as you can.
Press NEXT to begin the experiment or BACK to review
the stopping rules.

P.S.
If you forget some portion of the instructions,
HELP will be available during the experiment..

INSTRUCTIONS PROVIDED WHEN THERE IS AN

OVERBID OF TOTAL COST:

The group has overbid the total cost by the amount - - .
This amount is divided between an increase in the facility
size and a total rebate of work time in the ratio of _ to _.
Each member's share of this rebate is proportional to that
member's bid.

You have 1 trial left.

The group has reached a tentative joint decision. It is
now the group's job to decide whether or not to finalize
it.   You will vote "yes" if you want to accept your
current bid and the group's average proposal size, or
"no" to veto the decision.   The decision vote must be
unanimous to be valid. If it is unanimous, you will be
done and the current value of the group decision paid to
you in cash. You have the option to veto the joint solution and go for additional trials if you think you can
improve your position.

EXAMPLE:

Your current bid = 2.5   Your share of cost = 2.5

Your current proposal = 2   Average proposal size = 2.5

The current value to you of this decision = $ 4.50

Enter your vote on whether or not to accept the
current group decision and press NEXT.

≫

WHEN DOES MAJORITY RULE SUPPLY PUBLIC GOODS EFFICIENTLY?*

Ted C. Bergstrom

University of Michigan, Ann Arbor, Michigan, USA

Abstract

H. R. Bowen showed that majority voting leads to a Pareto efficient supply of a single public good if all voters have equal tax shares and if marginal rates of substitution for the public good are symmetrically distributed in the voting population. In general however, even if preferences are identical and tax shares equal, majority voting is not Pareto efficient if income is asymmetrically distributed. Here we formalize and generalize Bowen's theorem. In the process we propose a new idea of a public goods allocation system, a "pseudo-Lindahl equilibrium". Though it is Pareto efficient for an interesting class of societies, the informational requirements for implementing pseudo-Lindahl equilibrium are considerably less stringent than those for a true Lindahl equilibrium.

I. Introduction

From Wicksell (1896), who argued for approximate unanimity, to Arrow (1951) who showed the impossibility of a thoroughly satisfactory democratic decision mechanism, one finds little support in the literature of public finance for majority rule as an efficient means of determining supplies of public goods. A notable exception is Howard R. Bowen's *The Interpretation of Voting in the Allocation of Resources* (1943). Bowen shows that if there is a single public good, if the marginal rates of substitution for that public good are symmetrically distributed in an appropriate way and if taxes are divided equally among the population then majority rule leads to an efficient output of public goods. Although this is, as far as I know, the only theorem in the economic literature which specifies conditions under which majority rule is efficient, it has received little attention.[1] The reason for this neglect is probably that the assumptions of the theorem rarely are even approximately met. For example, in most

---

* The idea for this article was conceived while the author was a National Fellow at the Hoover Institution in Stanford, California. Its development was aided by useful conversations with Arthur Denzau of the University of Arizona and Robert Parks of Washington University, St. Louis, M.
[1] An interesting paper which independently pursues a closely related line of thought is Barlow (1970). See also Bergstrom (1973).

political jurisdictions, wealth is not symmetrically distributed and in consequence the symmetry which Bowen's theorem demands is not likely to be realized. Furthermore, most economists would argue that where incomes differ, some sort of income tax is more "equitable" than the "head tax" which is considered in Bowen's theorem. In this paper we show that for an interesting class of economies, Bowen's ideas can be extended to demonstrate that majority voting together with an appropriate tax system leads to Pareto efficient provision of the public good. As we will show, these ideas are closely related to Lindahl's (1919) solution to the public good problem, but suggest a notion of equilibrium that is somewhat closer to being practically implementable than Lindahl equilibrium.

II. Bowen's Model

The model presented here is essentially that of Bowen. We assume that there are n individuals, a single public good, and a single private good. Preferences of each individual i are represented by differentiable strictly quasi-concave utility function $U^i(X_i, Y)$ where X_i is i's consumption of private good and Y is the amount of public good produced. Individual i has an initial wealth of W_i units of private good. Public good can be produced at a constant unit cost of c units of private good. Letting the private good be the numeraire, suppose that individual i is taxed to pay the fraction $t_i \geqslant 0$ of the total cost of the public good. Thus if Y units of public good are produced, he will have the amount $X_i = W_i - ct_i Y$ of wealth left for private consumption. Conditional on this system of taxation, his preferences over amounts of public goods are represented by the induced utility function, $\tilde{U}^i(Y) = U^i(W_i - ct_i Y, Y)$. If U^i is strictly quasi-concave in X_i and Y, then $\tilde{U}^i$ is strictly quasi-concave in Y. A strictly quasi-concave function of a single variable is single-peaked in the sense of Duncan Black (1958). Let Y_i^* be the (unique because of single peakedness) value of Y which maximizes $\tilde{U}^i(Y)$ on the interval $[0, (1/c)\sum_i W_i]$ of feasible outputs of Y. Let $\hat{Y}^*$ be the median of the Y_i^*'s. Then it follows from Black's results on single peaked preferences that $\hat{Y}^*$ is the unique amount of public good supply that is stable under pairwise majority voting. Thus an interesting case can be made for $\hat{Y}^*$ as the natural outcome of many majoritarian public decision processes.

We call the allocation of resources that results from such a process a *Bowen equilibrium*. Thus for the model under consideration, we define a Bowen equilibrium as follows.

Definition

Let $t_i \geqslant 0$ be the tax share and $W_i > 0$ be the wealth of individual i and let $\sum_i t_i = 1$. Let Y_i^* maximize $U_i(W_i - t_i cY, Y)$ and let

$$\hat{Y}^* = \underset{i \in \{1, \dots, n\}}{\text{median}} \hat{Y}_i^*$$

and $X_i^{**} = W_i - t_i c \hat{Y}^*$. Then the allocation $(X_1^{**}, ..., X_n^{**}, \hat{Y}^*)$ is the *Bowen equilibrium* corresponding to the tax share distribution $(t_1, ..., t_n)$.

Bowen was able to assert the following quite remarkable result:

Theorem 1 (Bowen). *In the model described above,*

if median M.R.S.$_i$ $(\hat{Y}^*) = \dfrac{1}{n} \sum_{i=1}^{n}$ M.R.S.$_i$ $(\hat{Y}^*),$
$\scriptstyle i \in \{1, ..., n\}$

then a Bowen equilibrium in which $t_i = 1/n$ for each i is Pareto optimal.

Proof. Strict quasi-concavity of $\tilde{U}^i$ implies that M.R.S.$_i$ (Y) is a monotone decreasing function of Y. Therefore, where $Y_j^* = \hat{Y}^*$ is the median of $Y_1^*, ..., Y_n^*$, it must be that

$$\text{M.R.S.}_j (\hat{Y}^*) = \underset{i \in \{1, ..., n\}}{\text{median M.R.S.}_i} (\hat{Y}^*) = \frac{1}{n} \sum_{i=1}^{n} \text{M.R.S.}_i (\hat{Y}^*).$$

It must also be that

$$\frac{c}{n} = \text{M.R.S.}_j (\hat{Y}^*) = \frac{1}{n} \sum_{i=1}^{n} \text{M.R.S.}_i (\hat{Y}^*).$$

Therefore $c = \sum_{i=1}^{n} \text{M.R.S.}_i (\hat{Y}^*)$. But this is just the "Samuelson necessary condition" (Samuelson, 1954)) for efficient supply of public goods. As we demonstrate in the appendix, when U^i is quasi-concave, the Samuelson conditions are sufficient as well as necessary for Pareto optimality. It follows that the allocation $(X_1^{**}, ..., X_n^{**}, \hat{Y}^*)$ is Pareto optimal where $X_i^{**} = W_i - (c/n) \hat{Y}^*$ for each i.   Q.E.D.

The novel assumption for the Bowen theorem is, of course, the assumption that the mean of the marginal rates of substitution at $\hat{Y}^*$ is equal to the median of these rates. The most natural way of establishing such a condition appears to be to assume that the distribution among individuals of marginal rates of substitution given the amount of public goods and the tax system is symmetric. We illustrate by examples when this is more or less likely to be the case.

Example 1: The "transferable utility" case. For each i let $U_i(X_i, Y) = X_i + a_i f(Y)$ where $f'(Y) > 0$ and $f''(Y) < 0$ for all Y. Then if $t_i = 1/n$ for each i, it must be that $c/n = a_i f'(Y_i^*)$. Therefore $Y_i^* = f'^{-1}(c/na_i)$. Since $f''(Y) < 0$ for all Y, the inverse function, $f'^{-1}(\cdot)$ is monotone decreasing. It follows that Y_i^* is an increasing function of a_i and that $\hat{Y}^* = f'^{-1}(c/n\hat{a})$ where $\hat{a} = \text{median} \{a_1, ..., a_n\}$. Also, for any i, M.R.S.$_i$ $(\hat{Y}^*) = a_i f'(\hat{Y}^*)$. It follows that

median M.R.S.$_i$ $(\hat{Y}^*) = \hat{a} f'(\hat{Y}^*)$
$\scriptstyle i \in \{1, ..., n\}$

and $1/n \sum_i \text{M.R.S.}_i (\hat{Y}^*) = \bar{a} f'(\hat{Y}^*)$ where $\bar{a} = 1/n \sum_{i=1}^n a$. Thus if the a_i's are symmetrically distributed so that $\hat{a} = \bar{a}$, then the condition for the Bowen theorem is satisfied.

Example 2. Log linear utility and identical wealth. The previous example had the peculiar feature that the "income elasticity of demand" for the public good is zero. Thus Y_i^* is independent of W_i. Here we consider an example in which this is not the case. For each i, let $U_i = \ln X_i + a_i \ln Y$. If $t_i = 1/n$ for each i, then a bit of computation shows that $Y_i^* = (a_i/(1+a_i))(c/n) W_i$. If $W_i = \overline{W}$ for all i, then $\hat{Y}^* = \hat{a}/(1+\hat{a})(c/n) \overline{W}$ where

$$\hat{a} = \underset{i \in \{1, ..., n\}}{\text{median }} a_i.$$

Then $\text{M.R.S.}_i (\hat{Y}^*) = a_i (X_i^*/\hat{Y}^*) = a_i (\overline{W} - n\hat{Y}^*/\hat{Y}^*) = (a_i/\hat{a}) c/n$. Thus

$$\underset{i \in \{1, ..., n\}}{\text{median M.R.S.}_i (\hat{Y}^*)} = \frac{c}{n}$$

and

$$\frac{1}{n} \sum_{i=1}^n \text{M.R.S.} (\hat{Y}^*) = \frac{\bar{a}}{\hat{a}} \left(\frac{c}{n}\right)$$

where

$$\bar{a} = \frac{1}{n} \sum_{i=1}^n a_i.$$

Therefore if all individuals have the same wealth, and if the parameters a are symmetrically distributed, Bowen's theorem again applies.

Example 3. Identical log linear utility functions and different wealths. Now let us consider the case where preferences are as in example 2 but the a_i's are all the same, $a_i = \bar{a}$ for all i, and the W_i's differ. Then

$$\hat{Y}_i^* = \frac{1+\bar{a}}{\bar{a}} \left(\frac{n}{c}\right) W_i$$

and

$$\hat{Y}^* = \frac{\bar{a}}{1+\bar{a}} \left(\frac{n}{c}\right) \hat{W}$$

where

$$\hat{W} = \underset{i \in \{1, ..., n\}}{\text{median }} W_i.$$

Then

$$\text{M.R.S.}_i (\hat{Y}^*) = \bar{a} \frac{X_i^{**}}{\hat{Y}^*} = \bar{a} \left(\frac{W_i - (c/n) \hat{Y}^*}{\hat{Y}^*}\right).$$

Then computation shows that

$$\underset{i \in \{1, \ldots, n\}}{\text{median}} \text{M.R.S.}_{\cdot i}(\hat{Y}^*) = \frac{c}{n}$$

and

$$\frac{1}{n} \sum_{i=1}^{n} \text{M.R.S.}_{\cdot i}(\hat{Y}^*) = \left[(1 + \bar{a})\frac{\overline{W}}{\hat{W}} - \bar{a}\right]\left(\frac{c}{n}\right).$$

Thus the Bowen condition will be satisfied if and only if $\overline{W} = \hat{W}$, that is, median wealth equals mean wealth. If mean wealth exceeds median wealth, then

$$\frac{1}{n} \sum_{i=1}^{n} \text{M.R.S.}_{\cdot i}(\hat{Y}^*) > \frac{c}{n} \text{ so that } \sum_{i=1}^{n} \text{M.R.S.}_{\cdot i}(\hat{Y}^*) > c$$

It follows from a simple application of the calculus that if this is the case, $\hat{Y}^*$ is "too small" in the sense that it would be possible to collect revenue for an increased amount of public goods in such a way that everyone's utility would be increased.

III. A Median Voter Model with a Proportional Wealth Tax and Log Linear Utilities

Since there is evidence that in most political jurisdictions, mean income exceeds median income,[1] the result of example 3 suggests that if utility is approximately log linear, financing public goods by a "head tax" would result in a Bowen equilibrium with too little public goods. Thus we might consider a Bowen equilibrium where tax shares are positively related to wealth. As it turns out, if the distribution of "tastes" in the economy is appropriately symmetric and uncorrelated with wealth, we can show that a Bowen equilibrium with a proportional wealth tax is Pareto optimal.

Let there be n individuals. Individual i has preferences represented by $U^i(X_i, Y) = \ln X_i + a_i \ln Y$ and his initial wealth is $W_i > 0$. The public good is produced at constant unit cost c. Tax rates are proportional to wealth so that $t_i = W_i / \sum W_j$ is i's tax share. Where $\text{M.R.S.}_i(Y)$ is defined as

$$\frac{U_y(W_i - t_iY, Y)}{U_x(W_i - t_iY, Y)},$$

individual i determines his favorite amount Y_i^* of public good by solving the equation $\text{M.R.S.}_i(Y) = t_ic$. Solving this equation yields

$$Y_i^* = \left(\frac{a_i}{1 + a_i}\right)\frac{\sum_j W_j}{c}.$$

---

[1] See Bergstrom (1973).

Thus differences in Y_i^* between individuals are due only to differences in a_i and not to differences in W_i. Furthermore, the larger is a_i, the larger is Y_i^*. Therefore where $\hat{Y}^*$ is the the median of the Y_i^*'s and $\hat{a}$ is the median of the a_i's,

$$\hat{Y}^* = \frac{\hat{a}}{1+\hat{a}} \frac{\sum_j W_j}{c}.$$

Then

$$\text{M.R.S.}_i(\hat{Y}^*) = a_i \frac{W_i - ct_i\hat{Y}^*}{\hat{Y}^*} = \left(\frac{a_i}{\hat{a}}\right)\left(\frac{cW_i}{\sum_j W_j}\right).$$

Therefore $\sum_i \text{M.R.S.}_i(\hat{Y}^*) = c \sum_i a_i W_i / \hat{a} \sum_i W_i$. If the a_i's are uncorrelated with the W_i's then it must be that $\sum_i a_i W_i = \bar{a} \sum_i W_i$ where $\bar{a}$ is the mean of the a_i's. But then $\sum_i \text{M.R.S.}_i(\hat{Y}^*) = c(\bar{a}/\hat{a})$. Therefore if $\bar{a} = \hat{a}$, it must be that $\sum_i \text{M.R.S.}_i(\hat{Y}^*) = c$. But this is the Samuelson condition for efficiency. Therefore where $X_i^{**} = W_i - t_i c\hat{Y}^* = W_i/(1+\hat{a})$, the Bowen equilibrium allocation $(X_1^{**}, ..., X_n^{**}, \hat{Y}^*)$ is Pareto optimal. The results of this discussion are summarized by Theorem 2.

Theorem 2. *Let there be n individuals where individual i has preferences represented by $U_i = \ln X_i + a_i \ln Y$ and wealth W_i. Assume that the public good Y is produced at constant unit cost c. Let $t_i = W_i/\sum_i W_i$ for each i. If the a_i's are symmetrically distributed and uncorrelated with the W_i's, then the Bowen equilibrium is Pareto optimal.*

IV. Lindahl Equilibrium, Pseudo–Lindahl Equilibrium and Bowen Equilibrium

Here we seek to extend results of the previous section to find an equally satisfactory resolution for a more general class of preferences. In particular, we would like to find a practical way of assigning tax shares so that the corresponding Bowen equilibrium is Pareto efficient. For this purpose it is useful to consider the Lindahl theory of public expenditure determination. For a simple model of the kind discussed above, a Lindahl equilibrium is defined as follows.

Definition. A *Lindahl equilibrium* is a vector of tax shares $(t_1^*, ..., t_n^*) \geq 0$ such that $\sum_i t_i^* = 1$ and an allocation vector $(X_1^*, ..., X_n^*, Y^*)$ such that for each i, (X_i^*, Y^*) maximizes $U^i(X_i, Y)$ subject to $X_i + t_i cY \leq W$. Bergstrom (1973), Foley (1970), and others have shown that Lindahl equilibrium exists and is Pareto optimal for a rich class of models. Lemmas 1 and 2 state these results for the simple model studied here.

Lemma 1. *If utility functions are quasi-concave and continuous, and $W_i > 0$ for each i, then there exists a Lindahl equilibrium.*

Lemma 2. *If preferences are locally non-satiated, a Lindahl equilibrium is Pareto optimal.*

If tax shares are all set at their Lindahl equilibrium levels, then there is unanimous agreement about the appropriate amount of public goods. Therefore the Lindahl equilibrium quantity of public goods is also the Bowen equilibrium corresponding to Lindahl tax shares. If the conditions of Lemmas 1 and 2 are satisfied, then Lindahl equilibrium exists and is Pareto optimal. Therefore when these conditions are satisfied, there exist assignments of tax shares such that the corresponding Bowen equilibrium is Pareto optimal.

As has often been observed in discussions of the "free rider problem", computation of a true Lindahl equilibrium for a community would require a detailed knowledge of individual preferences which not only would swamp the data processing (and equilibrium computing) capabilities of any government, but would also, in general, require the individuals to reveal accurate information about their preferences, even though no mechanism can be devised which would give selfish individuals an incentive to do so; see for example, Gibbard (1973), Groves & Ledyard (1977) and Bergstrom (1976).

Our analysis of the previous section suggests an interesting possibility for resolving this difficulty. There we showed that if preferences are all log linear and appropriately symmetric, then a Bowen equilibrium with proportional wealth taxation is Pareto optimal. It is also true that if all individual preferences were identical and representable by the "average" utility function, $U(X_i, Y) = \ln X_i + \bar{a} \ln Y$, then the Lindahl tax would be a proportional wealth tax and the Lindahl quantity of public goods would be the same as the Bowen quantity $\hat{Y}^*$ found in the previous section. This suggests that more generally we could compute Lindahl equilibrium for a hypothetical community in which preferences are "averaged", ignoring individual eccentricities of tastes that are not easily observable. Under certain circumstances, the Lindahl equilibria so computed are Pareto efficient for the actual community and may also be Bowen equilibria.

Let there be m observable types of individuals. Let n_j be the number of type j individuals. Assume that all individuals of type j have the same wealth, W_j, and that preferences of the ith individual of type j are representable by a utility function $U^i(X_i, Y, a_j^i)$ where a_j^i is a parameter of i's preferences that need not be observable to anyone other than i.

For each j, let $\bar{a}_j = (1/n_j) \sum_i a_j^i$ and consider the hypothetical community in which all type j individuals have the same utility function, $U^j(X_i, Y, \bar{a}_j)$. Then under the assumptions of Lemma 1 there will exist a Lindahl equilibrium for the hypothetical economy and in this equilibrium, tax shares of all individuals of the same type will be the same.

Definition. Let l_j be the common Lindahl share of type j's, and $\bar{Y}$ the Lindahl equilibrium quantity of public goods for the hypothetical community described above. The allocation in which type j's consume $\bar{X}_j = W_j - t_j c \bar{Y}$ of private good and everyone enjoys $\bar{Y}$ of the public good will be called a *pseudo-Lindahl equilibrium* for the actual community.

Theorem 3. *Let variations in preferences within types be such that for each j there exists a function $M^j(X_i, Y)$, for which*

$$\frac{U_y^j(X_i, Y, a_j^i)}{U_x^j(X_i, Y, a_j^i)} = a_j^i M^j(X_i, Y).$$

Then a pseudo-Lindahl equilibrium is Pareto optimal. If, in addition, for each type j,

$$\bar{a}_j = \underset{i \in \{1, \dots, n_j\}}{\text{median}} \ a_j^i \equiv \hat{a}_j,$$

then a pseudo-Lindahl equilibrium is also a Bowen equilibrium.

Proof. Let t_j for $j = 1, \dots, m$ and $\bar{Y}$ be the pseudo-Lindahl equilibrium tax shares and quantity of public goods and let $\bar{X}_j = W_j - t_j c \bar{Y}$. Then $t_j c = \bar{a}_j M_j(\bar{X}_j, \bar{Y})$ for all j. Then

$$c = \sum_{j=1}^m n_j t_j c = \sum_{j=1}^m n_j \bar{a}_j M_j(\bar{X}_j, \bar{Y}) = \sum_{j=1}^m \sum_{i=1}^{n_j} a_j^i M_j(\bar{X}_j, \bar{Y}) = \sum_{j=1}^m \sum_{i=1}^{n_j} \frac{U_y^j(\bar{X}_j, \bar{Y}, a_j^i)}{U_x^j(\bar{X}_j, \bar{Y}, a_j^i)}.$$

Therefore the Samuelson condition is satisfied. It follows that pseudo-equilibrium is Pareto optimal.

If $\bar{a}_j = \hat{a}_j$ then

$$\bar{Y} = \underset{i \in \{1, \dots, n_j\}}{\text{median}} \ Y_{j \bullet}^i$$

where $Y_{j \bullet}^i$ is the quantity of public good that individual i of type j would most prefer given that his tax share is t_j. If $\bar{Y}$ is the median demand for each type, it is also the median over all types. Therefore where tax shares t_j are assigned to each member of j, $\bar{Y} = \hat{Y}^*$ where

$$\hat{Y}^* = \underset{\substack{j \in \{1, \dots, m\} \\ i \in \{1, \dots, n_j\}}}{\text{median}} \ Y_{j \bullet}^i.$$

It follows that $\bar{Y}$ is a Bowen equilibrium quantity.   Q.E.D.

A Lindahl equilibrium, though Pareto efficient, requires unobtainable information to be implemented. A Bowen equilibrium, while practically implementable is, in general, not Pareto efficient. Theorem 3 suggests that in an interesting class of cases, a pseudo-Lindahl equilibrium is Pareto optimal and is a Bowen equilibrium. When the number of individuals of each type is large, the informational requirements for implementing a pseudo-Lindahl equilibrium appear to be considerably less stringent than the requirements for a full Lindahl equilibrium. For example sampling procedures such as those suggested by Bergstrom (1974), Green & Laffont (1977) or Kurz (1974) could be used.

V. Extension to the Case of Many Public Goods

These results can be extended in a straightforward way to the case of several public goods. We can show that if variations in the marginal rates substitution take a multiplicative form as in Theorem 1, the multidimensional pseudo-Lindahl equilibrium is Pareto optimal. If, also, variations in preferences are symmetric, the pseudo-Lindahl equilibrium is an l dimensional Bowen equilibrium. This latter notion corresponds to the idea of a sophisticated voting equilibrium as defined by Kramer (1972).

These results are sketched more formally as follows. Let there be n consumers, one private good and l public goods. Each public good k is produced at constant unit cost c_k. Individual i has an initial endowment W_i of private good and a utility function $U^i(X_i, Y_1, ..., Y_l)$.

A Lindahl equilibrium consists of tax shares, $(T^*_{11}, ..., T^*_{nl})$ where T^*_{ik} is the share of the cost of the kth public good paid for by i, with $\sum_i T^*_{ik} = 1$, and an allocation vector $(X^*_1, ..., X^*_n, Y^*_1, ..., Y^*_l)$ such that for each i, $(X^*_1, Y^*_1, ..., Y^*_l)$ maximizes U^i subject to $X^*_i + \sum_{k=1}^l T^*_{ik} Y^*_k = W_i$.

Let there be m types of consumers and let there be n_j consumers of type j. Let all consumers of the same type have the same wealth. Let the marginal rate of substitution of the ith consumer of type j between public good k and the public good $a^i_{jk} M_{jk}(X_i, Y_1, ..., Y_l)$. Consider the hypothetical community where for all j and k, $a^i_{jk} = \bar{a}_{jk} \equiv (1/n_j) \sum_{i=1}^{n_j} a^i_{jk}$. Solve for a Lindahl equilibrium for this hypothetical economy and call it a pseudo-equilibrium for the actual economy. Using the same kind of argument employed in Theorem 3, it can be shown that pseudo-Lindahl equilibrium is Pareto optimal.

Conditional on a specified assignment of tax shares for each public good and for each individual, tax shares t^i_k define an n dimensional Bowen equilibrium to be an allocation $(X^{**}_1, ..., X^{**}_n, Y^*_1, ..., Y^*_l)$ such that if changes in the amounts of public good are voted on one good at a time, no change will receive majority approval. Equivalently, this allocation is a Bowen equilibrium if and only if conditional on the tax shares and the quantities of the other public goods being fixed, each $\hat{Y}^*_k$ is the median of the most preferred values for Y_k.

If the values a^i_{jk} are symmetrically distributed in each group j then it follows that for each population subgroup, the pseudo-Lindahl equilibrium quantity of each public good is the median of the preferred quantities conditional on the Lindahl tax shares and the amounts of the other public goods. Therefore the pseudo-Lindahl equilibrium is also an l dimensional Bowen equilibrium.

This result is encouraging and somewhat surprising, since as Kramer (1973) has pointed out, if there are two or more public goods, even with quasi-concave preferences there are in general likely to be Condorcet cycles in pairwise voting.

Appendix

Theorem 0 (Samuelson)

Let there be n individuals, one private good and m public goods. Let preferences of individual i be represented by a differentiable function, $U^i(X_i, Y_1, ..., Y_l)$ and let the set of feasible allocations be $(X_1, ..., X_n, Y_1, ..., Y_l) \geqslant 0$ such that $\sum_{i=1}^{n} X_i + \sum_{k=1}^{l} c_k Y_k = W$. Let

$$M_k^i(X_i, Y_1, ..., Y_l) = \frac{\dfrac{\partial U^i(X_i, Y_1, ..., Y_l)}{\partial Y_k}}{\dfrac{\partial U^i(X_i, Y_1, ..., Y_l)}{\partial X_i}}.$$

A necessary condition for the allocation $(\bar{X}_1, ..., \bar{X}_n, \bar{Y}_1, ..., \bar{Y}_l) > 0$ to be Pareto optimal is $\sum_{i=1}^{n} M_k^i(\bar{X}_i, \bar{Y}_1, ..., \bar{Y}_l) = c_k$ for all k. If U^i is quasi-concave for each i, this condition is also sufficient.

The proof of necessity is familiar (see Samuelson, 1954). Though the sufficient condition is widely believed to suffice, I have never seen a proof in print. The proof requires the following Lemma.

Lemma 0

Let $U: R_+^n \to R$ be a quasi-concave and differentiable and $DU(x^*) \neq 0$ where $DU(x^*)$ is the gradient of U at x^*. Then if $U(x) \geqslant U(x^*)$, $(x - x^*)DU(x^*) \geqslant 0$. If $x^* \gg 0$ and $U(x) > U(x^*)$, then $(x - x^*)DU(x^*) > 0$.

Proof of Lemma 0

Let $U(x) > U(x^*)$, $x(t) = tx + (1 - t)x^*$ and $f(t) = U(x(t))$. Quasi-concavity of U implies that f is monotone increasing in t for $0 < t < 1$. It follows from a simple application of calculus that

If $U(x) \geqslant U(x^*)$ then $(x - x^*)DU(x^*) \geqslant 0$. $\qquad\qquad$ (1)

We wish to show that (1) holds with strict inequalities. Suppose that $U(x) > U(x^*)$ and $(x - x^*)DU(x^*) \leqslant 0$. Since $x^* \gg 0$ and $x \geqslant 0$, $x(t) \gg 0$ for $0 < t < 1$. Also $(x(t) - x^*)DU(x^*) \leqslant 0$ and $U(x(t)) > U(x^*)$. Continuity of U ensures that there exists a neighborhood, N, of $x(t)$ such that $U(y) > U(x^*)$ for all $y \in N$. Since $DU(x^*) \neq 0$, y can be chosen so that $(y - x)DU(x^*) < 0$ and $U(y) > U(x^*)$. But this contradicts (1). Lemma 0 therefore must be true. $\qquad$ Q.E.D.

Proof of Sufficiency

Suppose $(\bar{X}_1, ..., \bar{X}_n, \bar{Y}_1, ..., \bar{Y}_l)$ satisfies the marginal conditions of the theorem and the feasibility equation and suppose $(X_1, ..., X_n, Y_1, ..., Y_l)$ is Pareto superior to $(\bar{X}_1, ..., \bar{X}_n, \bar{Y}_1, ..., \bar{Y}_l)$. The according to Lemma 0,

$$\frac{\partial U_i(\bar{X}_i, \bar{Y}_1, ..., \bar{Y}_l)}{\partial X_i}(X_i - \bar{X}_i) + \sum_k \frac{\partial U_i(\bar{X}_i, \bar{Y}_1, ..., \bar{Y}_l)}{\partial Y_k}(Y_k - \bar{Y}_{kj}) \geqslant 0$$

for all i with strict inequality for some i.

Therefore $\sum_i (X_i - \bar{X}_i) + \sum_i \sum_k M_k^i(\bar{X}_i, \bar{Y}_1, ..., \bar{Y}_l)(Y_k - \bar{Y}_k) > 0$. But since $\sum_i M_k^i(\bar{X}_i, \bar{Y}_1, ..., \bar{Y}_l) = c_k$, this implies that $\sum_i (X_i - \bar{X}_i) + \sum_k c_k(Y_k - \bar{Y}_k) > 0$. Since $\sum_i \bar{X}_i + \sum_k c_k \bar{Y}_k = W$, it follows that $\sum_i X_i + \sum_k c_k Y_k > W$. Therefore the Pareto superior allocation $(\bar{X}_1, ..., \bar{X}_n, \bar{Y}_1, ..., \bar{Y}_l)$ is not feasible. It follows that $(\bar{X}_1, ..., \bar{X}_n, \bar{Y}_1, ..., \bar{Y}_l)$ is Pareto optimal. Q.E.D.

References

Arrow, K.: *Social choice and individual values*, Wiley, New York, 1951.

Barlow, R.: Efficiency aspects of local school finance. *J.P.E. 78*, 1028–1040, 1970.

Bergstrom, T.: A note on efficient taxation. *J.P.E. 81*, 1973.

Bergstrom, T.: Collective choice and the Lindahl allocation method. In *Theory and Measurement of Economic Externalities* (ed. S. A. Y. Lin). Academic Press, New York, 1976.

Bergstrom, T.: *On the Free Rider problem.* Mimeo, University of Michigan, Department of Economics.

Bergstrom, T.: Regulation of externalities. *Journal of Public Economics 5*, 131–138, 1976.

Black, D.: *The theory of committees and elections.* Cambridge University Press, Cambridge, 1958.

Bowen, H.: The interpretation of voting in the allocation of economic resources. *Quarterly Journal of Economics 58*, reprinted in *Readings in welfare economics* (ed. K. Arrow and T. Scitovsky), Homewood, 1969.

Foley, D.: Lindahl's solution and the core of an economy with collective goods. *Econometrica 38*, January 1970.

Gibbard, A.: Manipulation of voting schemes; A general result. *Econometrica 41*, 1973.

Green, J. & Laffont, J.-J.: On the revelation of preferences for public goods. *Journal of Public Economics 8*, 79–94, 1977.

Groves, T. & Ledyard, J.: Some limitations of preference revealing mechanisms. *Public Choice 37*, 1977.

Kramer, G.: Sophisticated voting over multidimensional choice spaces. *Journal of Math Soc 2*, 165–180, 1972.

Kramer, G.: On a class of equilibrium conditions for majority rule. *Econometrica 41*, 285–299, 1973.

Kurz, M.: Experimental approach to the determination of demand for public goods. *Journal of Public Economics 3*, 329–348, 1974.

Lindahl, E.: *Die Gerechtigkeit der Besteuerung*, Lund, Part I, Chapter 4, "Positive Lösung", English Translation, "Just taxation a positive solution" appears in *Classics in the theory of public finance* (ed. R. Musgrave and A. Peacock), Macmillan Co., London, 1958.

Samuelson, P. A.: The pure theory of public expenditure. *Review of Economics and Statistics 36*, 387–389, 1954.

Wicksell, K.: Ein neues Prinzip der gerechten Besteuerung, Jena 1896, English translation, "A new principle of just taxation", appears in *Classics in the theory of public finance* (ed. R. Musgrave and A. Peacock), pp. 72–118. Macmillan Co., New York, 1958.

ON THE DIFFICULTY OF ATTAINING DISTRIBUTIONAL GOALS WITH IMPERFECT INFORMATION ABOUT CONSUMERS*

Jean-Jacques Laffont

Ecole Polytechnique, Paris and Université des Sciences Sociales de Toulouse, France

Eric Maskin

Massachusetts Institute of Technology, Cambridge, Mass., USA

Abstract

Recently, mechanisms which overcome the free rider problem and achieve Pareto optimality under imperfect information have been constructed. In this paper we provide various impossibility theorems which show the difficulty of achieving distributional goals when consumers' tastes are unknown. The results are developed for a particular game theoretic solution concept, that of dominant strategy; they could be extended if, instead, Bayesian equilibrium were the solution concept. As a way out we propose a second-best approach to welfare optimization.

I. Introduction

Recently a solution to the free rider problem proposed by Vickrey, Clarke and Groves has received a great deal of attention.[1] Mechanisms have been constructed to elicit private information; in particular, individuals' preferences for public goods.[2] These mechanisms use the information to optimize the welfare criterion corresponding to the sum of individuals' willingnesses to pay. In a model of public goods and a single private good (say, money) where utility functions are additively separable between the public and private goods and where all agents have the same constant marginal utility of money, this social objective function yields the same allocation of public goods as the Pareto optimum in which all individuals' utilities are given equal weight. Because our distribution goals may not be strictly utilitarian, however, we may be interested in optimizing social welfare functions (SWF) which are not simply sums of

* This work has been supported by the Sonderforschungsbereich 21 and the National Science Foundation.
[1] See, for example, Green & Laffont (1978) and Laffont (1979).
[2] Economies with a single private good are considered. True tastes are elicited as dominant strategies in the revelation game set up by the mechanisms.

utilities. In particular, we may wish to consider SWF's which take account of an agent's ability to pay as well as his willingness to pay for a public project. This paper investigates the extent to which this and other distributional goals are attainable. The results are, for most part, negative.

In Section II, we set up a framework in which to study these issues. Section III provides a general impossibility theorem which shows that under imperfect information no strictly concave Bergsonian SWF can be optimized. This result leaves us with essentially just the linear SWF's. Section IV extends this result to SWF's which are more general than the Bergsonian variety. It also elucidates the difficulties of optimizing SWF's—even linear SWF's—which incorporate information about abilities to pay for public projects. Section V illustrates comparable difficulties for the use of information which is not taste related.

The results of this paper are developed for a particular game theoretic solution concept—that of dominant strategies. We note in the conclusion that the results would all go through if, instead, Bayesian equilibrium were the solution concept; see Harsanyi (1968). As a way out of the pessimism of this paper, we propose a second-best approach to welfare optimization which we hope to pursue in future work.

II. The Model

We consider an economy with n $(n \geqslant 2)$ consumers, indexed by $i = 1, ..., n$, and two commodities, one public and one private. The utility function of consumer i, $u_i(K, x_i)$, is additively separable between the public good K and the private good x_i, $i = 1, ..., n$, and furthermore each agent is assumed to have the same constant marginal utility of private good. Hence,

$$u_i(K, x_i) = v_i(K) + x_i.^1$$

The family of utility functions is further restricted by:

Assumption 1. For $i = 1, ..., n$ let Θ_i be an open interval of $\mathbf{R}$ and let $v_i : \overset{0}{\mathbf{R}}_+ \times \Theta_i \rightarrow \mathbf{R}$ be a continuously differentiable function such that for any $\theta \in \Theta = \prod_{i=1}^{n} \Theta_i$, for any $\lambda = (\lambda_1, ..., \lambda_n)$ such that $\sum_{i=1}^{n} \lambda_i = 1$ and $\lambda_i \geqslant 0$, $i = 1, ..., n$, there exists $K^*(\theta) \in \overset{0}{\mathbf{R}}_+$ for which

(i) $\sum_{i=1}^{n} \lambda_i v_i(K^*(\theta), \theta_i) = \max_{K \in R_+} \sum_{i=1}^{n} \lambda_i v_i(K, \theta_i)$

(ii) $K^*(\theta)$ is continuously differentiable.

An agent is characterized by his valuation function, v_i, his taste characteristic, θ_i, and a vector, $\eta_i \in H_i$, of welfare relevant characteristics other than

---

[1] $v_i(K)$ is the *net* willingness to pay for the public good; i.e., the willingness to pay less the imputed cost share.

his tastes for the public good; η_i might represent, for example, endowment or productivity.

The functional forms $v_i(\cdot,\cdot)$ are assumed to be known publicly, but the true value $\hat{\theta}_i$ of the parameter θ_i is known only to agent i, *a priori*. Similarly, $\hat{\eta}_i$, the true value of η_i, is, at the beginning, strictly private information. A mechanism is a procedure where agents announce messages, on the basis of which a public good level is chosen. The purpose of a mechanism is to determine an "optimal" level of the public good. An optimal level is one which maximizes a given social welfare function. This paper studies the class of social welfare functions which can be optimized by mechanisms in which agents announce *characteristics* as messages and where revelation of true characteristics is a dominant strategy. A mechanism where agents announce characteristics (not necessarily their true characteristics) as strategies is a revelation mechanism.

A mechanism is formally defined as a mapping, $f = (d, t)$, from the strategy spaces $\prod_{i=1}^n H_i \times \prod_{i=1}^n \Theta_i$ into $\overset{0}{\mathbf{R}}_+ \times \mathbf{R}^n$, composed of a decision function, $d(\cdot)$, with range $\overset{0}{\mathbf{R}}_+$ and a n-tuple of transfer functions, $t(\cdot) = [t_1(\cdot), ..., t_n(\cdot)]$, each with range $\mathbf{R}$. $d(\cdot)$ associates to any $2n$-tuple of announced parameters a quantity of public good, while $t_i(\cdot)$ associates a transfer of private good to agent i, $i = 1, ..., n$.

A revelation mechanism is said to be C^1 when the function $f(\cdot)$ is continuously differentiable.

A revelation mechanism, $f(\cdot) = [d(\cdot), t(\cdot)]$ is said to be *strongly individually incentive compatible* (s.i.i.c.) if the truth is dominant strategy for each consumer, that is, if, for any i, any $(\eta, \theta) \in \prod_{j=1}^n H_j \times \prod_{j=1}^n \Theta_j$, and any $(\hat{\eta}_i, \hat{\theta}_i) \in H_i \times \Theta_i$

$$v_i(d(\hat{\eta}_i, \eta_{-i}, \hat{\theta}_i, \theta_{-i}), \hat{\theta}_i) + t_i(\hat{\theta}_i, \theta_{-i}, \hat{\eta}_i, \eta_{-i})$$

$$\geqslant v_i(d(\eta_i, \eta_{-i}, \theta_i, \theta_{-i}), \hat{\theta}_i) + t_i(\theta_i, \theta_{-i}, \eta_i, \eta_{-i}),$$

where

$$\theta_{-i} = (\theta_1, ..., \theta_{i-1}, \theta_{i+1}, ..., \theta_n)$$

and

$$\eta_{-i} = (\eta_1, ..., \eta_{i-1}, \eta_{i+1}, ..., \eta_n).$$

A social welfare function is a real valued function F of $[v_1(K, \hat{\theta}_1), ..., v_n(K, \hat{\theta}_n), t_1, ..., t_n, \theta_1, ..., \theta_n, \hat{\eta}_1, ..., \hat{\eta}_n]$.

We say that a social welfare function F is implementable if there exists a s.i.i.c. mechanism whose outcome maximizes F when everyone tells the truth.

From Green & Laffont (1978), we know that the social welfare functions $\sum_{i=1}^n \lambda_i v_i(K, \hat{\theta}_i)$ where the weights λ_i ($\sum_{i=1}^n \lambda_i = 1$, $\lambda_i > 0$, $i = 1, ..., n$) are constants, are implementable by the following obvious generalization of the Groves mechanisms:

$$d(\theta) \text{ maximizes } \sum_{i=1}^{n} \lambda_i v_i(K, \theta_i) \quad \text{in } K$$

$$t_i(\theta) = \frac{1}{\lambda_i} \sum_{j \neq i} \lambda_j v_j(d(\theta), \theta_j)$$

III. Bergsonian Social Welfare Functions

By a Bergsonian SWF, we mean a real-valued function of $v_1, ..., v_n, t_1, ..., t_n$. This is actually a more general formulation than the usual definition, which makes F a function only of $v_1 + t_1, ..., v_n + t_n$. We shall demonstrate that strictly concave F's are not implementable.

We adopt the following assumptions.

Assumption 2. F is twice continuously differentiable and its matrix of second order partial derivatives with respect to the v_j's is negative definite. Furthermore $\partial F / \partial v_i > 0$ for all i.

To prove an impossibility theorem, we can work with a small set of valuation functions, since any superset will then lead to impossibility *a fortiori*.

Consider the class V^Q of valuation function n-tuples consisting of functions which are quadratic with constant term:

$$V^Q = \left\{ \theta_1 K - \frac{K^2}{2} + \alpha_1, ..., \theta_n K - \frac{K^2}{2} + \alpha_n \middle| \theta \in \Theta \right.$$

$$= \prod_i \Theta_i, \ \alpha = (\alpha_1, ..., \alpha_n) \in \mathbf{R}^n, \ K \in \overset{0}{\mathbf{R}}_+ \right\}$$

$$= \{ v_1(K, \theta_1, \alpha_1), ..., v_n(K, \theta_n, \alpha_n) \mid \theta \in \Theta, \ \alpha \in \mathbf{R}^n, \ K \in \mathbf{R} \},$$

where Θ_i is a bounded open interval of the positive real line.

Assumption 3. $\forall \theta \in \Theta$, $\forall \alpha \in \mathbf{R}^n$, there exists a unique continuously differentiable $K^*(\theta, \alpha)$ which maximizes $F(v_1(K, \theta_1, \alpha_1), ..., v_n(K, \theta_n, \alpha_n), t_1(\theta, \alpha), ..., t_n(\theta, \alpha))$.

Theorem 1. *Under Assumptions 2 and 3, there exists no implementable Bergsonian SWF.*

Proof. We first parameterize v_i by rewriting it as

$$\bar{v}_i = \bar{\theta}_i K - \frac{K^2}{2} + \beta_i \bar{\theta}_i + \gamma_i, \quad \text{where } \bar{\theta}_i, \beta_i, \gamma_i \in \mathbf{R}$$

The class of valuation functions $\{\bar{v}_i\}$ is the same as the class $\{v_i\}$ so that nothing substantive has changed. Take

$$\theta_i = (\bar{\theta}_i, \beta_i, \gamma_i).$$

Suppose that F is a Bergsonian SWF satisfying Assumptions 2 and 3 and which is implemented by the mechanism $(K^*(\theta), t_1, ..., t_n)$. Agent i's maximization problem is

$$\max_{\bar{\theta}_i} \bar{v}_i(K^*(\theta), \bar{\theta}_i) + t_i(\theta).$$

The first-order condition in $\bar{\theta}_i$ is

$$\frac{\partial t_i}{\partial \bar{\theta}_i}(\theta) = -\frac{\partial \bar{v}_i}{\partial K}(K^*(\theta), \bar{\theta}_i)\frac{\partial K^*}{\partial \bar{\theta}_i}.$$

Evaluated at the truth, $\bar{\theta}_i = \hat{\theta}_i$, the second-order condition in $\bar{\theta}_i$ is:

$$\frac{-\partial^2 \bar{v}_i}{\partial K \partial \bar{\theta}_i}(K^*(\hat{\theta}_i, \theta_{-i}), \hat{\theta}_i)\frac{\partial K^*}{\partial \bar{\theta}_i}(\hat{\theta}_i, \theta_{-i}) < 0. \tag{1}$$

Since K^* maximizes F, $\sum_j \frac{\partial F}{\partial v_j}\frac{\partial \bar{v}_j}{\partial K} = 0$ when $K = K^*$.

Differentiating this last condition with respect to $\bar{\theta}_i$ and solving for $\partial K^*/\partial \bar{\theta}_i$, we obtain

$$\frac{\partial K^*}{\partial \bar{\theta}_i} = -\frac{\dfrac{\partial F}{\partial v_i}\dfrac{\partial^2 \bar{v}_i}{\partial K \partial \bar{\theta}_i} + \displaystyle\sum_{j=1}^{n}\dfrac{\partial \bar{v}_j}{\partial K}\dfrac{\partial^2 F}{\partial v_j \partial v_i}\dfrac{\partial \bar{v}_i}{\partial \bar{\theta}_i} + \displaystyle\sum_j\sum_s\dfrac{\partial \bar{v}_j}{\partial K}\dfrac{\partial^2 F}{\partial v_j \partial t_s}\dfrac{\partial t_s}{\partial \bar{\theta}_i}}{\displaystyle\sum_{j=1}^{n}\dfrac{\partial F}{\partial v_j}\dfrac{\partial^2 \bar{v}_j}{\partial K^2} + \displaystyle\sum_r\sum_s\dfrac{\partial \bar{v}_r}{\partial K}\dfrac{\partial^2 F}{\partial v_r \partial v_s}\dfrac{\partial \bar{v}_s}{\partial K}} \tag{2}$$

Let $D_i(\theta)$ be the denominator of the right-hand side of (2). Using the quadratic specification of the valuation functions, (1) can be rewritten as:

$$\hat{\beta}_i G_i(\hat{\theta}_i, \theta_{-i}) + H_i(\hat{\theta}_i, \theta_{-i}) < 0,$$

where

$$G_i(\hat{\theta}_i, \theta_{-i}) = \frac{\displaystyle\sum_{j \neq i}(\hat{\theta}_j - K^*)\frac{\partial^2 F}{\partial v_j \partial v_i} + (\hat{\theta}_i - K^*)\frac{\partial^2 F}{\partial v_i^2}}{D_i(\hat{\theta}_i, \theta_{-i})}$$

$$H_i(\hat{\theta}_i, \theta_{-i}) = \frac{\dfrac{\partial F}{\partial v_i} + \displaystyle\sum_{j \neq i}(\theta_j - K^*)\left[\dfrac{\partial^2 F}{\partial v_j \partial v_i}K^* + \displaystyle\sum_j\sum_s\dfrac{\partial^2 F}{\partial v_j \partial t_s}\dfrac{\partial t_s}{\partial \bar{\theta}_i}\right]}{D_i(\hat{\theta}_i, \theta_{-i})}$$

$$+ \frac{(\hat{\theta}_i - K^*)\left[\dfrac{\partial^2 F}{\partial v_i^2}K^* + \displaystyle\sum_s\dfrac{\partial^2 F}{\partial v_i \partial t_s}\dfrac{\partial t_s}{\partial \bar{\theta}_i}\right]}{D_i(\hat{\theta}_i, \theta_{-i})}$$

Now choose $\theta \in \Theta$ so that, for some $t, u \in \{1, ..., n\}$, $\hat{\theta}_t \neq \hat{\theta}_u$. Then because the matrix of second partials $(\partial^2 F/\partial v_s \partial v_r)$ is non-singular, the numerator of $G_i(\theta)$

does not vanish for some i. For such i, choose $\tilde{\beta}_i \in \mathbf{R}$ such that $\tilde{\beta}_i G_i(\theta_i, \theta_{-i}) + H_i(\theta_i, \theta_{-i}) > 0$.

Select $\tilde{\gamma}_i \in \mathbf{R}$ so that $\tilde{\gamma}_i + \tilde{\beta}_i \theta_i = \gamma_i + \beta_i \theta_i$. This implies that $\tilde{\beta}_i G_i(\tilde{\theta}_i, \tilde{\beta}_i, \tilde{\gamma}_i, \theta_{-i}) + H_i(\tilde{\theta}_i, \tilde{\beta}_i, \tilde{\gamma}_i, \theta_{-i}) > 0$. So second-order conditions are violated at $(\tilde{\theta}_i, \tilde{\beta}_i, \tilde{\gamma}_i, \theta_{-i})$, and, therefore, incentive compatibility cannot hold. Q.E.D.

IV. More General Social Welfare Functions

Theorem 1 demonstrates that if the family of possible valuation functions is large enough to include the quadratic class, one cannot implement Bergson SWF's which are strictly concave. This goes a long way toward ruling out non-linear SWF's. We next investigate the implementability of more general SWF's. That is, we shall consider SWF's which depend directly on the taste parameters θ. The results, however, are not much more positive than those for Bergson SWF's.

Consider again the class V^Q of quadratic valuation functions with constant terms. Let F be a real valued function of $v_1, ..., v_n, t_1, ..., t_n, \theta_1, ..., \theta_n, \alpha_1, ..., \alpha_n, K$, where $(v_1, ..., v_n) \in V^Q$.

Assumption 2′. F is twice continuously differentiable, and the matrices $(\partial^2 F / \partial v_i \partial v_j)$ and $(\partial^2 F / \partial \alpha_i \partial v_j)$ are negative definite. Furthermore $\partial F / \partial v_i > 0$ for all i.

Assumption 3′. $\forall \theta \in \Theta$, $\forall \alpha \in \mathbf{R}^n$, there exists a unique, continuously differentiable $K^*(\theta, \alpha)$ which maximizes $F(v_1(K, \theta_1, \alpha_1), ..., v_n(K, \theta_n, \alpha_n), t_1, ..., t_n, \theta_1, ..., \theta_n, \alpha_1, ..., \alpha_n, K)$.

Theorem 2. *No SWF satisfying Assumptions 2′ and 3′ is implementable.*

Proof. Almost identical to the proof of Theorem 1.

Theorem 2 is a strongly negative result but still does not bear on a large class of potentially implementable SWF's; viz., those that are linear in the valuation functions. For example, suppose the class of valuation functions is quadratic: $\theta_i K - (K^2/2)$, $\theta_i > 0$. Then the second order conditions for implementability becomes

$$\frac{\partial K^*}{\partial \theta_i}(\theta) > 0 \quad \forall \theta \, \forall i. \tag{4}$$

If (4) holds for K^*, then any SWF for which K^* is maximizing is implementable. In particular the following two-person SWF is implementable for v_1 and v_2 quadratic:

$$F \equiv \theta_2 v_1(K, \theta_1) + \theta_1 v_2(K, \theta_2).$$

The maximizing K for this SWF is

$$K^*(\theta) = \frac{2\theta_1\theta_2}{\theta_1 + \theta_2},$$

the fact that $(\partial K^*/\partial\theta_i) = (2\theta_i^2/(\theta_1 + \theta_2))^2 > 0$ implies implementability.

The transfer functions of the implementing mechanism are of the form

$$t_1(\theta) = \int \frac{2\theta_1\theta_2^2(\theta_2 - \theta_1)}{(\theta_1 + \theta_2)^3} \, d\theta_1 + h_1(\theta_2)$$

$$t_2(\theta) = \int \frac{2\theta_2\theta_1^2(\theta_1 - \theta_2)}{(\theta_1 + \theta_2)^3} \, d\theta_2 + h_2(\theta_1) \tag{5}$$

It may easily be verified that this mechanism is not of the Clarke–Groves variety. That is, the transfers are not chosen so as to make the individual and social maximands coincide.

This example should not, however, make us too sanguine about the possibility of implementability in the linear case. From Robert's paper in Laffont (1979), we know that if the class of valuation functions is entirely unrestricted, then only the SWF's of the form $\sum_i \lambda_i v_i$, where the λ_i's are constants, can be implemented.

This suggests a general result: the larger the class of valuation functions is, the less freedom one has to have the weights depend on the taste parameters. The conjectured result is illustrated by the following example.

Consider the SWF $\sum_{i=1}^n \lambda_i(\theta_i) v_i(K, \theta_i)$ in the quadratic case. K^* is defined by

$$\sum_{i=1}^n \lambda_i(\theta_i)(\theta_i - K^*) = 0$$

or

$$K^*(\theta) = \frac{\sum_{j=1}^n \lambda_j(\theta_j)\theta_j}{\sum_{j=1}^n \lambda_j(\theta_j)}$$

$$\frac{\partial K^*}{\partial\theta_i} = \frac{(\sum\lambda_j)[\lambda_i(\theta_i) + \theta_i\lambda_i'(\theta_i)] - (\sum\lambda_j\theta_j)\lambda_i'(\theta_i)}{(\sum\lambda_j)^2} \tag{6}$$

$$\text{sign } \frac{\partial K^*}{\partial\theta_i} = \text{sign } \sum_j \lambda_i\lambda_j\left[1 + \frac{\lambda_i'}{\lambda_i}(\theta_i - \theta_j)\right]$$

Suppose that $\lambda_i'/\lambda_i \neq 0$. When the range of θ_j is small enough, condition (4) is satisfied. However, when this range increases, sign $\partial K^*/\partial\theta_i$ becomes negative for some values of θ, showing that as the class expands the SWF of the type chosen here becomes non-implementable.

As we noted in the introduction, one question of particular interest is whether it is possible to implement SWF's that take account of an individual's *ability* (rather than desire) to pay for a public good. Taking account of abilities is a simple matter if these are known; one can simply arrange lump-sum transfers accordingly. Eliciting this information may be difficult, however, as the following argument suggests. Suppose that agent i's preferences can be represented by the utility function $v_i(K, \theta_i) + \lambda_i(\eta_i)t_i$, where $\lambda_i(\cdot)$ is a known function of the publicly unknown characteristic η_i. Taking the private good as *numéraire*, λ_i is the marginal utility of money. One might interpret η_i as marketable endowments (whether in human or physical form). λ_i is presumably lower the more richly endowed is i and is, therefore, a useful index of ability to pay. From Theorem 2, we know there is little point in considering SWF's which are strictly concave functions of the v_j's; so consider SWF's of the form

$$\sum_{j=1}^{n} \phi_j(\eta_j) v_j(K, \theta_j)$$

where $\phi_j > 0$ for all j.

Assumption 4. λ_i and ϕ_i are strictly positive, continuously differentiable functions for all i and there is a unique twice continuously differentiable function $K^*(\theta, \eta)$ such that $K = K^*(\theta, \eta)$ maximizes $\sum_{j=1}^{n} \phi_j(\eta_j) v_j(K, \theta_j)$.

Assumption 5.

$$\frac{\partial^2 v_i}{\partial K \partial \theta_i}(K^*(\theta, \eta), \theta_i) \neq 0 \quad \forall \theta, \eta.$$

Theorem 3. *Under Assumptions 1, 4, and 5, an SWF of the form $\sum_{i=1}^{n} \phi_i(\eta_i) v_i(K, \theta_i)$ is implementable if and only if*

$$\phi(\eta_i) = \frac{A_i}{\lambda_i(\eta_i)},$$

where A_i is a positive constant.

Proof. Maximizing $\sum_j \phi_j(\eta_j) v_j(K, \theta_j)$ leads to the first-order condition.

$$\sum_j \phi_j(\eta_j) \frac{\partial v_j}{\partial K}(K^*(\theta, \eta), \theta_j) = 0 \tag{7}$$

Differentiating (7), we obtain

$$\frac{\partial K^*}{\partial \eta_i} = \frac{-\frac{\partial \phi_i}{\partial \eta_i}\frac{\partial v_i}{\partial K}}{\sum_j \phi_j \frac{\partial^2 v_j}{\partial K^2}} \quad \text{and} \quad \frac{\partial K^*}{\partial \theta_i} = \frac{-\phi_i \frac{\partial^2 v_i}{\partial K \partial \theta_i}}{\sum_j \phi_j \frac{\partial^2 v_j}{\partial K^2}} \tag{8}$$

Incentive compatibility implies the identities

$$\frac{\partial t_i}{\partial \theta_i} \equiv -\frac{1}{\lambda_i}\frac{\partial v_i}{\partial K}\frac{\partial K^*}{\partial \theta_i}$$

$$\frac{\partial t_i}{\partial \eta_i} \equiv -\frac{1}{\lambda_i}\frac{\partial v_i}{\partial K}\frac{\partial K^*}{\partial \eta_i},$$

since the first-order conditions must be satisfied for any θ_{-i} and any true parameters.

Using the fact that $\partial^2 t_i/(\partial\theta_i\partial\eta_i)$ must equal $\partial^2 t_i/(\partial\eta_i\partial\theta_i)$ (Young's theorem), we obtain

$$\frac{\frac{\partial \lambda_i}{\partial \eta_i}}{\lambda_i}\frac{\partial v_i}{\partial K}\frac{\partial K^*}{\partial \theta_i} = \frac{-\partial^2 v_i}{\partial K \partial\theta_i}\frac{\partial K^*}{\partial \theta_i}. \tag{9}$$

Using (8) and invoking Assumption 5, we can reduce (9) to

$$\frac{\frac{\partial \lambda_i}{\partial \eta_i}}{\lambda_i} = \frac{\frac{-\partial \phi_i}{\partial \eta_i}}{\phi_i}$$

or

$$\phi_i(\eta_i) = \frac{A_i}{\lambda_i(\eta_i)}.$$

It remains only to check the second-order conditions. Since $v_i(K, \theta_i)$ is strictly concave in K, the matrix of second-order derivatives of agent i's objective function is negative semi-definite, implying pseudo-concavity. Thus the first-order conditions suffice.   Q.E.D.

Theorem 3 is a decidedly negative result for those who are equity minded. It states, in effect, that the only implementable SWF's which take into account ability to pay are those which weight richer agents more heavily than poorer.

V. On the Use of Non-Taste-related Information

Theorem 3 is discouraging as to the possibility of using information about endowments. As we formulated preferences, however, endowments entered the agent's utility function through his marginal utility of income. A natural inquiry is to ask whether characteristics which do not affect utility at all (but still may be relevant to social welfare) may be incorporated by an implementable SWF. Unfortunately, the answer is, once again, no, as we shall now demonstrate. In view of Theorem 1, we can immediately exclude SWF's which are strictly concave functions of the v_i's. Therefore, consider a linear SWF of the form:

$$F = \sum_i \lambda_i(\eta) v_i(K, \theta_i) \tag{10}$$

where $\eta = (\eta_1, ..., \eta_n)$, and η_i is a non-taste-related characteristic of individual i.

Assumption 6. Let V be a class of utility functions such that for all C^1-decision functions, $d(\eta, \theta)$ for which

$$\sum_{i=1}^{n} \lambda_i(\eta) v_i(d(\eta, \theta), \theta_i) = \max_{K>0} \sum_{i=1}^{n} \lambda_i(\eta) v_i(K, \theta),$$

$$\frac{\partial d}{\partial \eta_i}(\eta, \theta) \neq 0 \quad \text{and} \quad \frac{\partial^2 v_i}{\partial K \partial \theta_i}(d(\eta, \theta), \theta_i) \neq 0$$

for each i and almost any (η, θ).

The condition $\partial d/\partial \eta_i \neq 0$ guarantees that the optimal public decision is genuinely dependent on the parameters η_i, while $\partial^2 v_i/(\partial K \partial \theta_i) \neq 0$ ensures that the decision depends on the θ_i's. Assumption 6, therefore, serves only to rule out uninteresting cases.

Theorem 4. *If a class of valuation functions satisfies Assumptions 1 and 6, then if a SWF F on V satisfies (10), F is not implementable.*

Proof. Consider the maximization program of an agent i faced with a C^1-mechanism, $f(\cdot) = (d(\cdot), t(\cdot))$.

$$\max_{\theta_i, \eta_i} v_i(d(\eta, \theta), \hat{\theta}_i) + t_i(\eta, \theta)$$

The first-order conditions of this program are:

$$\frac{\partial v_i}{\partial K}(d(\eta_i, \eta_{-i}, \theta_i, \theta_{-i}), \hat{\theta}_i) \cdot \frac{\partial d}{\partial \eta_i}(\eta, \theta) + \frac{\partial t_i}{\partial \eta_i}(\eta, \theta) = 0$$

$$\frac{\partial v_i}{\partial K}(d(\eta, \theta), \hat{\theta}_i) \frac{\partial d}{\partial \theta_i}(\eta, \theta) + \frac{\partial t_i}{\partial \theta_i}(\eta, \theta) = 0$$

In order for the true values $(\hat{\eta}_i, \hat{\theta}_i)$ to be dominant strategies, the above conditions must hold as identities when evaluated at the truthful point. Thus,

$$\frac{\partial t_i}{\partial \eta_i}(\eta, \theta) \equiv \frac{-\partial v_i}{\partial K}(d(\eta, \theta), \theta_i) \cdot \frac{\partial d(\theta)}{\partial \eta_i}$$

$$\frac{\partial t_i}{\partial \theta_i}(\eta, \theta) \equiv \frac{-\partial v_i}{\partial K}(d(\eta, \theta), \theta_i) \cdot \frac{\partial d(\theta)}{\partial \theta_i}$$

The equality of the cross derivatives of $t_i(\eta, \theta)$ implies

$$\frac{\partial^2 v_i}{\partial K \partial \theta_i} \cdot \frac{\partial d(\theta)}{\partial \eta_i} \equiv 0$$

which is impossible from Assumption 6.   Q.E.D.

VI. Conclusions

This paper demonstrates that, even for highly restricted domains of preferences, the possibilities of implementing SWF's other than a weighted sum (with constant weights) of marginal rates of substitution between public and private goods are highly limited. In particular, SWF's which incorporate elicited information about ability to pay rather than willingness to pay for a public good appear impossible, in general, to implement.

Throughout, the solution concept we have imposed for implementing mechanisms is that of dominant strategies. One avenue for attaining more optimistic results would seem to be to weaken the solution concept. As we argued elsewhere,[1] Bayesian equilibrium[2] does not generally permit a wider range of SWF's to be implemented than does the dominant strategy equilibrium. Indeed, the four theorems of this paper all go through when Bayesian equilibrium become the solution concept.

Alternatively, one might adopt Nash equilibrium as the solution concept. More work needs to be done to determine the possibilities in this case. Maskin (1977) has shown that any social welfare function satisfying the properties of monotonicity and no veto power can be implemented by a Nash mechanism. On the other hand, Roberts[3] has shown that when valuation functions are unrestricted and the social welfare function has a unique optimum, it can be Nash-implemented only if it is dominant–strategy–implementable.

An alternative direction, which we hope to explore in future work, is second-best optimization. The results of this paper show that only a limited class of social welfare functions may be implemented. If a SWF of interest falls outside this class, one can "partially" implement it by optimizing instead the implementable SWF which best approximates it (in an expected welfare sense). Obviously, the worse the approximation, the more partial the implementation.

References

Green, J. & Laffont, J. J.: *Incentives in public decision making*. North-Holland, Amsterdam, 1978.

Harsanyi, J.: Games with incomplete information played by Bayesian players, I–III. *Management Science*, 1968.

Laffont, J. J. (ed.): *Aggregation and revela-tion of preferences*. North-Holland, Amsterdam, 1979.

Maskin, E.: Nash equilibria and welfare optimality. Mimeo, 1977.

Sen, A.: On weights and measures: Informational constraints in social welfare analysis. *Econometrica 47*, 1539–1572, 1977.

---

[1] See Laffont & Maskin, "A differential approach to expected utility maximizing mechanisms" in Laffont (1979).
[2] Sen (1977) discusses the use of non-utility components of social welfare functions.
[3] In Laffont (1979).

PROFESSED INEQUALITY AVERSION AND ITS ERROR COMPONENT

Louis Gevers, Herbert Glejser and Jean Rouyer *

Facultés Universitaires Notre-Dame de la Paix, Namur, Belgium

Abstract

In order to know better how people react when they are faced with a conflict between efficiency and equality in the distribution of disposable income, we asked
123 students to consider various ways of allocating fellowships to two hypothetical
recipients. Each questionnaire consisted of a series of binary choice experiments,
which led the respondents to disclose the amounts of equally distributed income
they considered equivalent to two reference distributions of fellowships. The questionnaire was re-administered to a subsample of students after six months. We
analyse the responses and the influence of the error term. It was found that envy
is very common when the reference income situation is one of affluence whereas
less extreme inequality aversion dominates strongly when the reference situation is
close to the one experienced by most respondents: in the latter case, the variance
as between individuals is also much smaller than in the former.

I. Introduction

In market economies where government expenditures are financed by distortionary taxation, it is usual to face a conflict between efficiency and equality
in the distribution of disposable income.

It is quite difficult to get a clear idea of the preference structure of the
participants in the political debate over taxation. Indeed, there is much uncertainty about the true shape of the set of possible states of the economy.
Secondly, pronouncements about preferences and even actual votes may, on
strategic grounds, fail to reflect true preferences. Thirdly, the preference structures themselves may be very involved, as they result from both egoistic and
altruistic motivations, while the latter combine judgements about desert and
vested rights with pure inequality aversion considerations.

---

* We wish to thank B. Jehin, Ph. Lambot and J. A. Morales for their helpful assistance.
We retain responsibility for errors.

For these reasons, we found it worthwhile to start an empirical investigation of preference structures in the context of the pure distribution problem.

We asked 123 students in economics to consider various ways of allocating fellowships to two hypothetical recipients. In answering our questionnaire, they were led to disclose the amounts of equally distributed income they considered equivalent to two distinct reference distributions of fellowships.

We have described elsewhere[1] our findings pertaining to the socioeconomic variables which influence inequality aversion among students.

One may however object that students who answered the questionnaire were unfamiliar with the choices they were asked to make. There may be a discrepancy between an actual answer and the answer the student would have arrived at if he had been familiar with such choices.

For this reason, we repeated our experiment after six months for a subsample of 54 students: this made it possible to estimate the variance of the error term in the students' answers, and how it evolved from one experiment to the next.

The remainder of this paper consists of three sections which deal successively with the questionnaire (Section II) and the data as well as the mean and dispersion of observed inequality aversion (Section III). In Section IV, we investigate some characteristics of the distribution of true inequality aversion, and we provide an estimate of the error term in the responses to both questionnaires.

II. Questionnaire Presentation

We asked 123 first and second year students at our Faculty of Economics and Social Sciences in Namur to consider the case of two hypothetical incoming students who did not know each other.

By assumption, they had the same needs. Each of them had to rely exclusively on a fellowship to support himself financially. The amount of money granted to each recipient was the object to be debated in the questionnaire. It was stipulated that each recipient would only know his monthly stipend; he would neither know how this figure had been selected, nor the amount received by the other student.

We first wanted to elicit from the respondents the amount of equally distributed income they considered equivalent to our two students getting respectively 70 and 100 (hundreds of B.F.) as monthly stipends. It was pointed out that the latter figure corresponded to an average student's expenditure, while the former was a lower bound under which regular studies would have to be disrupted.

---

[1] H. Glejser, L. Gevers, Ph. Lambot and J. A. Morales, "An econometric study of the variables determining inequality aversion students", *European Economic Review* 10, 173–188, (1977).

Our first list of questions consisted of two columns which contained respectively the reference figures 70–100 and the equally distributed amounts 85–85 (first line), 84–84 (line two), etc. down to 70–70.

Each respondent was asked to compare each uniform allocation with the reference figures, on the assumption that the loss of total income would benefit no one else in society.

Each respondent was requested to put a check mark on each line, on the side of his preferred allocation. We wanted to find out where check marks would jump across columns, as this would permit to locate the equally distributed allocation which, in the eyes of the respondent, was equivalent to the reference allocation. In case no jump was observed between 85 and 70, more lines were added until a jump would indeed occur.

The questionnaire contained another set of analogous questions, with reference figures 140 and 180 (instead of 70 and 100).

We were aware that respondents were unfamiliar with the type of questions we were raising. In order to ascertain the random error component in the answers, we asked a subsample of 54 students to answer the questionnaire again after six months had elapsed.

III. The Data

To facilitate comparison of our data, we shall make use of an index of inequality aversion (IA) which may be interpreted as the total amount of income which the respondent would be ready to let evaporate in order to obtain an equal distribution of fellowships, per unit of range of variation in the reference distribution.

Let us refer to fellowship recipients by means of a subscript which takes up values 1 and 2.

Let $x^s = (x_1^s, x_2^s)$ stand for a given reference distribution of fellowships, where s may take up values 0 and 1. The corresponding amount of equivalent equally distributed income, as inferred from a given questionnaire, will be denoted by v^s.

Thus, we define

$$IA^s = \frac{x_1^s + x_2^s - 2v^s}{\max x^s - \min x^s} \tag{1}$$

If the respondent does not care about inequality, the numerator vanishes, so that $IA^s = 0$.

If the respondent conforms to conventional utilitarian wisdom, a utility function u is defined on individual income, such that

$$2u(v^s) = u(x_1^s) + u(x_2^s).$$

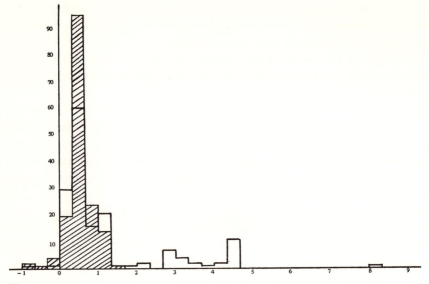

Fig. 1

By assumption, u is increasing, so that the indifference curve through x^s has negative slope. It follows that the numerator in (1) is not larger than the denominator, so that $IA^s \leqslant 1$.

Moreover, u is usually assumed concave. As a consequence, the indifference curve through x^s is convex towards the origin, and the numerator in (1) is non negative. It follows that $IA^s \geqslant 0$.

However, if a respondent believes that 70 is not enough to meet a student's subsistence requirements, he may consider that marginal utility is increasing at this level, so that his IA^0 may be negative.

Finally, when $IA^s > 1$, indifference curves are locally positively sloped. Either u is decreasing from some point on, or the recipient's utilities are interdependent, or the utilitarian framework must be abandoned.

In Fig. 1, we present in histogram form the distributions of IA^0 and IA^1, as computed from all our observations, so that both answers of the 54 students who were reinterviewed are included.

The calculated means and standard deviations of IA^0 are respectively 0.501 and 0.326. The corresponding figures for IA^1 are 1.159 and 1.393.

There is thus a significant and substantial increase in mean inequality aversion as the distribuend is roughly increased by 100%. Envy seems to be prevalent for $s = 1$, as the mean exceeds the critical value 1.

The increase in standard deviation appears even more drastic as we go from $s = 0$ to $s = 1$. This may indicate an increase in the dispersion of "true" inequality aversion, and/or an increase in the variance of the error term, at income levels much higher than those of most respondents. In the next section, we try, among other things, to disentangle the two effects.

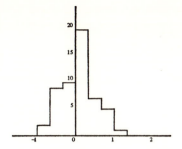

Fig. 2. Observed frequences, $IA_N^0 - IA_F^0$.

IV. True Inequality Aversion and Error Terms

When measurement is subject to random errors, repeated measurement tells something about the distribution of the error term. In this section, we concentrate on the 54 students who answered the questionnaire twice. We denote answers to the first and second survey by subscripts F and N, respectively.

The observed distributions of $(IA_N^s - IA_F^s)$ are presented in Figs. 2 and 3, while a few relevant statistics pertaining to the distributions are recorded in Table 1.

It does seem clear from Table 1 that mean income aversion did not change value from the first survey to the next.

We shall now assume that for both values of t and for both values of s, IA_t^s is the sum of two independent random variables, to be interpreted respectively as true inequality aversion (a^s) and an error term (e_t^s).

Having observed that mean inequality aversion looks stable in our subsample, we shall assume that all moments of the distribution of true inequality aversion remained stable. This is why a^s is written without subscript t.

For each s value, we further add the following assumptions:

$$E(e_t^s) = E(e_N^s \cdot e_F^s) = E(a^s \cdot e_t^s) = 0, \quad t = F, N. \tag{2}$$

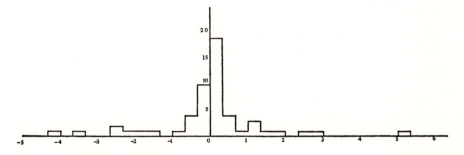

Fig. 3. Observed frequences, $IA_N^1 - IA_F^1$.

Table 1. *Mean and dispersion of* $(IA_N^s - IA_F^s)$

Variable	Mean	Standard deviation	Absolute mean deviation
$IA_N^0 - IA_F^0$	0.048	0.440	0.344
$IA_N^1 - IA_F^1$	−0.062	1.440	0.799

As a consequence, for each s value, we get:

$$\text{Var}(IA_t^s) = \text{Var}(a^s) + \text{Var}(e_t^s), \quad t \neq F, N. \tag{3}$$

$$\text{Cov}(IA_F^s \cdot IA_N^s) = \text{Var}(a^s). \tag{4}$$

Combining these equations with sample estimates of their left-hand side, we computed estimates of the standard deviations of a^s, e_F^s and e_N^s which are listed in Table 2.

Comparing rows first and columns afterwards, we can draw a number of conclusions from Table 2. Admittedly, they rest on the vanishing covariances assumption embodied in (2), an assumption we do not regard as innocuous.

(*a*) The standard deviation of true inequality aversion increases by 500 % as incomes roughly double.

(*b*) Under the same circumstances the standard deviations of the error term increase by 350 % and 200 %, respectively.

(*c*) On each line, the estimated standard deviation of a^s lies between the estimates pertaining to the error terms. As we go from the first questionnaire ($t = F$) to the new one ($t = N$), there is a sharp increase in the estimated standard deviation of e_t^s, which may be accounted for by the impatience of the re-interviewed students; the increase is particularly noticeable for $s = 0$, and this is also illustrated by the fact that the correlation coefficient between IA_F^0 and IA_N^0 amounts only to 0.275, while the corresponding figure is 0.523 for $s = 1$.

By combining our estimated mean and standard deviation of a^0 with the Tchebycheff inequality, we obtain an upper bound to the probability of getting a respondent who is truly envious ($a^0 > 1$) or who truly favors inequality ($a^0 < 0$). The probability amounts to 0.11 at most. If a^0 is normally distributed, the figure shrinks to a mere 0.0026. Thus, even though envy is very common when the reference income situation is one of affluence, it is exceptional when the reference situation is close to the one experienced by most respondents.

Table 2. *True inequality aversion and error terms; estimated standard deviations*

Reference income distribution	True inequality aversion (a^s)	Error term, (e_F^s)	Error term, (e_N^s)
$s = 0$	0.169	0.163	0.411
$s = 1$	1.022	0.711	1.236

OPTIMIZATION AND QUANTITATIVE ASSESSMENT OF CHILD ALLOWANCES*

Vidar Christiansen

University of Oslo, Oslo, Norway

Abstract

This paper illustrates a possible application of revealed social preferences. Welfare weights revealed to be implicit in the Norwegian system of indirect taxation in a previous paper, are adopted to explore whether child allowances in Norway are optimal given these welfare weights. A set of optimality conditions—which may be interesting in their own right—is established, and economic interpretations are presented. The empirical results indicate that the allocation of child allowances is inconsistent with the design of indirect taxation in pursuing distributional ends. A reallocation in favor of larger families seems advantageous given the implicit welfare weights.

I. Introduction

In public economics, social choice problems involving distribution policy are usually solved by maximizing a social welfare function. This implies that welfare weights are assigned to the marginal income of various individuals or households according to their income level, household size, and possibly other characteristics. Such distributive weights make it possible in principle to measure whether a marginal redistribution of income is advantageous. At optimum, of course, the government has to be indifferent towards any feasible, marginal redistribution. However, such optimality conditions are of very limited practical significance as long as the distributive weights are unknown parameters. A number of approaches have therefore been suggested to quantify welfare weights; for very good survey articles, see Johansen (1974) and Stern (1977).

One approach is the revealed preference method. Its starting-point is that many decisions are actually made in which various objectives and the interests of various groups are weighed against each other. Some kind of weighting system, whereby conflicting interests are traded off, is implicit in the

---

* Most of the research for this paper was carried out during my stay at the University of Warwick in 1977–78 and I am grateful for the hospitality shown by its Economics Department. I am greatly indebted to my friend Eilev Jansen, who has given a number of valuable comments on the draft manuscript. My thanks are also due to an anonymous referee.
3

decision-making. The purpose of the method is to reveal the implicit welfare weights in actual policy decisions. *The implicit welfare weights are defined as the welfare weights which make the actual policy optimal given these weights.* In practice, optimal in this context must be taken to mean optimal with a reasonable degree of approximation.

A previous paper, Christiansen & Jansen (1978), has revealed implicit social preferences in the Norwegian system of indirect taxation (including subsidies). We used a model of optimal commodity taxation in combination with tax and market data to estimate a number of implicit social valuation parameters. This analysis is referred to in the following as the revealed preference study. In the present paper we demonstrate how implicit distributive weights from the revealed preference study can be applied to make an assessment of actual child allowances in Norway.

The approach is to explore whether optimality conditions for child allowances are satisfied given the implicit distributive weights derived from commodity taxation, as they should be if the policies were based on consistent criteria. If they are not, inconsistencies between the two categories of decisions are revealed. In either case the information should be of interest in the current process of policy evaluation and revision.

In Norway excise taxes and subsidies are used to redistribute income in favor of families with children and households with low incomes. Child allowances are used to transfer income to families with children, and the main concern is obviously with low-income families with children. The purposes of the two policy categories are to promote the same kind of distributional objectives. Thus they constitute policies for which it seems appropriate to require that they be designed as if they were derived from the same underlying welfare criterion.

The consistency concept may need further comment. If there is a single decision-maker, the consistency concept is straightforward. With reasonable approximation this may include the case where the decisions are taken by a government or party of fairly homogeneous preferences, and the case where the policy proposals of such a party gain sufficient support to be accepted by the decison-making body. These are important cases.

In general, however, the consistency concept is more problematic when collective decison-making is considered. Suppose there are two or more opposing parties involved in designing the collective decisions. In this case the optimality criterion and hence the consistency concept are not clear. But even if the parties disagree about the desirable magnitude of redistribution, they may still want the policies, which after all are to be put into effect, to be consistent in the sense that they maximize a welfare criterion which ensures that the total policy is efficient, given the finally accepted level of redistribution. More precisely, what they could be expected to want is an outcome which is Pareto optimal from the points of view of the parties. Hence they would like to maximize a preference function which supports an appropriate Pareto optimum. However, it is difficult to formulate a preference function which is suitable for analysis of implicit preferences and can also be expected to support a Pareto optimal compromise decison. This question has been dealt with in a separate paper, Christiansen (1978b), and further discussion would be beyond the scope of the present article. A fairly simple preference function of the kind commonly used in distribution analysis might be a reasonable approximation no worse than other approximate functional forms in empirical studies.

Even if these problems are acknowledged, it does not imply that inconsistencies which may be revealed are uninteresting. Rather than being accepted quietly, they should stimulate discussion as to whether they are a necessary consequence of the conflicting preferences of several decision-makers or whether they simply reflect bad decisions.

Before an assessment of child allowances can be made, theoretical optimality conditions for a system of child allowances have to be derived. This is done in Section II. Apart from providing a basis for the empirical study, the theory may be interesting as such. The analysis brings out the kind of effects which should in general be taken into account when determining lump sum transfers which are part of a larger tax/transfer system including distortionary taxes. Of particular interest is the impact on the inefficiency of existing distortions.[1] Such lump sum transfers have received little attention in the theory of optimal taxation, although they are not without practical significance.

Section III is devoted to a brief introduction to the revealed preference study, and presents data for the empirical investigation. The empirical results are presented and discussed in Section IV.

II. Optimality Conditions for Child Allowances

We begin by working out optimality rules for child allowances derived from welfare maximization. We adhere to the standard approach to assessment of household welfare which takes household income and size into account, and considers households to be better off the greater the income and the smaller the size. This seems to be the prevailing viewpoint on which distribution policy is based.[2]

It is assumed that child allowances are optimized for the given population, and that possible effects on the future number of children are absent or assigned no weight. This implies that the analysis does not allow for optimum population arguments or any impact via the parents' choice of number of

---

[1] This point may easily be forgotten because of the much worshipped reputation of lump-sum transfers for non-distortive properties in a first-best economy. Whether the effect is important in concrete situations is, of course, an empirical question.
[2] Some alternative welfare judgements are discussed in Christiansen (1978a).

children on possible social externalities of a growing population density. Nor does it take into account the argument that child allowances are subsidies on children which may be regarded as having the same kind of distortion effect as any other subsidy. These assumptions allow us to treat child allowances as lump-sum transfers.

One problem encountered in designing the system of child allowances is whether or not the allowances should be income conditioned. There are no income qualifications in the Norwegian system. The child allowance received by a family depends solely on the number of children. In assessing different systems we should keep in mind that what matters both with regard to income distribution and distortion effects, is the *net* tax schedules faced by different types of households. A rule which states that households below a certain income limit are entitled to an allowance, while those above the limit are not, will introduce discontinuity into the net tax schedule which implies a marginal tax rate well above one. This violates the well-established optimal taxation rule that the marginal tax rate should not exceed unity. In addition there would have to be a costly administration to select the eligible applicants.

The most general optimization problem we might consider would be the optimal design of separate net tax schedules for the respective types of households. Our efforts here, however, are confined to the simpler problem of deriving optimality rules for child allowances in a system where, apart from allowances, families face a given tax schedule.

The problem is to establish conditions for optimal levels of the allowances granted for the first, second, etc. child in a family. We denote the levels of the respective allowances by $a_1, a_2, ..., a_M$, where M is the largest number of children in any family. A family with m children will thus qualify for a total grant equal to $\sum_{i=1}^{m} a_i$.

Children in this context are those who satisfy the age qualification for child allowances, which is taken as given. Let n_m denote the total number of families with exactly m children. Let N_m be the number of families with at least m children, which corresponds to the total number of families who are eligible for the allowance due to the mth child in a family. By definition $N_m = \sum_{i=m}^{M} n_i$. The total sum of child allowances then amounts to $\sum_{i=1}^{M} a_i N_i$.

All prices are assumed to be given. Each family is assumed to face a given wage rate and adjust its total labor supply. The role of this simplification is merely to avoid complications which would not contribute to the essential features of the analysis. Let q denote wage rate and L labor supply. Gross (pre-transfer) income is then $y = qL$. The net tax function is given by:

$$S_m = F(y; t) + T - \sum_{i=1}^{m} a_i. \tag{1}$$

S_m is the net income tax collected from a family with m children. Note that child allowances are not included in taxable income. t and T are parameters of the tax function. T is supposed to give the "level" of the tax function, while t determines its shape (degree of progressivity, etc.). t may well be interpreted as a vector.

T may well be negative and may ensure that no (positive) tax is imposed on taxpayers below a certain income level. $-T$ can then be interpreted as a uniform lump sum transfer. The analysis will consider increasing child allowances, $a_1, ..., a_M$, while T is adjusted to keep total tax revenue unchanged. This implies that the lump sum part of the tax/transfer system is differentiated according to number of children.

$$F' = \frac{dF}{dy} = \text{the marginal income tax.}$$

Disposable income, r_m, is defined by:

$$r_m = y - S_m = qL - S_m. \tag{2}$$

We do not have to distinguish between income tax and a general purchase tax since the latter is equivalent to an income tax. But we do have to allow for excise taxes on certain commodities. This includes subsidies as negative excise taxes. Assume that excise taxes are imposed on n commodities, and denote the quantities of these goods by $x^1, ..., x^n$. Let x denote the vector $(x^1, ..., x^n)$. Let s^i be the excise tax per unit of x^i, $i = 1, ..., n$, and z be a vector of quantities of other goods. A household is supposed to maximize its utility function $U(z, x, L; m)$ subject to the budget restriction that total expenditure on z and x is constrained by disposable income. All prices and the number of children are given. The optimization may be thought of as carried out in two stages. First, any disposable income must be optimally allocated among the various goods. That is, U is maximized for given L and r_m. This leads to ordinary demand functions:

$$z = Z(r_m, m)$$
$$x = X(r_m, m), \tag{3}$$

where Z and X are vector functions. As prices are taken as given throughout the analysis, they need not be specified.

(3) inserted into $U(\ )$ gives a quasi-indirect utility function:

$$V(r_m, L, m) = V(qL - S_m, L, m) = \max_{x,z} U(z, x, L, m)$$
$$\text{s.t. the budget constraint.} \tag{4}$$

Second, L must be chosen optimally by maximizing V with respect to L. This leads to the familiar optimality condition:

$$V_L = -V_r q(1 - F'), \tag{5}$$

where the subscripts denote partial derivatives with respect to the appropriate argument. The arguments of the V- and F-functions are left out to simplify the exposition.

(5) defines the family's labor supply function:

$$L\left(q, t, T - \sum_{i=1}^{m} a_i, m\right). \tag{6}$$

L_t and L_T denote the partial derivatives with respect to t and T.

Since disposable income becomes a function of the same arguments, we can write the demand functions:

$$X^i(r_m, m) = x^i\left(q, t, T - \sum_{i=1}^{m} a_i, m\right) \quad i = 1, \ldots, n. \tag{7}$$

Let $q_1, \ldots, q_k, \ldots, q_K$ be the existing wage rates. Subscripts k, m indicate wage rate and number of children. Thus $x_{k,m}^i$ is the consumption of commodity i by a household with wage rate q_k and m children, and $n_{k,m}$ is the number of families with wage rate q_k and m children. For simplicity we do not distinguish between different categories of families without children. The analysis can easily be extended in that direction.

We assume a net government revenue constraint requiring that net tax proceeds amount to $S°$:

$$\sum_{k=1}^{K} \sum_{m=0}^{M} \left[F\left(q_k L\left(q_k, t, T - \sum_{i=1}^{m} a_i, m\right); t\right) + T - \sum_{i=1}^{m} a_i \right] n_{k,m}$$

$$+ \sum_{i=1}^{n} s^i \sum_{k=1}^{K} \sum_{m=0}^{M} x_{k,m}^i\left(q_k, t, T - \sum_{i=1}^{m} a_i, m\right) n_{k,m} = S°. \tag{8}$$

This equation implicitly defines:

$$T = \theta(t, s, a_1, \ldots, a_M) \tag{9}$$

where s is the vector $(s^1, \ldots, s^n)$.

In deriving optimality conditions for $(a_1, a_2, \ldots, a_M)$, t and s are taken as given. This implies assuming that the tax changes required by marginal changes in child allowances are brought about by changing T alone. If the tax parameters are optimized in the situation under consideration, this is obviously a legitimate assumption because we are then indifferent to alternative tax parameter changes to raise a small amount of extra tax revenue. At the margin the welfare effect of using T alone is the same as the effect of using any other tax parameters. No matter what the tax parameter change actually is, it can be represented by a change in T alone. It does not seem reasonable to analyze optimal child allowances on the assumption that tax parameters are non-optimal because such lack of optimality should be corrected independently of the tax parameter changes which are necessary to finance changes in child allowances.

Social preferences are expressed by an additive social welfare function, which is given by:

$$W = \sum_k \sum_{m=0}^{M} V \left[q_k L \left(q_k, t, T - \sum_{i=1}^{m} a_i, m \right) - F \left(q_k L \left(q_k, t, T - \sum_{i=1}^{m} a_i, m \right); t \right) \right.$$

$$\left. - T + \sum_{i=1}^{m} a_i, L \left(q_k, t, T - \sum_{i=1}^{m} a_i, m \right), m \right] n_{k,m}. \tag{10}$$

V is taken to be a particular cardinalization of the individual utility indicator which, in addition to describing individual preferences, also expresses the distribution preferences of the government. The additive form of the welfare function has been discussed elsewhere; see for example Christiansen & Jansen (1978, Section 3). First-order conditions for an interior maximum with respect to $a_1, ..., a_M$ subject to (9) are easily derived. Since the individual households are optimally adjusted, we can make use of the envelope theorem. We get:

$$\frac{\partial W}{\partial a_j} = \sum_k \sum_{m=j}^{M} V_r n_{k,m} - \theta_j \sum_k \sum_{m=0}^{M} V_r n_{k,m} = 0 \quad \forall_j. \tag{11}$$

Again the arguments of the functions are omitted.

If negative child allowances are ruled out, and the possibility of hitting non-negativity constraints is allowed for, we obtain the optimality conditions:

$$\frac{\partial W}{\partial a_j} = 0 \quad \text{or} \quad \frac{\partial W}{\partial a_j} < 0 \quad \text{and} \quad a_j = 0. \tag{12}$$

Such corner solutions are by no means unlikely. It seems expedient, however, to give economic interpretations of the formulae without reference to corner cases. From (8) we find that:

$$\frac{\partial T}{\partial a_j} = \theta_j = \frac{\sum_k \sum_{m=j}^{M} F' q_k L_T n_{k,m} - \sum_i s^i \sum_k \sum_{m=j}^{M} e^i_{k,m} n_{k,m} + N_j}{\sum_k \sum_{m=0}^{M} F' q_k L_T n_{k,m} - \sum_i s^i \sum_k \sum_{m=0}^{M} e^i_{k,m} n_{k,m} + N} \quad \forall_j \tag{13}$$

where $e^i_{k,m} = -\partial x^i_{k,m} / \partial T$, i.e. the Engel derivative of the consumption of good i by a household of type (k, m) with respect to lump sum income.

To facilitate the interpretation of the optimality conditions, we introduce a term b_j which is defined as the average change in tax payments from families with at least j children because of their change in work effort and consumption induced by a marginal lump sum transfer:

$$b_j = \frac{1}{N_j} \sum_k \sum_{m=j}^{M} (\sum_i s^i e_{k,m}^i - F' q_k L_T) n_{k,m}. \tag{14}$$

Let B be the corresponding average for all families. b_j and B may be called *marginal propensities to pay taxes*.

Then (13) can be written as:

$$\theta_j = \frac{N_j(1-b_j)}{N(1-B)}. \tag{15}$$

The optimality conditions (11) can then be rewritten as:

$$N \sum_k \sum_{m=j}^{M} V_r n_{k,m} - N_j \frac{1-b_j}{1-B} \sum_k \sum_{m=0}^{M} V_r n_{k,m} = 0 \quad \forall_j. \tag{16}$$

(16) requires a balance at the margin between positive and negative welfare effects of child allowances. We see that the negative term is greater in absolute value, the greater the fraction which appears in it. This fraction captures the efficiency effects of the marginal redistribution under study. These effects are due to existing distortionary taxation. The effects are of the following nature.

If there is a (positive) tax on a commodity the marginal utility of the commodity exceeds its marginal production cost, and there will be a welfare gain from increased consumption of that commodity. If there is a subsidy on a commodity, the converse will be true. Thus if the redistribution of income we consider leads to more consumption of taxed commodities or less consumption of subsidized commodities, it gives a welfare improvement. If the opposite effects occur, there will be a welfare loss.[1] Normally there will be effects in both directions. Similarly, when the social marginal product of labor exceeds the private marginal product of labor because of a positive marginal tax rate, an increase in labor effort will increase economic efficiency, and a reduction in work effort will reduce economic efficiency. As we have just seen, a marginal rise in a_j will add a net lump sum to the disposable income of those with at least j children, while others will have their disposable income cut by an increased head tax. The former effect will normally reduce work effort, while the latter effect will normally increase work effort.

The net efficiency effect of raising a_j will be positive or negative, conditional on whether the total net proceeds from excise and income taxes tend to increase or decrease when income is transferred to families with at least j children. It follows that if the marginal propensity to pay taxes is higher

---

[1] Note that in this analysis the use of excise taxes to correct for externalities is not considered.

(lower) among families with at least j children than among households in general, there will be an efficiency gain (loss). This corresponds to $b_j > B(<B)$ and consequently $(1-b_j)/(1-B) < 1(>1)$. If the fraction is less than unity, it implies that the welfare loss due to income being taxed away from households is scaled down in (16) because there is also an efficiency gain which contributes to a rise in total welfare. If the fraction is greater than unity, there is an efficiency loss which adds to the welfare loss. If the fraction equals unity, (16) expresses pure income distribution effects. The distinction between welfare effects which are distribution effects and those which are efficiency effects may become clearer if we rewrite (16) as:

$$N \sum_k \sum_{m=j}^{M} V_r n_{k,m} - N_j \sum_k \sum_{m=0}^{M} V_r n_{k,m} + \left(1 - \frac{1-b_j}{1-B}\right) N_j \sum_k \sum_{m=0}^{M} V_r n_{k,m} = 0 \quad \forall_j. \quad (16')$$

The difference between the first and second terms expresses the distribution effect, while the third term captures the efficiency effect. As pointed out earlier, the process of increasing child allowances and adjusting T to keep total tax revenue unchanged is equivalent to differentiating a lump sum transfer according to the number of children. We see from (16') that the distribution effect of differentiating a marginal lump sum transfer according to the number of children depends on the correlation between marginal welfare of income and number of children.

When taxes, allowances and the number of children are given, there is normally a one-to-one correspondence between the wage rate and the disposable income of each type of family. We can therefore express the marginal welfare of income, V_r, as a function, w, of disposable income, r, and the number of children, m:

$$V_r = w(r, m). \quad (17)$$

Let us assume that disposable income can assume S different values $r_1, ..., r_S$, and let $h_{s,m}$ be the number of households with disposable income r_s and m children. The optimality conditions can then be written as:

$$\sum_{s=1}^{S} \sum_{m=j}^{M} w(r_s, m) h_{s,m} / N_j (1-b_j) = \sum_{s=1}^{S} \sum_{m=0}^{M} w(r_s, m) h_{s,m} / N(1-B) \quad \forall_j. \quad (18)$$

The left-hand side is the gross welfare effect of increasing a_j by $1/N_j(1-b_j)$ units. "Gross effect" means that the effect of raising the extra tax revenue necessary to pay out the additional child benefit is not taken into account. We notice that in order to finance this increase in a_j it is necessary to raise T by $\theta_j/N_j(1-b_j)$ units, which equals $1/N(1-B)$ for all j according to (15). The tax change which is required is the same for all j. Obviously, the welfare loss because of the tax change will then be the same for all j, and equals the right-hand side of (18). Thus, at optimum, the gross welfare effect of increasing child allowances by amounts that require equal tax changes must be the same for all a_j and equal to the welfare loss because of the tax change.

Let us denote the left-hand side of (18) by μ_j:

$$\mu_j = \sum_s \sum_{m=j}^M w(r_s, m) h_{s,m}/N_j(1 - b_j). \tag{19}$$

Optimal allocation of a given amount of tax revenue to be paid out as child allowances requires that the shadow value μ_j is the same for all j. (Apart from corner cases.) The purpose of the empirical part of this study is to test whether this is the case.

It may be useful at this stage to anticipate one of the problems in the empirical analysis, namely that estimates of the Engel derivatives, e^i, are hardly available. (For simplicity subscripts are omitted.) What we have are estimates of the expenditure derivatives:

$$d^i = \partial x^i/\partial r. \tag{20}$$

By means of (1) and (2) we find:

$$e^i = -\frac{\partial x^i}{\partial r} \cdot \frac{\partial r}{\partial T} = -d^i \left[\frac{\partial y}{\partial T}(1 - F') - 1 \right] \tag{21}$$

which shows how d^i deviates from e^i. The deviation is zero if the Engel derivative of labor supply is zero.

III. The Implicit Welfare Weights and Other Data

In the empirical analysis we apply the theory to child allowances in Norway using data from 1975, as was done in the revealed preference study. In Norway child allowances are granted for all the children in a family. According to the government budget for 1975, government transfers as child allowances amounted to a total of 1 390 million Nkr. The allowance per child is listed in Table 1.

We see from the formulae established in Section II that we need data on distributive weights, the distribution of households by size and income, tax rates and derivatives of demand functions.

We use estimated implicit distributive weights derived from the use of excise taxes and subsidies on consumption goods in Norway in 1975, as reported in Christiansen & Jansen (1978). A model of optimal commodity taxes was combined with tax and market data to estimate certain social valuation parameters of a specified welfare function. Three variants were considered. Variant II, which we considered to be the most realistic and reliable, is used in this context.

Optimality conditions were established by maximizing a social welfare func-

Table 1. *Child allowances. Yearly grants in Norway, 1975*

Grants per child	Nkr
For the first child	550
For the second child	1 650
For the third child	2 400
For the fourth child	2 620

tion with respect to excise taxes on 15 good categories subject to a tax revenue constraint. The optimality conditions were (op. cit. formula (9)):

$$- \sum_i w^i x_k^i + \sum_j w_j \left(\frac{\partial x_j}{\partial p_k} \right) - \varkappa T_k = 0 \quad \forall_k.$$

Superscripts indicate households and subscripts indicate commodities subject to excise taxes. w^i is the welfare weight given to the marginal income of household i, x_k^i is household i's consumption of good k, w_j is the marginal welfare effect of external social costs associated with commodity j, $\partial x_j / \partial p_k$ is the appropriate price derivative of market demand, $\varkappa$ is the shadow price of the tax revenue constraint, and T_k is the marginal effect on tax revenue of the excise tax on commodity k.

For each type of household, actual income was transformed into equivalent one-person income by means of consumer unit numbers derived by Bojer (1977).

We used close approximations of Bojer's figures given by a convenient functional form. The equivalent income scales by which the actual incomes are deflated to obtain the equivalent one-person income are presented in Table 2. The corresponding distributive weights, w, are given by the iso-elastic marginal welfare function $D r_e^d$ where r_e is equivalent one-person income, d is a constant parameter measuring inequality aversion, and D determines the choice of welfare unit.

d and a number of social cost parameters, w_j (associated with wine and liquor, beer, tobacco and petrol) were estimated. An error term was introduced on the right-hand side of each optimality condition to allow for random

Table 2. *Equivalent income scales*

Household size	Equivalent income scales
Single adult	1
Two adults	1.72
Two adults and one child	2.12
Two adults and two children	2.52
Two adults and three children	2.97
Two adults and four children	3.50

Table 3. *Distributive weights for households of type* $(r, m)^a$

m	r 8 400	15 400	21 100	30 100	45 200	62 300	82 700	131 400
1	3.6161	2.1377	1.6369	1.1955	0.8403	0.6363	0.4976	0.3331
2	4.2069	2.4870	1.8927	1.3908	0.9776	0.7401	0.5789	0.3875
3	4.8515	2.8681	2.1827	1.6040	1.1274	0.8535	0.6676	0.4468
4	5.5901	3.3048	2.5150	1.8482	1.2990	0.9835	0.7693	0.5149

[a] Based on the estimates of variant II in Christiansen & Jansen (1978).

errors, and (nonlinear) least-squares estimates were obtained by minimizing the total sum of squares of the left-hand sides of the optimality conditions with respect to the parameters. d was estimated to be -0.87. D is adjusted to make the distributive weight given to a family consisting of two adults and whose disposable income is 30 100, equal to unity. Using these parameters and consumer unit numbers, the implicit distributive weights can be computed. The distributive weights for the income levels to be used in the analysis are shown in Table 3 above. r still denotes the actual disposable income of a household, and m denotes the number of children in a family with two adults.

As the reader will soon see, most of the data used in the present analysis were also essential data in the revealed preference study. We therefore confine this presentation to the data needed in the present context. More details about the revealed preference analysis may be obtained from the original paper; see Christiansen & Jansen (1978).

We let disposable income be represented by consumption expenditure. The percentage distribution of different types of households by disposable income is derived from the Survey of Consumer Expenditure in 1973[1] by assuming that the relative growth in nominal consumer expenditure was the same for every type of household from 1973 to 1975 and equal to 22 per cent. The data which have been available in practice give the income distribution by income brackets. The distribution by income levels presented in Table 4 assumes that all households in each income bracket have an income equal to the average income in that bracket. This distribution was also used in the revealed preference analysis. The total number of families with a given number of children used here is the average of the number at the end of 1974 and the number at the end of 1975 as reported in CBS (1975b) and CBS (1976a). Single supporters are simply excluded under the assumption that general child allowances are not determined out of consideration for these people who may be and are helped by special allowances.[2] The same thing applies to children in institu-

[1] See CBS (1975a).
[2] For instance, they receive allowances for a number of children which is one more than the actual number.

Table 4. *Percentage distribution of families with various numbers of children by income levels in 1975*

Number of children in the families, m	Disposable income, r								
	8 400	15 400	21 100	30 100	45 200	62 300	82 700	131 400	Σ
1	0.357	3.214	6.786	25.714	31.429	16.786	8.929	6.786	100
2	0.254	1.777	2.792	20.558	34.772	19.035	12.944	7.867	100
3	0	0.487	2.925	18.044	36.093	19.022	15.606	7.146	100
4 and more	0	1.188	2.386	17.854	36.906	19.052	15.479	7.146	100

Source: Christiansen & Jansen (1977), Table B.2. For more details and references to primary sources see also op. cit., pp. 31–32.

tions. The families with more than four children are added to the families with four children, and they are all treated as families with four children (in line with what was done in the revealed preference study). The error which may be committed because of this is commented on in Section IV.

The simultaneous distribution of families by disposable income and number of children is found by combining Tables 4 and 5.

It is neither manageable nor desirable to specify all the basic goods on which excise taxes are imposed. Therefore they are aggregated into 16 consumption categories. Choosing certain representative commodities within each group, a Laspeyres price index may be constructed for each group. If the excise taxes on all goods in a certain group were removed, the corresponding price index would change. We let the relative change in the price index define the excise rate on the index good as a share of consumer price, as was done in the revealed preference analysis; see Christiansen & Jansen (1977, pp. 22–26). Such indices have been established by the Central Bureau of Statistics of Norway; see CBS (1976b, p. 143). The weights of the indices are based on the Survey of Consumer Expenditure, 1973; see CBS (1975a). In the analysis all indices are normalized to unity in 1975. The quantities of the goods in 1975 are thus measured by current expenditure on the respective goods.

The consumption data which were used in the revealed preference study, and which are required to compute the expenditure derivatives needed in this study, are originally derived from the Survey of Consumer Expenditure 1973

Table 5. *Average distribution of families by number of children in 1975*

1	2	3	4 and more
192 361	191 609	86 759	34 020

Sources: CBS (1975b, Table 394) and CBS (1976a, Table 403).

Table 6. *Excise rates as a share of consumer price for the good categories included in the analysis*

Category	Excise rate as a share of consumer price, s^i
Flour and grains	−0.8192
Bread, cake, etc.	−0.1104
Meat and eggs	−0.2740
Fish	−0.1144
Canned foods	−0.2024
Milk, cream, etc.	−0.7590
Cheese	−0.4302
Butter	−0.2652
Margarine, etc.	−0.2713
Chocolate	0.1760
Non-alcoholic beverages	0.1305
Beer	0.2955
Wine and liquor	0.7579
Tobacco	0.5414
Petrol and oil	0.4495
Cosmetic articles	0.2170

carried out by the Central Bureau of Statistics (CBS). The expenditure data were constructed by Erik Biørn and Erik Garaas of the CBS. Total consumption in the Survey of Consumer Expenditure is divided into 45 commodity groups; 16 of these are identical to the commodity groups included in this analysis. Biørn and Garaas employed a method of data reduction by fitting 45 expenditure functions—one for each commodity group—to the complete sample of household reports. Their next step was to use this condensed information on the structure of consumption in 1973 to make a projection of the corresponding consumption figures in 1975. For this purpose they relied on the Frisch method for estimating a complete set of price elasticities; see Frisch (1959). A detailed record is given in CBS (1976b).

The expenditure derivatives for various goods by household types and income levels to be used in this analysis are derived from the expenditure functions estimated by Biørn & Garaas.[1]

IV. Empirical Results and Comments

The main purpose of the empirical analysis is to assign empirical values to the shadow prices $\mu_1, ..., \mu_4$ in formula (19). One problem was that firm knowledge about labor supply reactions is practically non-existent. Since possible effects on relative shadow prices may—as far as we know—go in

[1] I am indebted to Erik Biørn for providing necessary data for this project.

Table 7. *Computed marginal propensities to pay excise taxes, b_j*

Average figures for families with at least j children

b_1	b_2	b_3	b_4
0.018	0.017	0.014	0.009

either direction, we chose the simplest solution to the problem by assuming away possible labor supply reactions. This approach is to some extent supported by the fact that the usual judgement in Norway seems to be that such reactions are not of great importance. Later on we discuss whether reasonable effects on work effort may convert our results. We now set $L_T = 0$.

The marginal propensities to pay taxes are then reduced to marginal propensities to pay excise taxes. We may begin by presenting these figures separately since they may be interesting as such.

We observe that the average marginal net propensities to pay excise taxes differ between household categories. The larger the household, the lower the marginal net propensity to pay excise taxes. The reason is that larger households are less inclined to use marginal income on goods which are subject to (positive) excise taxes and more inclined to use marginal income on subsidized goods than smaller households.

We also observe that the marginal tax propensities are quite small. Only about 1 to 2 per cent of a marginal income unit is paid out as net excise tax.[1] The effects on the shadow values of child allowances are therefore likely to be small.

An implication of these two observations is that reallocation of child allowances towards larger households will reduce the inefficiency of existing distortions, but the effect will be very small.

Since it may be interesting to single out the effect of taking excise taxes into account, we present two sets of computed shadow values of child allowances, one which includes excise taxes, and one which excludes them. The shadow values are found by applying the data presented in Section III to formula (19); see Table 8. The values obtained by setting $s \equiv 0$, i.e. $b_j \equiv 0$, are indicated by superscript o. Relative figures may be more illustrating; see Table 9.

Even bearing in mind the likely presence of data errors, we seem justified in arguing that significant shadow price discrepancies prevail given the implicit welfare weights from the study of indirect taxation. This is especially true when families with three and more children are considered. Given the welfare weights used here, there would be a social gain from marginal realloca-

---

[1] If we deducted the non-distortionary part of some excise taxes levied in order to reflect social costs, the figures would be even smaller.

Table 8. *Computed shadow values of child allowances*

For actual excise taxes	For no excise taxes
$\mu_1 = 1.017$	$\mu_1^0 = 0.999$
$\mu_2 = 1.053$	$\mu_2^0 = 1.036$
$\mu_3 = 1.139$	$\mu_3^0 = 1.125$
$\mu_4 = 1.264$	$\mu_4^0 = 1.252$

tion of child allowances towards larger families. For example, the gain from reallocating one unit from allowances for the first child to allowances for the fourth child, would be equivalent to a family of two adults with an income of 30 100 receiving a gift of approximately 0.25 income units. (Recall that welfare is measured in marginal income units for this type of household.) If a marginal income unit is reallocated from allowances for the first child to allowances for the second child, its welfare contribution will increase by 3.5 per cent, and if reallocated to allowances for the third child, it will contribute 12 per cent more to social welfare.

When we compare $\mu_1, ..., \mu_4$ with $\mu_1^0, ..., \mu_4^0$, we see that the effect of taking distortionary excise taxes into account is almost negligible. This is a useful piece of information since excise taxes complicate the formulae, the data collecting and the computations significantly. When interested in numerical values, we may just as well consider $\mu_1^0, ..., \mu_4^0$ when convenient.

It may be argued that our figures underestimate the welfare effects by treating families with more than four children as if they had only four. If a term were added to allow for this argument, it would clearly add Δ/N_1 to μ_1^0, Δ/N_2 to μ_2^0 and so on. As N_k decreases with k, the addition would increase with k, and this would only make the shadow price differences even more substantial.

The welfare weights used here stem from the main variant (Variant II) of the revealed preference study. In another variant (Variant III) implicit equivalent income scales were also estimated (in addition to the parameters mentioned before) to replace Bojer's figures reported in Table 2. It may be interesting to know that the corresponding distributive weights show greater differences between household sizes, and are thus more favorable to larger

Table 9. *Computed relative shadow values of child allowances*

For actual excise taxes	For no excise taxes
$\mu_2/\mu_1 = 1.035$	$\mu_2^0/\mu_1^0 = 1.037$
$\mu_3/\mu_1 = 1.120$	$\mu_3^0/\mu_1^0 = 1.126$
$\mu_3/\mu_1 = 1.243$	$\mu_4^0/\mu_1^0 = 1.253$

households.[1] If these implicit welfare weights are applied in the computation of $\mu_1, ..., \mu_4$, shadow price discrepancies are considerably enlarged. However, we regard Variant III of the revealed preference study mostly as an experiment with very uncertain estimates, which does not warrant strong positive conclusions. What we can conclude with respect to our interest in this context is that there is no evidence to suggest that the shadow value discrepancies reported above arise because the applied equivalent income scales deviate from those which are actually (implicitly) used in tax policy. The suggestion is rather that discrepancies are underestimated.

If distribution policy by commodity taxation and by child allowances were designed on the basis of consistent welfare maximization, the welfare weights which make commodity taxation optimal would also make child allowances optimal. However, as far as the underlying assumptions are accepted, *our findings strongly indicate that from the point of view of welfare maximization the actual use of child allowances is inconsistent with the actual use of excise taxes and subsidies in distribution policy.*

An interesting question is whether actual child allowances could be justified by special welfare considerations which are omitted from the analysis. Throughout the analysis arguments related to population policy have been left out. Let us try and see how this might have affected the results if it had been desirable to keep down population growth. The total grant for child allowances would then have been lower than it would otherwise have been. What has been analyzed above, however, is the allocation of a given amount of tax revenue to be paid out as child allowances. It is more difficult to say how this allocation would have been affected. It may seem reasonable to assume that most families want to have one or two children without giving much attention to economic incentives, whereas decisions about whether to have more children are likely to be more sensitive to economic incentives. This may be a possible reason for being more moderate in giving child allowances to larger families than one would expect from distribution considerations.

On the other hand, we cannot expect all families to be optimizing. Since lack of optimization will normally lead to too many children, it may seem reasonable to assume that the proportion of non-optimizing families, whose behavior is rather insensitive to economic incentives, increases with size category. This would clearly be an argument in the opposite direction.

My conjecture is, however, that considerations about possible effects on the number of children have not been essential in designing distribution policy. If they had been, they should not only have been allowed for in analyses of child allowances, but, of course, also in analyses of subsidies and commodity taxes. Then our estimates of implicit welfare weights in the system of indirect taxation would also have been affected.

---

[1] Christiansen & Jansen (1978, Table 3).

It has been assumed that the allocation of child allowances is not influenced by (dis)incentives to work effort, as there is very little knowledge about such effects. We now deal with this problem in more detail. It may be that a family with few children is less constrained in its choice of work effort, and therefore more sensitive to economic incentives in choice of work effort than a family with a greater number of children.[1] If this were true, more care would be taken not to give disincentives to work effort to families with few children than to families with more children. This would strengthen the argument for higher allowances to larger families and lower allowances to smaller families.

On the other hand, it may be argued that supporters of larger families may feel a greater need to work overtime or take extra jobs, which is the kind of work effort that is likely to be more sensitive to economic incentives than more regular working hours. This would be an argument in the opposite direction. Another argument in this direction is that larger families on the average pay somewhat higher marginal tax rates because of higher income.

As we have seen, it makes practically no difference whether or not excise taxes (positive and negative) are taken into account. This will certainly be true even if we allow some change in labor supply. Let us therefore forget about excise taxes for the moment, i.e. set $s \equiv 0$.

We can now calculate what the effects via disincentives to work effort would have to be in order to make actual child allowances optimal given the implicit welfare weights. To simplify in the following exposition we define:

$$d_j = \sum_k \sum_{m=j}^{M} F' q_k L_T n_{k,m}/N_j. \tag{22}$$

From (14) we see that $d_j = -b_j$ (when $s \equiv 0$), and from (19) we have:

$$\mu_j = \mu_j^0/(1+d_j). \tag{23}$$

$(1+d_j)$ is the average *total* change in tax payment from families with at least j children when a marginal head tax unit is imposed, i.e. the sum of the head tax unit and the induced change in tax payment because of labor supply reactions. Equality of shadow values now requires that

$$\mu_j^0/(1+d_j) = \mu_1^0/(1+d_1)$$

or

$$\frac{1+d_j}{1+d_1} = \frac{\mu_j^0}{\mu_1^0} \quad \forall_j. \tag{24}$$

The required values of these fractions are already known from Table 9. We see for instance that $1+d_3$ must exceed $1+d_1$ by 12.6 per cent, and $1+d_4$ must exceed $1+d_1$ by 25.3 per cent. These are substantial differences in average

[1] This is especially relevant when the working opportunities of both parents are considered.

tax reactions between the various types of households. Suppose that $1 + d_1 = 1.2$, then it is required that $1 + d_4 \simeq 1.5$. That is, if a marginal head tax unit induces households with at least one child (including those with four and more children) to increase their work effort so as to pay 0.2 units extra income tax, it must induce households with at least four children to increase their work effort so as to pay 0.5 units extra income tax.

We see that in order to have the actual policy as optimal given the implicit welfare weights, larger households must be assumed to increase their tax payments in response to a marginal head tax much more than smaller households. But in this case a warning is necessary in that the assumptions made about labor supply reactions in the revealed preference study[1] may have to be changed, thereby destroying some of the basis for the present analysis. However, there is no reason to believe that tax reactions increase substantially with household size. On the basis of the arguments considered above, differences between household categories may—as far as we know—go in either direction. In my judgement it is a plausible assumption in order to peg the gap in our data, that households of different size do not show very different tax reactions.

V. Conclusion

The most important aspect of this paper has been to demonstrate how implicit welfare weights from revealed social preference studies can be used in the process of policy assessment. We have explored whether the allocation of child allowances in Norway in 1975 was optimal according to implicit welfare weights derived from subsidy and excise tax policy, as it should be if the two categories of distribution policy were consistent. The results indicate that such optimality did not obtain, which implies that inconsistency is revealed.

References

Bojer, H.: The effect on consumption of household size and composition. *European Economic Review 9*, 169–194, 1977.

CBS: *Survey of consumer expenditure 1973.* NOS A705. Central Bureau of Statistics, Oslo, Norway, 1975a.

CBS: *Statistical Yearbook of Norway 1975*, Central Bureau of Statistics, Oslo, Norway, 1975b.

CBS: *Statistical Yearbook of Norway 1976*, Central Bureau of Statistics, Oslo, Norway, 1976a.

CBS: *Taxation of income and consumption from a distributional point of view—a model for empirical analysis.* (In Norwegian with an English summary.) Samfunnsøkonomiske Studier 30, Central Bureau of Statistics, Oslo, Norway, 1976b.

Christiansen, V.: A theoretical and empiri-

[1] It was assumed that the optimal structure of indirect taxation is not altered by neglecting labor supply reactions.

cal analysis of child allowances. *Memorandum from the Institute of Economics,* University of Oslo, 15 October 1978 *a.*

Christiansen, V.: The social welfare function as a compromise. *Memorandum from the Institute of Economics,* University of Oslo, 15 December 1978 *b.*

Christiansen, V. & Jansen, E. S.: Implicit social preferences in the Norwegian system of indirect taxation. *Memorandum from the Institute of Economics,* University of Oslo, 13 August 1977.

Christiansen, V. & Jansen, E. S.: Implicit social preferences in the Norwegian system of indirect taxation. *Journal of Public Economics 10,* 217–245, 1978.

Frisch, R.: A complete scheme for computing all direct and cross demand elasticities in a model with many sectors. *Econometrica 27,* 177–196, 1959.

Johansen, L.: Establishing preference functions for decision models. Some observations on Ragnar Frisch's contributions. *European Economic Review 5,* 41–66, 1974.

Stern, N. H.: Welfare weights and the elasticity of the marginal valuation of income. In *Studies in modern economic analysis: The proceedings of the AUTE Conference in Edinburgh 1976* (ed. M. J. Artis and A. R. Nobay). Blackwell, Oxford, 1977.

DISTRIBUTIONAL OBJECTIVES SHOULD AFFECT TAXES BUT NOT PROGRAM CHOICE OR DESIGN

Aanund Hylland and Richard Zeckhauser *

Harvard University, Cambridge, Mass., USA

Abstract

A society can redistribute income through the tax system, and through the choice and design of government programs. Neither type of redistribution is as efficient as lump-sum transfers would be, if feasible. In practice, however, both taxes and government programs serve redistributional goals. The question becomes how best to integrate them to achieve an optimal outcome, maximizing the redistributional effect for a given efficiency cost. The following conclusions are reached. If total benefits are independent of the income distribution and relative benefits are determined by before or after-tax income, those projects that yield the greatest total of unweighted benefits across the population should be selected. If benefits depend on the distribution of income, the optimal program will be one which produces maximal net benefits at the income distribution which is being induced. Redistribution is a concern, but is carried out solely through the tax system.

I. Introduction

A society can redistribute income through the tax system, and through the choice and design of government programs. Neither type of redistribution is as efficient as lump-sum transfers would be, if feasible. In practice, however, both taxes and government programs serve redistributional goals. The question becomes how best to integrate them to achieve an optimal outcome, maximizing the redistributional effect for a given efficiency cost.

The design of a society's tax schemes and other government programs should perhaps be thought of as a constrained maximization problem. It could take various forms—for instance, provide the minimum acceptable level of welfare to each citizen at the least cost to the citizens who would be providing resources. Or, given the political and financial constraint imposed by the willingness of non-poor citizens to redistribute funds, generate the maximum welfare level for the poor. On the other hand, a society may make these decisions as if it were maximizing some social welfare function and therefore making trade-

* Hylland's work is supported by a fellowship from the Norwegian Research Council for Science and the Humanities (NAVF); Zeckhauser's work is supported by NSF Grant SOC 77-16602 to Harvard University. Albert Nichols gave us helpful comments.

offs among the welfares of different groups. In any case, the pursuit of optimality in redistribution is critical to more fundamental normative investigations: Given some criterion of social welfare, derived perhaps from philosophical investigation, but in any case for our analysis assumed to be exogenously given, how should the potential institutions of society for transferring resources be arranged?

A fundamental issue in the literature on the expenditure side of public finance has been how to take account of distributional consequences in the choice and design of government programs. This problem is a subsidiary question in our more general analysis of optimality in redistribution. The central question we shall pursue is how to design taxes and government programs to maximize any arbitrary criterion for social welfare. This formulation is sufficiently general to include any of the problems mentioned above.

This paper adopts the approach of the optimal income tax literature in a number of respects. It assumes that individuals have differentiated ability levels which affect their opportunities for earning, that is, their wage rates. It assumes that each individual will react in a rational, self-interested manner to whatever system of taxes and government programs is enacted. Income, but neither leisure nor ability, can be observed and taxed. The formal model on which the optimal income tax theory is based is presented in Section II, where we also comment briefly on the theory and some results from the literature.

We have diverged from optimal income tax discussions in making government programs a major element of our model. To do so, we have assumed that benefits from such programs can be converted into an increased income equivalent. This increased income equivalent is computed assuming that an individual's money income is known.

The government programs we consider have distributional consequences; that is, benefits depend on income. This suggests as well that these programs have redistributional capabilities.

In our principal model we assume that the total of benefits all individuals receive from a particular program is independent of the income distribution in society. This total may depend on the ability distribution, which is exogenously given. For a particular program, the relative levels of benefits for various income groups are assumed to be known or derivable.

The critical question is how to design expenditure and tax programs in concert so as to maximize the social welfare criterion. Intuition might suggest that redistributional purposes should be pursued in both areas. That is, in addition to implementing a tax mechanism that promotes redistribution, a government program which is somewhat inefficient in the sense that it does not maximize unweighted net benefits might nevertheless be adopted because of its distributional effects. For example, given that we are pursuing distributional objectives, it might seem reasonable, when choosing among governmental programs, to attach different weights to the benefits going to different income groups.[1]

For our model, we prove this intuitive conclusion wrong. In the optimal arrangement, distributional objectives are achieved through the tax system alone. Government programs are chosen solely on the basis of efficiency criteria, that is, total net benefits are maximized. Individuals' benefits from the government programs are then taken account of, in a straightforward way, through design of the tax system. The proof of this result is not difficult and can be readily grasped, although the conclusion, we believe, runs contrary to the conventional wisdom in most liberal democracies.

It is often argued that we should redistribute through taxes rather than government programs because the latter entail great inefficiencies in the form of administrative costs or giving individuals goods they would not themselves have purchased. Whatever the merits of these arguments, they are irrelevant in our analysis, since we examine programs on the basis of net cash-equivalent benefits to individuals.

Our result holds regardless of whether the benefits an individual receives depend on income before or after taxes (Section V). There are various cases in which the arguments do not apply or only apply in part (Section VI); further study is needed here to see if related results can be obtained. These cases include those in which:

(*a*) Total benefits from a program depend on the income distribution.

(*b*) Benefits to an individual depend on ability, instead of or in addition to income.

(*c*) Benefits from programs are complementary to leisure, that is, the money-equivalent benefit may depend on the amount of leisure consumed as well as on income.

(*d*) Benefits depend on income in a non-deterministic way, so that there are differences in the benefits the members of an income group receive.

Our model does not consider a number of political factors which are important in real-life decision making with respect to redistribution. Some of these factors are discussed in Section VII.

II. The Theory of Optimal Taxation

The idea that the income tax scheme should be designed so as to maximize total social utility (or some more general function of individual utilities), is an old one. Musgrave (1959), Chapter 5, reviews the classical discussion,

---

[1] There is a rich literature within economics, indeed an entire subfield of the expenditure side of public finance theory, which pursues this mode of approach. Sometimes efficiency and distributional benefits are separated; other times total benefits are simply computed on a weighted basis. Much of this literature seems to be based on an assumption like the one mentioned in the text. (Other interpretations are possible, because the tax system need not be treated as a control variable.)

describing various criteria of social welfare, or equivalently, various ways of measuring the total sacrifice imposed by the tax levy. In general, this literature does not consider the possible effects of the tax system on people's choices of how much to work. The contribution of the modern optimal income tax theory has been to take this effect explicitly into account. Zeckhauser (1969) pursued this approach and solved the problem in a simple case. Mirrlees (1971) and Fair (1971) attacked the problem on a higher level of generality, and from their works an entire literature has emerged. We follow the tradition established in this literature in presenting the basic model.

Individuals are characterized by a single non-negative parameter, called ability and denoted a. The number a is the productivity of one unit of the person's labor. We assume perfectly competitive labor markets, so that the person is also paid a per unit of labor. Individuals know their own ability, but ability cannot be observed by the government and hence cannot be made the basis for taxation or other administrative decisions. The distribution of ability in the population is known; we assume that the distribution is absolutely continuous with density function f and finite expectation.[1] An individual derives utility from consumption goods and leisure. We assume that the effect on utility of all consumer goods can be captured by making after-tax income, denoted x, an argument of the utility function.[2] The effect of leisure is accounted for by making the amount of labor provided, y, an argument. Hence the utility function is of the form $u(x, y)$; it is the same for all individuals and is defined for all $x > 0$ and $0 \leqslant y < 1$. (The restriction on y amounts to choosing the unit of labor such that 1 is the physical maximum. When the unit of ability is chosen, the unit of income is then given.) The function is assumed to be strictly increasing in x, strictly decreasing in y, strictly concave and continuously differentiable; $\lim_{x \to 0+} u(x, y) = -\infty$ for all y and $\lim_{y \to 1-} u(x, y) = -\infty$ for all x.

The government raises revenue by taxing individuals. An individual's gross income is the only variable which can be observed by the government and which therefore can be made the basis for taxation. This income can be observed without error. Let T be the tax scheme; then a person with ability a who provides y units of labor has a gross income of ay and pays a tax of $T(ay)$. We write $z = ay$ for gross income and allow $T(z)$ to be positive or negative. A negative value of $T(z)$ represents a welfare grant or subsidy.[3]

---

[1] The continuity assumption is made in order to simplify notation and is not essential.

[2] This assumption clearly holds in an economy with only one private good. For economies with many private goods, the utility function in our model must be interpreted as an indirect utility function; it is based on the assumption that people chose an optimal bundle of private goods for any level of after-tax income. An alternative model, not considered here, would have the utility function depend directly on consumption of the various goods.

[3] A negative $T(z)$ for low values of z is a feature of many existing tax and welfare systems. It is usually referred to as a welfare grant or the like, but could as well be called a "negative income tax", a term that seems more natural in the context of our model.

When the tax schedule is given, the utility-maximizing individual with ability a will face the following problem:

Find y with $0 \leqslant y < 1$ to maximize $u(ay - T(ay), y)$.   (1)

The way we have expressed the utility function, it is clear that all after-tax income will be consumed; hence y is the only decision variable. If the function T satisfies some weak conditions, this maximization problem will always have a solution.[1] We will also assume that the solution is unique. Let y_a be the optimal value; it obviously depends both on a and T. The optimal before-tax and after-tax income and utility level will be denoted $z_a = a y_a$, $x_a = z_a - T(z_a)$, and $u_a = u(x_a, y_a)$.

Revenue is required for programs outside the tax system. The revenue requirement is exogenously given and equal to R. Presumably, $R > 0$; it is not necessary, however, to assume this. (One can imagine the government having other sources of income, so that the income tax system can be allowed to run a deficit.) T must be chosen so that the net revenue from the income tax system is at least R, that is

$$\int_0^\infty T(z_a) f(a) \, da \geqslant R,$$ (2)

where z_a depends on a as described above.

The government's objective is represented by some criterion of social welfare, which depends on everybody's utility level. For simplicity of notation, we assume that the criterion can be expressed by some social welfare function; hence the government's objective is to

maximize $\Phi(u_a; a \geqslant 0)$ (3)

for a given function Φ. Note that the argument of Φ is the infinite-dimensional vector of numbers u_a for $a \geqslant 0$. Later, we will write $\bar{u}$ for this argument.[2] The formulation (3) is quite general, but it does imply that social welfare depends only on individuals' utilities and abilities. It does not depend directly on income and amount of labor provided. We expect Φ to be monotone, that is, $\Phi(\bar{u}) \geqslant \Phi(\bar{u}')$ if $u_a \geqslant u_a'$ for all $a \geqslant 0$. (Not all arguments below depend on monotonicity of Φ, however.)

In the discussion below, we are not actually going to compute optimal tax schemes; hence we may as well keep the general formulation (3) of the social welfare function. Some comments about possible forms of the functions are, however, in order.

---

[1] Continuity of T will suffice; for a weaker sufficient condition, see Mirrlees (1971) p. 177.
[2] Formally, the argument is a function from the set of non-negative real numbers into the real numbers; thus Φ itself is a functional. Of course, the criterion of social welfare should be allowed to depend not only on the numbers u_a, but also on how many people have each ability level a. Since the latter is exogenously given (by the function f), it can be incorporated into the functional form Φ.

For one thing, the different versions of constrained maximization problems mentioned in the introduction can be expressed in this model. One possibility is to construct Φ so that it has negative values when the constraint is not satisfied and non-negative values when it is satisfied, while it otherwise represents the chosen social welfare criterion. (In general, this implies that Φ will have a discontinuity corresponding to the constraint.) Alternatively, we can carry an explicit constraint through the entire argument below. It should be noted that the introduction of a constraint, in either of the two formulations, adds to the computational problems of actually finding optimal tax schemes, but does not raise any basic conceptual issues.

Possible Incorporation of Altruistic Concerns. Our assumptions concerning the form of the utility function u imply that everybody is completely selfish. This assumption, however, is not essential for the subsequent discussion. Under an alternative interpretation, u can be viewed not as a utility function capturing everything which is relevant to the individual, but merely as an index of personal satisfaction. The person's utility is then given by $v = v(u_e, \bar{u}_{-e})$, where u_e is the person's own level of satisfaction, and $\bar{u}_{-e}$ is the vector of these levels for everybody else. The function v specifies the degree of selfishness; one extreme case is given by $v(u_e, \bar{u}_{-e}) = u_e$, at the other extreme, u_e contributes to the functional value in exactly the same way as any component of $\bar{u}_{-e}$. It is assumed that the functional forms of u and v are the same for everybody, and that v is increasing in u_e and treats the components of $\bar{u}_{-e}$ symmetrically. This does not mean that the level of satisfaction of everybody else in any sense must be given equal weight; it is quite possible, for example, to pay more attention to the less well off. But the identity of other individuals cannot be taken into account. Neither can v depend directly on the consumption of goods and leisure of other people; only their satisfaction levels matter.

In this setting, the rational individual will still choose y according to (1). This is so because the individual in no way controls $\bar{u}_{-e}$; hence maximizing v is equivalent to maximizing u. The social objective would be to

$$\text{maximize } \Psi'(v_a; a \geqslant 0) = \Psi'(\bar{v}) \tag{3'}$$

for some function Ψ', where v_a is the utility level achieved by a person of ability a when everybody acts according to (1). The number v_a depends on the entire vector $\bar{u}$. The vector of numbers v_a for $a \geqslant 0$ is denoted $\bar{v}$.

The formulation (3'), however, is no more general than (3). For given v and Ψ', one can simply set $\Phi(\bar{u}) = \Psi'(\bar{v})$, which is well-defined by the symmetry assumption we have imposed on the function v. Monotonicity of Φ implies some restrictions on the functions v and Ψ'; these will, for example, be satisfied if Ψ' is monotone in $\bar{v}$ and $v = v(u_e, \bar{u}_{-e})$ is monotone in $\bar{u}_{-e}$. The latter condition rules out such possibilities as $v(u_e, \bar{u}_{-e})$ depending on the relative position of u_e among the components of $\bar{u}_{-e}$.

The Expected Utility Approach or Utilitarianism. Classical utilitarianism corresponds to

$$\Phi(\bar{u}) = \int_0^\infty u_a f(a) \, da \tag{4}$$

This is the criterion by which people would evaluate tax rules if they were ignorant of their own ability and knew only the probability distribution f, provided that u really captures everything which matters to the individual and represents attitude towards risk. That is, u must be a von Neumann–Morgenstern utility function. (Elsewhere in the paper we need only assume that u is a value function representing preferences under certainty.) This contractual formulation does not correspond to any real-world decision-making situation. In practice, at the time decisions are made, much of the uncertainty about an individual's ability has been resolved. Assuming self interest, those who thus far have been fortunate will favor a less progressive tax scheme and vice versa. A question of importance for both policy and philosophical investigation is: To what extent should arguments about this hypothetical "state of ignorance" influence real-world decision-making?[1]

Preference for Equality. The utilitarian formulation does not rule out a preference for equality; such a preference emerges if u exhibits risk aversion in income and hours of work. What is ruled out, is a desire for equality over and above what is implied by risk aversion. Such an additional preference for equality (or for more general distributional criteria) is captured by using the formulation involving the function v. The social welfare function is then given by

$$\Psi'(\bar{v}) = \int_0^\infty v_a f(a) \, da. \tag{4'}$$

This is a special case of (3') and therefore of (3), but it is more general than (4). In particular, (5)–(7) below can be obtained from (4') by appropriate choice of v.[2]

If we want to promote equality as such, whether justified by an argument like the one behind formula (4') or in some other way, we should pay more attention to the u-values of the less fortunate. This can be achieved by using a social welfare function of the form

$$\Phi(\bar{u}) = \int_0^\infty u_a g(a) f(a) \, da, \tag{5}$$

where g is a positive and decreasing weighting function,[3] or

$$\Phi(\bar{u}) = \int_0^\infty h(u_a) f(a) \, da, \tag{6}$$

---

[1] See Zeckhauser (1974) for some discussion of this issue.

[2] Harsanyi (1977), Chapter 4, argues that social welfare functions should always be of the form (4').

[3] It is easy to see that $a > a'$ implies $u_a > u_{a'}$; therefore, giving more weight to individuals with low ability implies giving more weight to the utility of the less fortunate.

where h is increasing and concave. A limiting case of (5) and (6) is the maximin rule, given by

$$\Phi(\bar{u}) = u_0, \tag{7}$$

provided that there exist individuals with ability arbitrarily close to 0.[1]

The Solution. When the social welfare function has been specified, the government's problem is: For given u and R, find the tax scheme T which maximizes (3) subject to (1) and (2). This is not at all a trivial problem, as the literature on the subject clearly shows. In general, we do not even know that an optimal solution exists.[2] In a sense, our discussion below presupposes that this problem has been solved. But this is not as important a restriction as it may seem. Provided that there is an upper bound on the achievable values of Φ, our results will essentially hold even if one can only find tax schemes which approximate the upper bound on Φ, which is likely to be an easier problem. See discussion at the end of Section III below.

The model just described makes strong simplifying assumptions. In addition to more formal simplifications, some of these are: Differences in tastes are ignored. The population is fixed; hence in and out migration is assumed to be impossible. Income can be perfectly observed, and the cost of administering the system is independent of the tax scheme. The time frame is ignored, and no attention is paid to the problem of defining the consumption unit. Finally, and perhaps most importantly, the work/leisure choice is assumed to be a pure problem of utility maximization, and productivity and wage rates are independent of the choices people actually make. This rules out, for example, any kind of institutional constraints such as standard working hours, or a feedback between hours worked and productivity.

Therefore, conclusions drawn from the model should not be interpreted as firm policy recommendations, but rather as indications of what an optimal solution might look like and how it will depend on the parameters. For further discussion of the problems and for a number of results in special cases, we refer to Mirrlees (1971), Fair (1971), Atkinson (1973) and Feldstein (1973).

III. Government Programs with Income-related Benefits

The general question we want to ask is: What is the optimal simultaneous choice of tax schemes and government programs when the latter have distributional effects? In this section, we address the simpler problem of designing the

---

[1] In general, we can define $a_0 = \inf \{a \mid \int_0^a f(\alpha) d\alpha > 0\}$. The number a_0 is then essentially the lowest existing ability, and the maximin social welfare function is $\Phi(\bar{u}) = u_{a_0}$.

[2] Mirrlees considers social welfare criteria of the form (6), of which (4) is a special case. From relatively weak conditions on the utility function u, he succeeds in proving the existence of an optimal tax scheme and deriving some general properties. But more specific results are obtained only when particular forms of u are assumed. Other authors have simplified the problem by restricting T to particular functional forms. Thus they derive, for example, the optimal linear tax scheme.

tax scheme when the government program is given. Here we assume that the benefits people derive from the program depend on before-tax income. The case of benefits depending on after-tax income is technically a little more complicated, and is considered in Section V.

A government program P is characterized by: B, a real number, representing the total (monetary) benefits from the program; C, a real number, representing the costs to the government of implementing the program; β, a function, defined for all $z \geqslant 0$, such that $\beta(z)$ represents the relative benefit from the program to a person whose before-tax income is z, as described in eqs. (8) and (9) below. (Since β represents relative benefits, nothing is changed if all values of β are multiplied by some positive constant.)

The entities are supposed to represent net benefits and costs; hence we can include in the model activities which are partially financed by user fees or the like. Our terminology might be thought to imply that B, C and $\beta(z)$ are all non-negative, but nothing in the formal derivations requires that this be the case. Therefore, we can also include programs which save money for the government by imposing income-related costs on individuals.[1]

We have defined β as a *relative* benefit function since we assume that B, the total program benefits, is fixed. If $\beta(z)$ were defined as the absolute value of benefits to a person with gross income z, the implication would be that the total benefits produced by the program would depend on the income distribution; in particular, if β has a maximum at z_0, total benefits could be increased by more people earning z_0. (Note that the income distribution is endogenous, it is determined by individual optimization according to (1) when the tax scheme is given.) We assume instead that the total benefits to all individuals are constant and independent of the income distribution. That is, we assume that some kind of a divide-the-spoils or congestion effect occurs if there is an increase in the number of people in the income group which receives the highest relative benefits from the program. (A more general formulation is discussed in Section VI.)

In an individual's utility, the benefits from the program are supposed to have the same effect as an increase in income proportional to $\beta(z)$, where z is before-tax income. (It does not matter whether the benefit is added to before-tax or after-tax income.) If z_a is the before-tax income of a person with ability a, that person's benefits will be

$$b(z_a) = b_0 \beta(z_a),\tag{8}$$

where b_0 is a number which satisfies

$$\int_0^\infty b_0 \beta(z_a) f(a)\, da = B.\tag{9}$$

---

[1] The military draft can perhaps be seen as such a program.

When a tax scheme T' and the function b of benefits are given, an individual with ability a will choose the amount of work to provide by solving the problem[1]

Find y with $0 \leqslant y < 1$ to maximize $u(ay - T'(ay) + b(ay), y)$.   (10)

As before, let y_a be the solution to this maximization problem for a given a, and let z_a, x_a and u_a be optimal before-tax income, after-tax income and utility. If the government's revenue requirements for other purposes than the program under consideration are R_0, the tax scheme must be chosen so that

$$\int_0^\infty T'(z_a) f(a) \, da \geqslant R_0 + C.$$ (11)

When the tax scheme T' is given, the benefit function and the income distribution will be mutually dependent on each other through eqs. (10) and (8)–(9); hence they must be determined simultaneously. When they are computed, we can check whether (11) holds. Alternatively, we can say that the functions T' and b, the constant b_0 and the income distribution must be chosen simultaneously so as to satisfy (8)–(11).

As before, the objective is to maximize a certain social welfare function given by (3) or one of the special forms (4)–(7). The achievable levels of social welfare with and without the program P, are related in the following way.

Proposition 1. Connection between tax schemes in the presence and absence of programs

Let u, B, C, β and R_0 be as described above. Suppose that T is a tax scheme such that in the absence of P, (2) is satisfied with $R = R_0 - B + C$. Then there exists a scheme T' which satisfies (8)–(11) such that every individual reaches equal utility levels when T' is used and P is implemented and when T is used and P is not implemented. Conversely, if T' satisfies (8)–(11), there exists a T which raises at least $R_0 - B + C$ in revenue when P does not exist, such that T without P and T' with P leads to the same utility level for everybody.

Proof

Let T be given. Via (1), T induces an income distribution $\tilde{z} = (z_a; a \geqslant 0)$. Compute b_0 and b from this distribution by (9) and (8). Define, for all $z \geqslant 0$,

$$T'(z) = T(z) + b(z).$$ (12)

Now (1) and (10) are exactly the same expressions for all values of a and y. Hence the solution is the same for each a, and T and T' will induce the same

---

[1] The formulation assumes that the individual regards the function b as constant, although in fact b depends on people's behavior via (8) and (9). This corresponds to the usual assumption in economics of price-taking or competitive behavior, an assumption which is reasonable when any one individual's action has only a negligible impact on society.

distribution of gross income. Therefore, (8) and (9) hold when the income distribution resulting from T' is used. By assumption, (2) holds with $R = R_0 - B + C$; hence (9) and (12) imply (11). Finally, it is clear from (1) and (10) that the resulting utility level u_a is the same under the two regimes, for any a.

Conversely, assume that T' satisfies (8)–(11) for some constant b_0 and some function b. Define $T(z) = T'(z) - b(z)$. Again, expressions (1) and (10) become equal, and an argument similar to the one used above will apply. The proof is complete.

Hence the problem of finding an optimal tax scheme in the presence of a government project with income-related benefits is reduced to the corresponding problem in the absence of such programs. As has been pointed out earlier, the latter problem is non-trivial. If the set of achievable values of Φ is bounded from above, it may be substantially easier to find tax schemes which approximate the least upper bound of the set. By Proposition 1, the set of achievable values of Φ must be the same in the situation with the program and in the appropriate situation without it, and an approximation of the upper bound in the latter case can immediately be transformed into an equally good approximation in the former case.

Then one can ask whether such approximations represent a satisfactory solution to the optimization problem, and whether the condition that the achievable range of Φ be bounded from above is an important restriction. (This question applies equally well to the original optimal income tax problem as to our extension of it.) If we view Φ solely as a representation of our ordinal preferences on social utility distributions, then this restriction is vacuous; it is always possible to find an order-preserving transformation of Φ which makes it bounded. But if Φ is interpreted this way, it is not at all clear that approximating the upper bound on Φ in any real sense implies coming close to an optimal solution. We would, on the other hand, like to interpret Φ as some kind of cardinal measure of social welfare, however vaguely that concept might be defined. Then the boundedness condition follows from assuming that society's resources and ability to achieve its goals are limited, an assumption probably accepted by most people. Under this interpretation, one can reasonably claim that approximate solutions of the type considered here are satisfactory.

IV. Comparison of Alternative Programs

Now assume that P_1 and P_2 are two programs of the type described in the previous section, characterized by numbers and functions B_1, C_1, β_1 and B_2, C_2, β_2, respectively. The functions β_1 and β_2 can be different, hence the two programs can distribute the benefits in widely different ways among income groups. The general form of our social welfare function (3) allows us to differentially evaluate benefits to different income groups; in particular, we are allowed to put a higher weight on benefits to people who are relatively worse off. Our major result is that in spite of this, if optimal taxation is available we should choose between competing government programs P_1 and P_2 solely on basis of their net benefits $B_1 - C_1$ and $B_2 - C_2$.

Proposition 2. Comparison of alternative programs

Let programs P_1 and P_2 be given, and assume $B_1 - C_1 \geqslant B_2 - C_2$. Then the optimal social welfare level which can be achieved under P_1 is at least as high as the optimal level under P_2.

Proof

This is immediate from Proposition 1. Suppose that a certain level ϕ of social welfare can be achieved under P_2, and let T'' be the corresponding tax scheme. By the second half of Proposition 1, a tax scheme T exists which satisfies (2) with $R = R_0 - B_2 + C_2$ and which, in the absence of both programs P_1 and P_2, gives all individuals the same utility level as they get in the situation with P_2 and T''. Hence the social welfare level when T is used is ϕ. By assumption, $R_0 - B_1 + C_1 \leqslant R_0 - B_2 + C_2$; hence T also satisfies (2) with $R = R_0 - B_1 + C_1$. The first half of Proposition 1 then implies the existence of a tax scheme T' which, when P_1 is implemented, produces social welfare level ϕ. The optimal level under P_1 is therefore at least ϕ. The proof is complete.

In fact, we have proved something which is stronger than the statement of Proposition 2, namely the following: Let $B_1 - C_1 \geqslant B_2 - C_2$, and let $\bar{u}''$ be any vector of individual utility levels which can be achieved under P_2 and some tax system T''. Then there exists a tax system T' such that the vector of individual utility levels becomes $\bar{u}'$ under P_1 and T', and $u_a' \geqslant u_a''$ for all a.

Formally, Proposition 2 only considers the comparison between two alternative programs. But the result implies the existence of a consistent way of ranking mutually exclusive programs. An optimal decision rule will simply be: Choose the program with highest net benefits. Alternative ways of designing what is basically the same project can formally be seen as different programs; therefore, the result also implies that when designing a project, the configuration which maximizes net benefits should be chosen. The alternative "no program" can be viewed as one element of the set of alternative programs; it is characterized by $B = C = 0$ and β arbitrary. If we are presented with a set of potential government programs which are not mutually exclusive, we can let every technically feasible subset of this set be a "program" in the sense of our model. This allows for complementarities in benefits and costs among the original programs, as long as all composite programs fit the model of Section III.

One can ask whether a program with higher net benefits actually leads to a higher achievable social welfare level. This is equivalent to asking whether a relaxation of the constraint (2) in the ordinary optimal income tax problem leads to a strict increase in the optimal value of (3). Under reasonable conditions on u and Φ this will be the case. We will not state and prove any formal result to this effect but only argue informally that it is likely to be true: Let T satisfy (2) for a given R, and let $r > 0$ be the amount by which the revenue requirement is reduced. For some small number $t > 0$, define T^* by $T^*(z) = T(z) - t$ for all z. If T^* is substituted for T and people do not change the amount of labor they provide, the revenue loss is t. Work decisions will in fact change, and this can increase the revenue loss. If individual decisions are continuous in t, the revenue loss is also continuous, and the loss can be restricted to r by choosing t small enough but positive. We assume that it is possible to choose t so that it depends only on r and not on T, at least as long as T is optimal or almost optimal. (This amounts to a regularity condition on u.) Everybody's utility has increased because of the change from T to T^*, and the increase is at least equivalent to a lump-sum monetary transfer of t. For all reasonable social welfare criteria, this leads to an increase in the value of Φ; in fact, it leads to an increase of at least ε, where $\varepsilon > 0$ depends only on t. (The latter, stronger statement holds for all the special forms (4)–(7).) If now T is chosen so that the value of Φ is closer than ε to the upper bound when the revenue requirement is R, then T^* demonstrates that the social welfare level increases strictly when the requirement is reduced to $R - r$.[1] Note that we have not assumed that there actually exist optimal tax schemes; we have only assumed that the optimum can be approximated.

Even if the argument of the previous paragraph fails, our main result is still true. Proposition 2 implies that maximizing net benefit is *an* optimal decision rule, though it need not be the only optimal rule.

V. Programs Whose Benefits Depend on After-Tax Income

In the model presented above, relative benefits from a program depend on before-tax income; alternatively one can assume that they are determined by after-tax income. Formally, this amounts to a change in eqs. (8)–(10) in Section III. If s_a is the after-tax income of a person with ability a, when a certain tax scheme T' is used and P is implemented, eqs. (8) and (9) are replaced by

$$b(s_a) = b_0 \beta(s_a), \tag{13}$$

where b_0 satisfies

$$\int_0^\infty b_0 \beta(s_a) f(a) \, da = B. \tag{14}$$

---

[1] This does not imply that the across-the-board tax cut represented by T^* is the optimal response to a reduction in required revenue; it is just one possible response which will increase social welfare.

A person with ability a must solve the following problem, which corresponds to (10):

Find y with $0 \leqslant y < 1$ to maximize
$$u(ay - T'(ay) + b(ay - T'(ay)), y). \qquad \left. \right\} \qquad (15)$$

In the same way as before, (13)–(15) and (11) should be viewed as a set of conditions which must be simultaneously satisfied by T', b, b_0 and the income distribution s_a.

Provided that β satisfies certain regularity conditions to be specified below, a result similar to Proposition 1 can now be proved. An equivalent of Proposition 2 then follows directly.

To outline the proof, let T satisfy the premise of the first half of Proposition 1. T induces a certain distribution of after-tax income, given by x_a for $a \geqslant 0$. For a given number $b_0 \geqslant 0$, find s_a for $a \geqslant 0$ such that

$$s_a + b_0 \beta(s_a) = x_a. \qquad (16)$$

If β is continuous and bounded, this equation always has a solution. The number s_a will represent after-tax income in the presence of P; therefore, we would like s_a to be non-negative for all x_a and b_0 that actually occur. (Formally, we can permit s_a to be negative, provided that β is defined on negative arguments.) Under any optimal or almost optimal tax scheme, there will be a positive lower bound on after-tax income. That is, for any T we want to consider, $T(0)$ is a non-negligible negative number, and $x_a \geqslant -T(0)$ for all a. Hence the condition $s_a \geqslant 0$ is not very restrictive. Also, we would like the solution of (16) to be unique. (On the formal level, this is not essential either; if there are several solutions, we just choose one of them.) This amounts to requiring that β not decrease too fast; in particular, if β is differentiable we must have $\beta'(s) > -1/b_0$ for all s and all b_0 which are being considered. (Intuitively, this is equivalent to saying that the benefits from the program should not fall so fast as income increases that the benefits lost outweigh the income gained.)

For any b_0, we now compute

$$\int_0^\infty (x_a - s_a) f(a) \, da.$$

For $b_0 = 0$, this is equal to 0. Under the conditions outlined above, the expression is an increasing function of b_0. Now we find b_0 such that

$$\int_0^\infty (x_a - s_a) f(a) \, da = B. \qquad (17)$$

Such a b_0 will exist, provided that β is positive over a non-negligible range and B is not too large compared to the aggregate after-tax income. By the above, (17) determines b_0 uniquely.[1] Note that the larger we have to choose b_0, the more restrictive are the conditions discussed above.

When b_0 is determined and s_a is defined by (16), we define T' such that, for all a

$$T'(z_a) = z_a - s_a. \tag{18}$$

Here z_a is the before-tax income of a person with ability a who acts according to (1). If $z \neq z_a$ for all a, we let $T'(z)$ be some large number, for example, $T'(z) = 2z$. (The point is that nobody shall want to have gross income z.)

Now it is easy to see that (1) and (15) have the same solution y_a for every a. The other properties of T' required in the conclusion of Proposition 1 are also established in a straightforward manner.

The proof of the second half of the Proposition is less complicated and does not require extra assumptions. Let T' satisfy the premise. Then a function b and a number b_0 are also given, such that (13)–(15) and (11) hold. We define

$$T(z) = T'(z) - b(z - T'(z)), \tag{19}$$

and the conclusion follows immediately.

VI. Problems for Further Study

In this section, we present a number of cases in which the arguments of Propositions 1 and 2 do not apply or apply only in part. In these situations, it is possible that redistributional objectives should affect the choice and design of programs and not only the construction of the tax system. Whether and to what extent this will be true should be the object of further study.

Total Benefits Depend on the Income Distribution. We have assumed that the total benefits derived from a program are independent of the endogenously determined income distribution. More generally, one could have total benefits depend on this distribution. This is equivalent to saying that benefits to an individual with income z are $b(z, \bar{z})$, where b is an arbitrary function and $\bar{z} = (z_a; a \geqslant 0)$ is the income distribution. When such a function b is given, one can compute the total benefits $B(\bar{z})$ given any distribution $\bar{z}$. We have considered the special case in which b is such that B becomes a constant function. Another special case has $b(z, \bar{z})$ depend only on z; this implies the absence of congestion effects or the like.

In this model, the problem of designing an optimal tax system, given certain government programs, can be reduced to the similar problem in the absence of such programs. That is, we have a result which in a sense is similar to Proposition 1. To be precise, we have the following: Let T' be a tax scheme

---

[1] The discussion so far has assumed $B > 0$ and $\beta(s) \geqslant 0$ for all s. The case $B < 0$ and $\beta(s) \leqslant 0$ for all s can also be taken care of. But we cannot allow β to change sign.

which is feasible in the presence of a program P and leads to income distribution $\bar{z}$. Define $T(z) = T'(z) - b(z, \bar{z})$. If T is used and P does not exist, the income distribution will again be $\bar{z}$. Moreover, the revenue generated will be at least $R_0 - B(\bar{z}) + C$, and everybody's utility level will be the same as in the presence of T' and P. Conversely, if T leads to income distribution $\bar{z}$ and revenue no less than $R_0 - B(\bar{z}) + C$, we can construct a scheme T' which is feasible when P exists and such that the same kind of utility equivalence holds. Hence finding an optimal income tax when P is implemented is equivalent to solving the problem of Section III with the revenue constraint (2) replaced by

$$\int_0^\infty T(z_a)\, f(a)\, da + B(\bar{z}) \geq R_0 + C.$$

But it does not follow that the solution T in itself is an optimal tax scheme for any particular level of the revenue requirement R.

Programs cannot be compared directly on the basis of the net benefits $B - C$, as was done in Proposition 2, since B is not fixed. But a similar result does obtain. Assume that a program P_2 is implemented together with a tax scheme T'', such that the revenue constraint is satisfied and the income distribution $\bar{z}$ is induced. Then assume that there exists a program P_1 such that $B_1(\bar{z}) - C_1 \geq B_2(\bar{z}) - C_2$. That is, assume that P_1 has at least as high net benefits as P_2, when measured at the income distribution induced by P_2 and T''. Then we can prove, by an argument similar to the proof of Proposition 2, that there exists a tax scheme T' such that the combination P_1 and T' is at least as good, according to Φ, as P_2 and T''. If $B_1(\bar{z}) - C_1 > B_2(\bar{z}) - C_2$, it will normally be strictly better; see the discussion at the end of Section IV. The optimal configuration of a tax scheme T and a program P must therefore have the property that P is the program which maximizes net benefits, when benefits are measured at the income distribution resulting from P and T.

Benefits Depend on Ability. Next we consider the case in which total benefits from a program are constant, but individual's relative benefits depend not on income but on the unobservable variable ability (or that they depend both on income and ability). The proof of Proposition 1 cannot be applied. The tax system T' was constructed so as to "tax away" all benefits from the program, thereby eliminating any distributional effect. This is impossible when benefits depend on ability.

Normally, we would expect income to be a strictly increasing function of ability, provided that the tax system is optimal and people act rationally.[1]

---

[1] In the lower part of the ability range this cannot be expected to hold; under reasonable social welfare functions and optimal taxation there will exist a constant $a_0 > 0$ such that individuals with ability less than or equal to a_0 do not work and hence have the same before-tax income. (This is proved by Mirrlees in his model.) For ability level above a_0, if income is not strictly increasing in ability, income plays a role similar to that of a Giffen good. This possibility does not contradict our assumptions, but is certainly something out of the ordinary.

Then ability can be inferred from income, and one can ask whether that fact can be used to obtain a result equivalent to Proposition 1. The answer is no, for the following reason: Let a tax scheme T be given, as in the proof of the Proposition. Since ability can be inferred from income, one can construct a function b such that $b(z)$ is the benefit received from the program P by a person with income z, provided that the income distribution is the one induced by T. Then T' can be defined by (12). The expression the individual will maximize is not (10) but $u(ay - T'(ay) + b'_a, y)$, where b'_a is the benefits which accrue to a person with ability a. This is not equivalent to (1), and the proof breaks down. By working a little more or a little less, an individual will be perceived by the tax scheme as having a little higher or lower ability. This influences the "benefit part" $b(z)$ of the tax given by (12), but benefits are related to ability and do not change; hence the incentives are distorted.

Benefits Are Complementary to Leisure. The assumption that benefits are equivalent to an income-related increase in income, essentially rules out programs which are complementary to leisure. A way of removing this restriction is to let benefits depend on the amount of leisure consumed. But leisure is an unobservable variable, and we run into the same difficulties as we did above in considering ability-related benefits. For any level of gross income, leisure can be seen as a function of ability and vice versa. Hence the two cases are equivalent.

Benefits Differ among Members of an Income Group. Thus far, we have assumed that two individuals who are equal in income and other factors relevant to the model receive the same benefits from a program. More generally, and clearly more realistically, one could have benefits depend on income in a non-deterministic way. This can be incorporated into the formal model by assuming that for each $z \geqslant 0$, there is a known probability distribution of relative benefit levels received by individuals with income z. In an important special case there are, for each income group, only two possible benefit levels, namely 0 and a positive level. This corresponds to programs which do not reach the entire target group, but which benefit equally all individuals with the same income who actually participate. Rate of participation and benefits to participants can depend on income.

In this model, a program has two kinds of distributional effects, corresponding to differences in benefits within and among income groups. The income tax scheme can in no way be used to compensate for differences of the first type; therefore, our previous arguments do not apply. Suppose that the social welfare function implies a preference for equality. (This will be the case, for example, if we use the expected utility formulation (4) and the utility function u displays risk aversion.) Other things equal, we would then prefer a program for which the differences in benefits within income groups are small. That is, we would be willing to make a sacrifice in total benefits in order to achieve greater homogeneity within income groups. In particular, we would accept lower average benefits for any one group if they were more evenly spread among the members of that group. More definite statements about this type of trade-offs can only be made if further assumptions are introduced concerning the programs, the utility function and the social welfare function. This is an area for further study.

Next we turn to the differences among income groups. One would perhaps expect that these differences could be eliminated through the tax system and therefore should not influence the choice of program, exactly as in our main model. In fact, the situation is more complicated. When there are differences in benefits within a group, risk is imposed on the members of that group. (Equivalently, they are subjected to variation in utility level.) Everybody is not equally able to bear risk, and this is a factor which should be taken into account when programs are designed and chosen.

Let us present an example: Suppose that the social welfare function is given by (4) while the utility function u displays decreasing absolute risk aversion in money. That is, everybody is risk-averse, but the rich are less so than the poor. Moreover, assume that every feasible program reaches half the population in every income group; the other half receives nothing. There is a choice between a program which concentrates the benefits in the upper end of the income scale and one which mainly benefits the poor; total net benefits are approximately equal for the two programs. Then we shall choose the former program, the one which mainly benefits the rich. This way we avoid placing any significant risk on the lower-income individuals, who are most strongly risk-averse. Instead, the risk is borne by people with higher income, who are better able to do so. The purely distributional aspect of the programs, that is, the fact that one of them directs the benefits towards the rich and the other one towards the poor, should not influence the choice between them. This effect is compensated for through the tax system, as in our main model.[1] Again, further study should be devoted to a detailed examination of more general cases.

In addition to the possibility that benefits from a program vary randomly within an income group, one can clearly imagine programs for which benefits depend on identifiable criteria other than income. Examples are programs which help victims of accidents or others who are "needy" in a sense not solely related to money. If the target group is well-defined and easily recognized, such a program obviously can achieve its goal in a more efficient manner than programs of the type considered earlier. In order to incorporate such programs into the model, we must let the common utility function depend on

---

[1] To be precise, this is merely a sketch of an example. We have assumed that people make their work decisions before they know whether they will benefit from the program. The risk they have to bear will affect these decisions, and a full analysis should consider this complication. The conclusion is unlikely to be affected, however.

other arguments than income and hours of work. No difficulties arise in our tax schemes if all of these other arguments are readily monitored and can be made bases for taxes.

VII. Political Aspects of Distributional Decisions

Our entire discussion has assumed that society is making one grand decision in which taxes and government programs are simultaneously determined. Hence the conclusions apply to a situation in which a constitutional contract is being designed, and to an ideal form of government which makes comprehensive decisions about all sides of government policy and is aware of and takes account of all interrelationships between different areas and activities. In these cases, the conclusion is clear: Distributional considerations should be taken into account when the tax system is designed and only then; therefore, political groups which have distributional objectives should focus their attention on the tax system. Conversely, if one is not satisfied with the level of redistribution which can be achieved through the tax system, programs of the type considered here cannot improve matters; one must look elsewhere.

Real-life politics is of course not like this. Government decisions are made one by one; they may influence each other, but not in the comprehensive way described above. If decisions about programs and taxes were completely independent, a group with distributional goals should pursue them in both areas. If there is an incomplete relationship between the two areas, our results suggest that the group should emphasize tax strategies, but other programs should not necessarily be neglected.

There are other features of the political system that may tend to diminish the relevance of our conclusions. We will not attempt to discuss this issue in any detail, but a few points will be raised.

For one thing, groups with distributional objectives will often find—or at least believe—that their goals can more easily be reached in one area than in another. For example, a group which works for increased well being for the poor may achieve greater success by urging subsidies for low-income housing than by advocating cash grants to the same low-income groups. That is, the former type of support may be more acceptable to the higher-income people who will have to pay the subsidy. This claim can be seen as an argument against the use of a social welfare function of the form (3). Social welfare, it can be argued, does not depend only on individual utility, but directly on the levels of individual consumption of various goods, at least as far as certain basic necessities are concerned. (A more general formulation which takes account of this possibility can still employ social welfare functions of the form (3′) or (4′), but the arguments of the utility function v must include everybody's consumption of the basic goods, or at least some measure of how these goods are distributed.) Indeed, it is often asserted that in some modern industrial societies citizens are more "goods egalitarians" than "income egalitarians". If this is true, elimination of direct transfer programs would have relatively little impact on the progressivity of the tax system and on balance would harm the poor; if it is wrong, significantly increased progressivity in the tax system would be accepted if transfer programs were abolished.

Moreover, some programs benefit identifiable groups, not defined by income but by some criterion which may be related to income, such as blindness or residence in a particular area. These people are not likely to be swayed by an argument that their income group as a whole would be better served by different programs or general transfers through the tax system. From the point of view of various subgroups of low-income people, economic transfers have the character of a public good. Our results indicate that the income class as a whole should prefer that the most efficient programs be adopted and transfers made through the tax system. But each subgroup will prefer that the particular program which benefits that group be implemented. The program may reduce the willingness of higher-income groups to make other transfers, but this effect is spread out over all low-income people, and the subgroup has made a net gain.

Finally, it should not be forgotten that those who provide government services have a say in the political process. This is yet another reason why the outcome is not always what our model of rational and simultaneous decision making predicts.

VIII. Concluding Remarks

The implications of this analysis do not lead, as they do not for the "traditional" optimal income tax literature, to firm policy recommendations. They do, however, suggest the nature of optimal arrangement in some fairly general classes of circumstances.

Our positive results can be briefly summarized. If total benefits are independent of the income distribution and relative benefits are determined by before- or after-tax income, one should select those projects that yield the greatest total of unweighted benefits across the population. If benefits depend on the distribution of income, the optimal program will be one which produces maximal net benefits at the income distribution which is being induced. Redistribution is a concern, but is carried out solely through the tax system.

References

Atkinson, A. B.: How progressive should income tax be? Chapter 6 in M. Parkin and A. R. Nobay (eds.), *Essays in modern economics*, 1973.

Fair, R. C.: The optimal distribution of income. *Quarterly Journal of Economics 85*, 551–579, 1971.

Feldstein, M.: On the optimal progressivity

of the income tax. *Journal of Public Economics 2*, 357–376, 1973.

Harsanyi, J. C.: *Rational behavior and bargaining equilibrium in games and social situations.* Cambridge University Press, 1977.

Mirrlees, J. A.: An exploration in the theory of optimum income taxation. *Review of Economic Studies 38*, 175–208, 1971.

Musgrave, R. A.: *The theory of public finance.* McGraw-Hill, New York, 1959.

Zeckhauser, R.: Uncertainty and the need for collective action. In *The analysis and evaluation of public expenditures: The PPB system.* Joint Economic Committee, U.S. Congress, 1969. Reprinted as Chapter 4 in R. Haveman and J. Margolis (eds.), *Public expenditure and policy analysis.* Markham, Chicago, 1970.

Zeckhauser, R.: Risk spreading and distribution. In H. M. Hochman and G. E. Peterson (eds.), *Redistribution through public choice.* Columbia University Press, New York, 1974.

ISSUES IN THE MEASUREMENT OF POVERTY*

Amartya Sen

Nuffield College, Oxford, England

Abstract

The paper is concerned with discussing some of the basic issues in the measurement of poverty. The measurement of poverty can be split into two distinct operations, viz. *identification* (who are the poor?) and *aggregation* (how are the poverty characteristics of different people to be combined into an aggregate measure?). The nature of the exercise of poverty measurement is examined in Section I. Section II is devoted to the identification issue, including the fixation of a "poverty line". Section III goes into the aggregation problem. Some concluding remarks are made in the last section.

I. The Nature of Poverty Measurement

I.1. *A Value Judgment?*

The view that "poverty is a value judgment" has been presented forcefully by many authors. It seems natural to think of poverty as something that is disapproved of, the elimination of which is regarded as morally good. A consequence of this approach is to argue with Mollie Orshansky, an outstanding authority in the field, that "poverty, like beauty, lies in the eye of the be-holder".[1] The exercise would, then, seem to be primarily a subjective one, un-leashing one's morals on the statistics of deprivation.

I would like to argue against this approach. There is a difference between saying that the exercise is itself a prescriptive one from saying that the exercise must *take note of* the prescriptions made by members of the community. To describe a prevailing prescription is an act of description, not prescription. It may be the case that poverty, as Eric Hobsbawn (1968) puts it, "is always defined according to the conventions of the society in which it occurs" (p. 398). But this does not make the exercise of poverty assessment in a given society a value judgment, or even a subjective exercise of some other kind. For the person studying and measuring poverty, the conventions of society are matters of *fact* (what *are* the contemporary standards?) and not issues of *morality* or

---

* The paper draws partly on the analysis to be presented in a forthcoming book, *Poverty and Famine*, prepared for the ILO World Employment Programme. While that book is chiefly concerned with the causation of starvation and famines, it begins by analysing the more general concept of poverty.

[1] Orshansky (1969, p. 37). For a critique of this position, see Townsend (1974).

of *subjective search* (what *should be* the contemporary standards? what *should be* may values? how do I *feel* about all this?).[1]

The point was brought out very clearly by Adam Smith more than two hundred years ago:

By necessaries I understand not only the commodities which are indispensably necessary for the support of life, but what ever the custom of the country renders it indecent for creditable people, even of the lowest order, to be without. A linen shirt, for example, is, strictly speaking, not a necessary of life. The Greeks and Romans lived, I suppose, very comfortably though they had no linen. But in the present times, through the greater part of Europe, a creditable day-labourer would be ashamed to appear in public without a linen shirt, the want of which would be supposed to denote that disgraceful degree of poverty which, it is presumed, nobody can well fall into without extreme bad conduct.[2]

In a similar vein Karl Marx (1887) argued that while "a historical and moral element" enters the concept of subsistence, "nevertheless, in a given country, at a given period, the average quantity of the means of subsistence necessary for the labourer is practically known" (p. 150).

It is possible that Smith or Marx may have overestimated the extent of uniformity of views that tends to exist in a community on the content of "subsistence" or "poverty". Description of "necessities" may be very far from ambiguous. But the presence of ambiguity in a description does not make it a prescriptive act—only one of ambiguous description. One may be forced to be arbitrary in eliminating the ambiguity, and if so, that arbitrariness would be worth recording. Similarly, one may be forced to use more than one criteria because of non-uniformity of accepted standards, and look at the *partial* ordering generated by the criteria taken together (reflecting "dominance" in terms of all the criteria).[3] But the partial ordering would still reflect a descriptive statement rather than a prescriptive one.

I.2. *A Policy Definition?*

A related issue is worth exploring in this context. The measurement of poverty may be based on certain given standards, but what kind of statements do these standards themselves make? Are these standards of public policy, reflecting either the objectives of actual policy, *or* views on what the policy should be? There is little doubt that the standards must have a good deal to do with some broad notions of acceptability, but that is not the same thing as reflecting precise policy objectives—actual *or* recommended. On this subject too a certain amount of confusion seems to exist. For example, the United

---

[1] This does not, of course, in any way deny that one's values may implicitly affect one's assessment of facts, as indeed they very often do. The statement is about the nature of the exercise, viz., that it *is* concerned with assessment of facts, and not about the way it is typically performed and the psychology that lies behind that performance.

[2] Smith (1776, pp. 351–2).

[3] Sen (1973, Chapters 2 and 3).

States' President's Commission on Income Maintenance (1969) argued thus for such a "policy definition" in its well-known report *Poverty amid Plenty*:

> If society believes that people should not be permitted to die of starvation or exposure, then it will define poverty as the lack of minimum food and shelter necessary to maintain life. If society feels some responsibility for providing to all persons an established measure of well-being beyond mere existence, for example, good physical health, then it will add to its list of necessitites the resources required to prevent or cure sickness. At any given time a policy definition reflects a balancing of community capabilities and desires. In low income societies the community finds it impossible to worry much beyond physical survival. Other societies, more able to support their dependent citizens, begin to consider the effects that pauperism will have on the poor and non-poor alike.[1]

There are at least two difficulties with this "policy definition". First, the actual making of public policy depends on a number of influences of which the prevalent notions of what should be done is only one. Policy is a function of political organisation, and depends on a variety of factors including the nature of the government, the sources of its power, and the forces exerted by other organisations. Second, even if "policy" is taken to stand not for actual public policy, but for policy recommendations widely held in the society in question, there are problems. There is clearly a difference between the notion of "deprivation" and the idea of what should be eliminated by "policy". For one thing, policy recommendations must depend on an assessment of feasibilities ("ought implies can"[2]), but to concede that some deprivations cannot be immediately eliminated is not the same thing as conceding that they must not currently be seen as deprivations.

I would submit that the "policy definition" is based on a fundamental confusion. It is certainly true that with economic development there are changes in the notion of what counts as deprivation and poverty, and there are changes also in the ideas as to what should be done. But while these two types of changes are interdependent and also intertemporally correlated with each other, neither can be *defined* entirely in terms of the other. Oil-rich Kuwait may be "more able to support their dependent citizens" with its new prosperity, but the notion of what is poverty may not go up immediately to the corresponding level. Similarly, war-devastated Netherlands may keep up its standard of what counts as poverty and not scale it down to the level commensurate with its predicament.[3]

If this approach is accepted, then the measurement of poverty must be seen as an exercise of description assessing the predicament of people in terms of the prevailing standards of necessities. It is primarily a *factual* rather than an ethical exercise, and the facts relate to what is regarded as deprivation, and not *directly* to what policies are recommended.

[1] U.S. President's Commission on Income Maintenance (1969, p. 8).
[2] Cf. Hare (1963, Chapter 4).
[3] Cf. Stein, Susser, Saenger & Marolla (1975).

I.3. *Standards and Aggregation*

This still leaves two issues quite untouched. First, in comparing the poverty of two societies, how can a common standard of necessities be found, since such standards would vary from society to society? There are actually two quite distinct types of exercises in such inter-community comparisons. One is aimed at comparing the extent of deprivation in each community in relation to their respective standards of minimum necessities, and the other is concerned with comparing the predicament of the two communities in terms of some given minimum standard, e.g., that prevalent in either community. There is, indeed, nothing contradictory in asserting both of the following pair of statements:

(i) there is *less* deprivation in community A than in community B in terms of some *common* standard, e.g., the notions of minimum needs prevailing in community A (or in B);

(ii) there is *more* deprivation in community A than in community B in terms of their *respective* standards of minimum needs, which are a good deal higher in A than in B.

It is rather pointless to dispute which of these two senses is the "correct" one, since it is quite clear that both types of questions are of interest. The important thing to note is that the two questions are quite distinct from each other.

Second, while the exercise of "identification" of the poor can be based on a standard of minimum needs, that of "aggregation" requires some method of combining deprivations of different people into some over-all indicator. In the latter exercise some relative scaling of deprivations is necessary. The scope for arbitrariness in this is much greater since conventions on this are less firmly established and the constraints of acceptability would tend to leave one with a good deal of freedom.

In this context of arbitrariness of "aggregate description", it becomes particularly tempting to redefine the problem as an "ethical" exercise, as has indeed been done in the measurement of economic inequality.[1] But the ethical exercises involve exactly similar ambiguities, and furthermore end up answering a different question from the descriptive one that was originally asked.[2] There is very little alternative to accepting the element of arbitrariness in the description of poverty, and making that element as explicit as possible. Since the notion of the poverty of a nation has some inherent ambiguities, one should not have expected anything else.

II. Minimum Needs and the Poverty Line

II.1. *Deprivation: Absolute and Relative*

Since "necessities" include "things which established rules of decency have rendered necessary", the notion of "minimum needs" must, in an obvious

---

[1] See Dalton (1920) and Atkinson (1970), two of the outstanding contributions in this tradition.

[2] See Bentzel (1970), Hansson (1977), and Sen (1978*b*).

sense, be relative rather than absolute. The concept of "relative deprivation", much used in the sociological literature,[1] has thus an immediate relevance to the economic measurement of poverty. Deprivation has to be judged in comparison with the experience of others in the society.

Relative deprivation cannot, however, be the only basis of judging poverty. A famine, for example, will be readily accepted as a case of acute poverty no matter what the relative standards are. Indeed, there is an irreducible core of "absolute deprivation" in the notion of poverty which translates reports of starvation, severe malnutrition and visible hardship into a diagnosis of poverty without waiting to ascertain first the relative picture.[2] Thus the approach of relative deprivation supplements rather than supplants the analysis of poverty in terms of absolute dispossession.

This is particularly worth emphasizing in view of the recent tendency among some sociologists to view the problem of poverty as essentially indistinguishable from that of inequality. As Miller & Roby (1971) argue:

> Casting the issues of poverty in terms of stratification leads to regarding poverty as an issue of inequality. In this approach we move away from efforts to measure poverty lines with pseudo-scientific accuracy. Instead, we look at the nature and size of the differences between the bottom 20 or 10 per cent and the rest of the society.[3]

Studies of the difference between the bottom decile (or the bottom two deciles) and the rest do throw light on the nature of inequality in the economy in question,[4] but to identify that picture as one of poverty amounts to an exclusive concentration on relative as opposed to absolute deprivation (as well as quantifying relative deprivation in a very specific way). If an economic crisis leads to a general reduction of incomes with the relative pattern unchanged, then this approach of "poverty as inequality" may not diagnose any increase in the extent of poverty despite possibly dramatic rise in starvation and hunger. To ignore such information as hunger and hardship is not just an abstinence from "pseudo-scientific accuracy", but blindness to important parameters of the common understanding of poverty. There is, of course, a good deal of common ground between inequality and poverty, but the two cannot be treated as identical without impoverishing at least one of these two primitive notions.[5]

---

[1] See, for example, Runciman (1966) and Townsend (1971, 1974).
[2] Cf. Engels (1892). On related issues, see also Weisbrod (1965), Jackson (1972), Stewart & Streeten (1976), Drewnowski (1977), and Beckerman (1977).
[3] Miller & Roby (1971, p. 143).
[4] See, for example, Wiles (1974).
[5] It is also worth noting that there are many measures of inequality, of which the gap between the bottom 10 % and the rest is only one (and rather a blunt one at that, completely insensitive to many types of changes). Also the question of economic inequality is not merely a matter of examining the size distribution of income but of investigating contrasts between different sections of the community from many different perspectives (e.g., in terms of relations of production, as done by Marx (1887)). Finally, for the concept of relative deprivation, the choice of "reference group" is important and a contrast with the average level may not be adequate.

II.2. *The Direct Method vs. the Income Method*

Even with a given set of minimum needs in terms of which poverty is to be measured, there are complex issues of methodology to be resolved. In the exercise of identifying the poor *vis-à-vis* that set of minimum needs, it is possible to use at least two alternative methods. One is simply to check the set of people whose actual consumption baskets happen to leave some minimum need unsatisfied. This we may call the "direct method", and it does not involve the use of any income notion, in particular not that of a poverty-line income. In contrast, in what may be called the "income method", the first step is to calculate the minimum income π at which all the specified minimum needs are satisfied. The next step is to identify those whose actual incomes fall below that poverty line π.[1]

In an obvious sense the direct method is superior to the income method, since the former is not based on particular assumptions of consumption behaviour which may or may not be accurate. Indeed, it could be argued that *only* in the absence of direct information regarding the satisfaction of the specified needs can there be a case for bringing in the intermediary of income, so that the income method is at most a second best.

However, this is not all there is to the contrast of the two methods. The income method can also be seen as a way of taking note of individual idiosyncrasies without upsetting the notion of poverty based on deprivation. The ascetic who fasts on his expensive bed of nails will be registered as poor under the direct method, but the income method will offer a different judgement in recognition of his level of income at which typical people in that community would have no difficulty in satisfying the basic nutritional requirements. The income of a person can be seen to be not merely a rough aid to predicting a person's actual consumption, but also as capturing a person's *ability* to meet his minimum needs (whether or not he, in fact, chooses to use that ability).

There is a difficult line to draw here. If one were to look merely for the ability to meet minimum needs without being bothered by tastes, then one would, of course, set up a cost-minimizing programming problem and simply check whether someone's income falls short of that minimum cost solution. Such minimum cost diets are typically very inexpensive,[2] but exceedingly boring and quite unacceptable. (In Indira Rajaraman's (1974) pioneering work on poverty in Punjab, in an initial round of optimization, unsuspecting Punjabis were subjected to a deluge of Bengal grams.) Taste factors can be introduced through constraints (as Rajaraman did, and others do), but it is difficult to decide how pervasive and severe these constraints should be. In the extreme case the constraints determine the consumption pattern entirely.

---

[1] The distinction relates to Seebohm Rowntree's (1901) contrast between "primary" and "secondary" poverty, but is not exactly the same.
[2] See, for example, Stigler's (1945) astonishing estimates of the cost of subsistence.

But there is, I believe, a difference in principle between taste constraints that apply broadly to the entire community and those that essentially reflect individual idiosyncrasies. If the poverty-level income π can be derived from typical behaviour norms of society, a person with a higher income but choosing to fast on a bed of nails can be, with some legitimacy, declared to be non-poor.

The "direct method" and the "income method" are, in fact, not two alternative ways of measuring the same thing, but represent two alternative conceptions of poverty. The direct method identifies those whose actual consumption fails to meet the accepted conventions of minimum needs, while the income method is after spotting those who do not have the ability to meet these needs within the behavioural constraints typical in that community. Both concepts are of some interest on their own in diagnosing poverty in a community, and while the latter is a bit more remote in being dependent on the existence of some typical behaviour pattern in the community,[1] it is also a bit more refined in going beyond the observed choices into the notion of ability. A poor person, on this approach, is one whose income is not adequate to meet the specified minimum needs in conformity with the conventional behaviour pattern.

The income method has the advantage of providing a metric of *numerical* distances from the "poverty line", in terms of income short-falls. This the "direct method" does not provide. On the other hand, the income method is more restrictive in terms of preconditions necessary for the "identification" exercise. First, if the pattern of consumption behaviour has no uniformity, there will be no specific level of income at which the "typical" consumer meets his or her minimum needs. Second, if prices facing different groups of people differ, e.g., between social classes or income groups or localities, then π will be group-specific, even when uniform norms and uniform consumption habits are considered.[2] These are real difficulties and cannot be wished away.

II.3. *Family Size and Equivalent Adults*

Another difficulty arises from the fact that the family rather than the individual is the natural unit as far as consumption behaviour is concerned. In calculating the income necessary for meeting the minimum needs of families of different size, some method of correspondence of family income with individual income is needed. While the simplest method of doing this is to divide the family income by the number of family members, this overlooks the economies of large scale that operate for many items of consumption, and also the fact that the children's needs may be quite different from those of adults. To cope with these issues, the common practice both for poverty estimation as well as for social security operations is to convert each family into a certain number of "equivalent

[1] The income method is based on two different sets of conventions, viz., (i) those used to identify the minimum needs, and (ii) those used to specify behaviour and taste constraints.
[2] For evidence of sharp differences in income-group-specific price deflators in India, see Bardhan (1973), Vaidyanathan (1974), and Radhakrishna & Sharma (1975), among others.

adults" by the use of some "equivalence scale", or, alternatively, to convert the families into "equivalent households".[1]

There tends to be a lot of arbitrariness in any such conversion. Much depends on the exact consumption patterns of the people involved, and their perception of their own relative position. Indeed, both the minimum needs of children as well as variations of consumption behaviour of families with variations of the number and age composition of children are complex fields for empirical investigation.

There are also different *bases* for deriving appropriate equivalence of needs.[2] One approach is to take the nutritional requirements for each age group separately and then to take the ratios of their costs given established patterns of consumer behaviour. A second approach is to examine how the people involved regard the equivalence question themselves, viz. how much extra income do they think is needed to make a larger family have the same standard of well-being as a smaller one. Empirical studies of these "views" have shown considerable regularities and consistency.[3] A third way is to examine the actual consumption behaviour of families of different size and to treat some aspect of this behaviour as an indicator of welfare. For example, the fraction of income spent on food has been treated as an indicator of poverty: two families of different size are regarded as having "equivalent" incomes when they spend the same proportion of their incomes on food.[4]

No matter how these equivalent scales are drawn up, there remains the further issue of the weighting of families of different size. Three alternative approaches may be considered: (i) put the same weight on each household irrespective of size, (ii) put the same weight on each person irrespective of the size of the family to whom they belong, and (iii) put a weight on each family equal to the number of equivalent adults in it.

The first method is clearly unsatisfactory since the poverty and suffering of a large family is, in an obvious sense, greater than that of a small family at a *per capita* poverty level judged to be equivalent to that of the former. The third alternative might look like a nice compromise, but it is, I believe, based on a confusion. The scale of "equivalent adults" indicates conversion factors to be used to find out how well off members of that family are, but ultimately we are concerned with the sufferings of *everyone* in the family and not of a hypothetical equivalent number. If two can live as cheaply as $1\frac{1}{2}$ and three as cheaply as 2, these facts must be taken into account in comparing the relative well-beings of two-member and three-member families, but there is no reason why the suffer-

[1] See Orshansky (1965), Abel-Smith & Townsend (1965), and Atkinson (1969), among others.
[2] For an illuminating account of these methods and their underlying logic, see Muellbauer (1978).
[3] See, for example, Goedhart, Halberstadt, Kapteyn & Van Praag (1977).
[4] See Muellbauer (1977b). The method goes back to Engel (1895). See also Friedman (1952), Brown (1954), Prais & Houthakker (1955), Barten (1964), Nicholson (1976), Muellbauer (1977a), Kakwani (1977), among others.

ing of two three-member families should receive any less weight than that of three two-member families at the same level of illfare. There is, thus, a good case for using procedure (ii) after the personal level of well-being or poverty has been ascertained by the use of equivalent scales taking note of the size of the families to which they belong.

III. Aggregate Poverty

III.1. *Poverty Gaps and Relative Deprivation*

The income short-fall of a person whose income y_i is less than the poverty line π can be called his "income gap" $(\pi - y_i)$. In the aggregate assessment of poverty, these income gaps must be taken into account. But does it make a difference as to whether or not a person's shortfall is unusually large compared with those of others? It seems reasonable to argue that any person's poverty cannot really be independent of how poor the others are.[1] Even with exactly the same absolute shortfall $(\pi - y_i)$, a person may be thought to be "poorer" if the other poor have shortfalls smaller than his, in contrast with the case in which his shortfall is less than that of others. Quantification of poverty would, thus, seem to need the marrying of considerations of absolute and relative deprivation even *after* a set of minimum needs and a poverty line have been fixed.

The question of relative deprivation can be viewed also in the context of a possible transfer of a unit of income from a poor person—call him 1—to another—christened 2—who is richer but still below the poverty line and remains so even after the transfer. Such a transfer will increase the absolute shortfall of the first person by exactly the same amount by which the absolute shortfall of person 2 will be reduced. Can one then argue that the overall poverty is unaffected by the transfer? One can dispute this, of course, by bringing in some notion of diminishing marginal utility of income, so that the utility loss of the first may be argued to be greater than the utility gain of the second. But such cardinal utility comparisons for different persons involves the use of a rather demanding informational structure with well-known difficulties. In the absence of cardinal comparisons of marginal utility gains and losses, is it then impossible to hold that the over-all poverty of the community has increased? I would argue that this is not the case.

Person 1 is relatively deprived compared with 2 (and there may be others in between the two who are more deprived than 2 but less so than 1). When a unit of income is transferred from 1 to 2, it *increases* the absolute shortfall of a more deprived person and *reduces* that of someone *less* deprived, so that in a straightforward sense the over-all relative deprivation is increased.[2] And this is the

---

[1] Cf. Scitovsky (1976) and Hirsch (1976).

[2] A complex problem arises when the transfer makes person 2 cross the poverty line—a possibility that has been deliberately excluded in the postulated case. This case involves a reduction in one of the main parameters of poverty, viz., the identification of the poor,

case quite irrespective to whether absolute deprivation is measured by income shortfalls, or (taking utility to be an increasing function of income) by utility shortfalls, from the break-even poverty line. One does not, therefore, have to introduce an interpersonally comparable *cardinal* welfare scale to be able to say that the transfer specified will increase the extent of relative deprivation.

In the "aggregation" exercise the magnitudes of absolute deprivation may have to be supplemented by considerations of relative deprivation. Before this exercise is studied, it will be useful to review the standard measures of poverty used in the literature and to examine their shortcomings.

III.2. *Critique of Standard Measures*

The commonest measure of over-all poverty is what may be called the head-count measure H given by the proportion of the total population that happens to fall below the specified poverty line π. If q is the number of people who are identified as being poor and n the total number of people in the community, then the head-count measure H is simply:

$$H = q/n \tag{1}$$

This index has been widely used—explicitly or by implication—ever since quantitative study and measurement of poverty began (see Booth (1889), Rowntree (1901)). It seems to be still the mainstay of poverty statistics on which poverty programmes are based (see Orshansky (1965, 1966), Abel-Smith & Townsend (1965)). It has been extensively utilised recently both for intertemporal comparisons as well as for international contrasts.[1]

Another measure that has had a fair amount of currency is the so-called "poverty gap", which is the aggregate shortfall of income of all the poor from the specified poverty line π.[2] The index can be normalized by being expressed as the percentage shortfall of the average income of the poor from the poverty line. This measure—denoted I—will be called the "income-gap ratio". With the poverty line income π and income of person i being y_i, the income-gap of person i is: $g_i = \pi - y_i$. The "income-gap ratio" I is given by the following when $S(\pi)$ stands for the set of people with income no higher than π:

$$I = \sum_{i \in S(\pi)} g_i/q\pi \tag{2}$$

---

and while there is an arbitrariness in attaching a lot of importance to whether a person actually crosses the poverty line, this is an arbitrariness that is implicit in the concept of poverty itself based on the use of a breakeven line. The question is investigated further in section 3.4.

[1] See, for example, the lively debate on the time trend of Indian poverty: Ojha (1970), Dandekar & Rath (1971), Minhas (1970, 1971), Bardhan (1970, 1971, 1973), Mukherjee, Bhattacharya & Chatterjee (1972), Vaidyanathan (1974), and Lal (1976). For international comparisons, see Chenery, Ahluwalia, Bell, Duloy & Jolly (1974).

[2] The poverty gap has been used by the U.S. Social Security Administration. For a discussion of the poverty-gap approach, see Batchelder (1971). See also Kakwani (1977) and Beckerman (1977).

The income-gap ratio I is completely insensitive to transfers of income among the poor so long as nobody crosses the poverty line by such transfers. It also pays no attention whatever to the number or proportion of poor people below the poverty line, concentrating only on the aggregate shortfall, no matter how it is distributed and among how many. These are damaging limitations.

The head-count measure H is, of course, not insensitive to the number below the poverty line; indeed for a given society it is the only thing to which H is sensitive. But H pays no attention whatever to the extent of income shortfall of those who lie below the poverty line: it matters not at all whether someone is just below the line, or very far from it in acute misery and hunger.

Furthermore, a transfer of income from a poor person to one who is richer can never increase the poverty measure H—surely a perverse feature. The poor person from whom the transfer takes place is, in any case, counted in the value of H, and no reduction of his income will make him count any more than he does already. On the other hand, the person who *receives* the income transfer cannot, of course, move below the poverty line as a consequence of this. Either he was rich and stays so, or was poor and stays so, in both cases the H measure remains unaffected; or he was below the line but is pulled above it by the transfer, and this makes the measure H fall rather than rise. So a transfer from a poor person to one who is richer can *never* increase poverty as represented by H.

There are, thus, good grounds for rejecting the standard poverty measures in terms of which most of the analyses and debates on poverty have traditionally taken place. The head-count measure in particular has commanded implicit support of a kind that is quite astonishing. Consider A. L. Bowley's (1923) famous assertion: "There is, perhaps, no better test of the progress of the nation than that which shows what proportion are in poverty" (p. 214). The spirit of the remark is acceptable enough but surely not the gratuitous identification of poverty with the head-count measure H.

What about a combination of these poverty measures? The head-count measure H ignores the extent of income shortfalls, while the income-gap ratio I ignores the numbers involved: why not a combination of the two? This is, alas, still inadequate. If a unit of income is transferred from a person below the poverty line to someone who is richer but who still is (and remains) below the poverty line, then both the measures H and I will remain completely unaffected. Hence any "combined" measure based only on these two must also show no response whatsoever to such a change, despite the obvious increase in aggregate poverty as a consequence of this transfer in terms of relative deprivation.

There is, however, a special case in which a combination of H and I might just about be adequate. Note that while individually H is insensitive to the extent of income shortfalls and I to the numbers involved, we could criticise the *combination* of the two only for their insensitivity to variations of distribution of income among the poor. If we were, then, to confine ourselves to cases in which all the poor have precisely the same income, it may be reasonable to expect that H and I together may do the job. Transfers of the kind that have been considered above to show the insensitivity of the combination of H and I will not then be in the domain of our discourse.

The interest of the special case in which all the poor have the same income does not arise from its being a very likely occurrence. Its value lies in clarifying the way absolute deprivation *vis-à-vis* the poverty line may be handled when there is not the additional feature of relative deprivation *among* the poor.[1] It helps us to formulate a condition that the required poverty measure P should satisfy when the problem of distribution among the poor is assumed away by postulating equality. It provides *one* regularity condition to be satisfied among others.

III.3. *Axiomatic Derivation of a Poverty Measure*

The absolute shortfall of income of a person i lying below the poverty line is given by g_i. We may begin by taking the poverty measure P to be a weighted sum of the shortfalls of all people who are judged to be poor, i.e., the set $S(\pi)$.[2] This is done in a very general way with provision for normalization in any way we like, and with weights that can be functions of other variables so that the superficially additive form is not a real constraint.

$$P = A(\pi, q, n) \sum_{i \in S(\pi)} g_i v_i \qquad (3)$$

So far not much has been said, since both the weights v_i and the parameter A have been left unspecified, and not much exclusion has been achieved as yet.[3] The interesting questions arise when we start characterizing the weights v_i and the parameter A.

If we wished to base the poverty measure on some quantification of the sum-total loss of utility arising from the penury of the poor, then v_i should be derived from the familiar utilitarian considerations. If, additionally, it is assumed that the utility of each person depends only on his own income, then v_i too will depend only on the income y_i of that person, and not also on the incomes of others. This will provide a "separable" structure, each person's component of

---

[1] As was discussed in Section II.1, the question of relative deprivation *vis-à-vis* the rest of the community is involved also in the fixing of minimum needs on which the choice of the poverty line is based, so that the estimation of "absolute" deprivation *vis-à-vis* the poverty line involves implicitly some considerations of *relative* deprivation as well. The reference in the text here is to issues of relative deprivation that remain *even after* the poverty line has been drawn, since there is the *further* question of how deprived one is compared with others who are also deprived.

[2] In fact, it is convenient to define the poor as those with income *no higher than* π. So, formally, $S(\pi) = [i \,|\, y_i \leqslant \pi]$.

[3] To return to the head-count measure H, choose $v_i = 1/g_i$ and $A = 1/n$, where n is the total number of people in the community. For the income-gap ratio, use $v_i = 1$, and $A = 1/q\pi$, where q is the number of people who are poor, i.e., belong to $S(\pi)$.

the overall poverty being derived without reference to the conditions of the others. But this use of the traditional utilitarian model will miss the idea of relative deprivation, which—as we have already argued—is rather central to the notion of poverty. Furthermore, there are difficulties with such cardinal comparisons of utility gains and losses, and even if these were ignored, it is no easy matter to secure agreement on using one particular utility function among so many that can be postulated, all satisfying the usual regularity conditions such as concavity requirements.

Instead, the concentration here will be precisely on aspects of relative deprivation. Let $r(i)$ be the rank of person i in the ordering of all the poor in the decreasing order of income, e.g., $r(i) = 12$ if i is the 12th worst off among the poor. If more than one person has the same income, they can be ranked in any arbitrary order: the poverty measure must be such that it should not matter which particular arbitrary order is chosen among those with the same income. Clearly, the poorest poor has the largest rank value q, when there are q people altogether on this side of the poverty line, while the least poor has the rank value of 1. The greater the rank value the more is the person deprived in terms of relative deprivation with respect to others in the same category.[1] It is, thus, reasonable to argue that a poverty measure capturing this aspect of relative deprivation must make the weight v_i on a person's income shortfall increase with his rank value $r(i)$. As a functional relation this leads to:

$$v_i = f(r(i)), \text{ with } f \text{ an increasing function.} \tag{4}$$

A rather distinguished and simple case of such an increasing function f is the identity mapping which makes v_i equal the rank value $r(i)$. This makes the weights equi-distanced, and the procedure is in the same spirit as Borda's (1781) famous argument for the rank-order method of decisions, choosing equal distances in the absence of a convincing case for any alternative assumption. While this too is arbitrary, it captures the notion of relative deprivation in a simple way, and leads to a transparent procedure making it quite clear what precisely is being assumed.[2]

Axiom R (Ranked Relative Deprivation). The weight v_i on the income short-fall of person i is given by the income rank of person i among the poor, i.e.,

$$v_i = r(i) \tag{4.1}$$

This axiom, which focuses on the distribution of income among the poor, may be combined with the kind of information that is presented by the head-count measure H and the income-gap ratio I in the special case in which every-one below the poverty line has the same income (so that there is no distribution problem among the poor). H presents the proportion of people who are de-

---

[1] Cf. Runciman (1966), and Townsend (1971, 1974).

[2] It is, in fact, possible to derive the characteristic of equi-distance from other—more primitive—axioms (see Sen (1973b, 1974)).

prived in relation to the poverty line π, and I reflects the proportionate amount of absolute income deprivation *vis-à-vis* π. It can be argued that H catches one aspect of overall deprivation, viz. how many (never mind how much), while I catches another aspect of it, viz. how much on the average (never mind suffered by how many). In the special case when all the poor have the same income, H and I together may give us a fairly good idea of the extent of poverty in terms of overall deprivation. Since the problem of relative distribution among the poor does not arise in this special case, we may settle for a measure that boils down to some function of only H and I under these circumstances. A simple representation of this, leading to a convenient normalization, is the product HI.

Axiom A (Normalized Absolute Deprivation)[1]. If all the poor have the same income, then $P = HI$.

If these two axioms are accepted, then a precise measure of poverty emerges axiomatically (see Sen (1973b, 1976a)):

If the number of the poor is large, then the only poverty measure satisfying Axioms R and A is given by:

$$P = H[I + (1 - I)G], \tag{5}$$

where G is the Gini coefficient of the income distribution among the poor.

For formal proofs of results essentially equivalent to this one, the reader is referred to Sen (1973b, 1976a). Here I confine myself to giving a heuristic view of what P stands for.[2] When there is no inequality among the poor, clearly G is zero, and P will then stand for HI, consisting of the product of two indicators of "absolute" deprivation, viz. the proportion of people who are deprived (H) and the proportionate average deprivation of those who are deprived (I). With the same number of poor and the same average deprivation, if the income among the poor is redistributed with some becoming poorer and others richer (though still poor), it would clearly lead to more relative deprivation. The poorer a person is, the larger his income shortfall g_i, and under Axiom R this shortfall will receive a greater weight than the shortfall of a person who is relatively richer.[3] Thus a transfer from a poorer person (call him 1) to a richer person (call him 2) will reduce the shortfall of 2, which has a lower weight, by

---

[1] It should be remembered that in fixing the poverty line considerations of relative deprivation have already played a part, so that absolute deprivation *vis-à-vis* the poverty line is non-relative only in the limited context of the "aggregation" exercise. As was discussed earlier, the concepts of absolute and relative deprivation are both relevant to *each* of the two exercises in the measurement of poverty, viz., identification and aggregation. Axioms A and R are each concerned exclusively with the aggregation exercise.

[2] For empirical applications of this measure of poverty to data of different countries and interesting discussions of related conceptual issues, see Ahluwalia (1978), Alamgir (1976), Anand (1977), Bhatty (1974), Dutta (1978), Kakwani (1977), Osmani (1978), Sastry (1978), Seastrand & Diwan (1975), among others.

[3] This approach relates closely to the evaluation of real national income in terms of "named good vectors" presented in Sen (1976b). The relationship between the two types of exercises has been analysed in depth by Osmani (1978).

the same amount as the increase in the shortfall of 1, which has a higher weight. This will, of course, increase the overall measure of poverty with weights based on the notion of relative deprivation. In some ways, this increase in inequality among the poor with an unchanged average gap I is equivalent to an increase in that average gap with unchanged distribution. To the absolute deprivation I is, thus, to be added a bit from the rest, i.e., from $(1-I)$, in proportion to the measure of inequality among the poor given by the Gini coefficient. This "equivalent" absolute shortfall is, thus, given by the actual shortfall I *plus* the additional equivalent bit reflecting the impact of the inequality among the poor $(1-I)G$. If we now take the product of this aggregate "equivalent" short-fall $[I+(1-I)G]$ with the other aspect of absolute deprivation given by the head-count measure H, then we indeed get the poverty measure P as expressed in (5).

III.4. *Alternatives and Variations*

Axioms A and R can be varied in certain ways that are not unreasonable. Ambiguities in the notion of poverty permit such plurality (see section 1 above). One idea is to modify the income-gap element I in the measure of deprivation by taking the *per capita* gap not as a percentage of the poverty level income π but as a percentage of the mean income of the community: where μ is the mean income of the entire community.

$$I^* = \sum_{i \in S(\pi)} g_i/q\mu \tag{2*}$$

HI^* clearly equals the ratio of the aggregate poverty gap to total national income or GDP:[1]

$$HI^* = \sum_{i \in S(\pi)} g_i/n\mu \tag{2**}$$

Axiom A* (Alternative Normalized Absolute Deprivation). If all the poor have the same income, then $P = HI^*$.

It is easily checked that Axioms A^* and R lead to a modified poverty measure P_1, which has been proposed and extensively explored by Sunhir Anand[2], and which differs from P by a multiplicative constant reflecting normalization per unit of national mean income rather than the poverty line income:

$$P_1 = P\pi/\mu \tag{6}$$

P_1 has the feature of being sensitive to the income of the non-poor as well. A rise in the income of a non-poor person, given other things, will reduce I^* and obviously will also reduce the modified poverty measure P_1. A rise in the

---

[1] Beckerman (1977) puts this measure to good use as an indicator of the relative burden of poverty, but also warns against reading too much into this ratio (p. 12).
[2] See Anand (1977).

income of anyone can be taken to be, in some ways, a reduction of the poverty of the nation; P_1 will show this directional response, while P will not budge if the income rise is of a person who is above the poverty line. Another way of defending the use of P_1 rather than P is to note that HI^* expresses the percentage of national income that would have to be devoted to transfers if poverty were to be wiped out by redistribution, and in some sense, HI^* does, therefore, reflect the *relative burden* of poverty on the nation compared with its aggregate income.

On the other hand, it can be argued that assessing the relative burden of poverty is really a different exercise from the description of poverty in terms of prevailing notions of deprivation. More importantly, P_1 has the characteristic that some increase in the income shortfall of the poor may be compensated by a sufficiently high rise in the income of the non-poor. And this can be objected to on the ground that poverty is a characteristic of the poor, and a reduction of the incomes of the poor must increase the measure of poverty, no matter how much the incomes of the non-poor go up at the same time. P satisfies this condition, but not P_1.

The choice of the index must, of course, depend on the purpose for which such a measure is sought. For descriptive exercises on "the state of the poor" (to quote the title of the famous treatise of F. M. Eden (1797)) P would have an obvious advantage over P_1. But if, on the other hand, the intention is to check the country's potential ability to meet the challenge of poverty, P_1 has a clear advantage. The two versions, therefore, describe two rather different things.

Variants of Axiom R may also be considered. Nanak Kakwani (1977) has provided various measures closely related to the measure P. An especially interesting one—we may call it P_2—makes the weight v_i on the income shortfall of person i depend not on the number of people among the poor *vis-à-vis* whom i is relatively deprived, but on the aggregate *income* of these people. P_2 has the merit of making i's sense of deprivation take note of the actual incomes enjoyed by those who are richer than him, but lying below the poverty line. On the other hand, P_2 takes no note of how the aggregate income of these people is divided among them, and more importantly, no note even of the number of persons among whom this aggregate income is divided. The sense of relative deprivation is made to depend on the sum-total of income of those who—while poor—are better off than the person in question, and no other information is used regarding the disposition of that sum-total.

In another contribution, Kakwani (1978) modifies Axiom R in a different way to provide a more general structure than Axiom R would permit. Essentially, Kakwani's axiom makes the weight v_i the kth power of the income rank of person i among the poor.

Axiom R^*. The weights v_i in (3) are given by:

$$v_i = r(i)^k \tag{4.2}$$

For the poverty measure—call it P_3—derived from this, the sensitivity of between-poor income distribution will depend on the value of k. The poverty measure P obtained earlier corresponds to $k = 1$, making it, as Kakwani (1978) puts it, "equally sensitive to a transfer of income at all income positions" (p. 7). The generalization involved in P_3 permits various alternative assumptions about transfer sensitivity, e.g., giving more weight to transfers of income at the lower end of the distribution of income.

A different generalization based on a reinterpretation of the poverty index P has been proposed by Blackorby & Donaldson (1978). They note that the measure P, as given by (5), can be seen as the product of the head count ratio H and the proportionate gap between the poverty line income π and the Atkinson-Kolm "equally distributed equivalent income", e^g, of the incomes of the poor when the evaluation is done with the Gini social evaluation function.[1]

$$P = H[(\pi - e^g)/\pi]. \tag{5.1}$$

If the social evaluation function is changed, a new poverty measure would emerge correspondingly, with e the equally distributed equivalent income according to that social evaluation function.[2]

$$P_4 = H[(\pi - e)/\pi]. \tag{5.2}$$

Blackorby & Donaldson choose an *ethical* interpretation of the poverty measures. The value of e reflects that level of income which if shared by all the poor would be judged by the social evaluation function to be exactly as good as the actual distribution of income among the poor. But it is easily seen that the format permits a *descriptive* interpretation as well, viz. e standing for that level of income which if shared by all the poor will be regarded as displaying as much overall poverty as the actual distribution of income among the poor. The issues involved in the choice between descriptive and ethical interpretations of poverty have been discussed elsewhere (Sections I.1 and I.2 above),[3] and will not be pursued further. The poverty measures, not merely in the generalized form P_4, but also in the original form P, can be mathematically interpreted in either way, and the real question is one of relevance of the exercise to the motivation that leads to the search for a measure of poverty.

A particular descriptive characteristic of the poverty measure P has been the subject of some detailed investigation. While it is clear that the measure P of poverty *must* record a rise when there is a transfer of income from a poorer

---

[1] For the concept of equally distributed equivalent income, see Kolm (1969) and Atkinson (1970). For the relation of the poverty measure P to the Gini evaluation function, see Sen (1976a), and related matters in Sen (1974, 1976b).

[2] Blackorby & Donaldson (1978) point out the need for some assumptions about the general characteristics of such a social evaluation function, especially its homotheticity, and strict separability of a kind that permits one to rank the distributions of income among the poor independently of the incomes of those who are richer.

[3] See also Sen (1978b).

person to one who is richer provided this does not make the richer person cross the poverty line, exactly the opposite *can* happen—depending on the exact values—when such a crossing does take place (see Sen (1977*a*, p. 77)). It is arguable whether a poverty measure should not show *increased* poverty *whenever* some income is transferred from a poorer to a richer person *no matter* whether this makes the richer person cease to be regarded as poor because of his crossing the poverty line. Dominique Thon (1978) has analysed the analytical relations involved in such monotonic transfer sensitivity, and has proposed a variation of *P* that would ensure that the poverty measure records an increase whenever there is a transfer of income from a person who is poor to one who is richer. He modifies Axiom *R* to make the weight v_i on poor *i*'s income gap g_i equal his income rank $R(i)$ among *all* the people in the community and not merely among the poor (as under Axiom *R*).

Axiom R^{**}. The weights v_i in (3) are given by:

$$v_i = R(i) \tag{4.3}$$

Combined with the original structure with slight modifications, Axiom R^{**} precipitates Thon's variant—we may call it P_5—of the poverty measure satisfying this montonic transfer property.[1]

There remains, of course, the substantial issue as to whether a poverty measure should always register an increase whenever there is such a transfer even when the transfer actually reduces the number of the poor.[2] In so far as the index of poverty is interpreted to represent the condition of the poor in the nation—their prevalence and their penury—a good case can perhaps be made for permitting the possibility that a reduction of the prevalence of poverty might under some circumstances compensate a rise in the extent of penury of those who remain below the poverty line. The old measure *P* admits this, while Thon's P_5 does not. If, however, the focus is on the general poverty of the nation and not merely of the predicament of people below the poverty line, then the monotonic transfer axiom would make a good deal of sense, since the poverty-alleviating role of crossing the poverty line would be then rendered less crucial. Again, the variation proposed has merits that are conditional on the purpose for which the poverty measure is being sought.

---

[1] $P_5 = [2/\pi n(n+1)] \sum_{i=1}^{q} g_i R(i)$. This contrasts with the poverty measure *P*, which can be written as:

$P = [2/\pi n(q+1)] \sum_{i=1}^{q} g_i r(i)$.

[2] The "transfer axiom" considered (but not used in the derivation of *P*) in Sen (1976*a*) demanded: "Given other things, a pure transfer of income from a person below the poverty line to anyone who is richer must increase the poverty measure" (p. 219). In Sen (1977*a*), this was modified to the less demanding requirement: "Given other things, a pure transfer of income from a person below the poverty line to anyone richer must strictly increase the poverty measure unless the number below the poverty line is strictly reduced by the transfer" (p. 77). This contrast is the central one between *P* and P_5. It is worth noting that the traditional measures of poverty, such as *H* and *I*, which were shown to violate the original transfer axiom continue to violate this modified transfer axiom.

Another interesting variant of the poverty measures P has been proposed by Takayama (1978), and the approach used in that derivation has been extensively explored by Hamada & Takayama (1977). From the actual income distribution a "censured" income distribution is obtained by replacing the incomes that exceed the poverty line $(y > \pi)$ by incomes exactly equalling the poverty line (π). Takayama (1977) then takes the Gini coefficient G_C of the censured income distribution as the measure of poverty—we may call it P_6—and other measures of inequality are applied to the censured distribution to derive corresponding measures of poverty in Hamada & Takayama (1977).

The approach has some clear merits. The Gini coefficient of the censured distribution is a much neater—and closer—translation of the Gini measure of inequality into a poverty measure. It doctors the income distribution itself by ignoring the information on the actual incomes of the people who are not poor, but counts them in with poverty line incomes. Takayama (1978) has also provided an interesting axiomatization of his measure of poverty G_C, and Hamada & Takayama (1977) have suggested derivations for similar poverty measures based on other inequality indexes applied to the censured distribution.

The main drawback of this approach lies in its robust violation of the requirement that a reduction of income of anyone below the poverty line—given everything else—must *increase* the poverty measure to be used (the "monotonicity axiom" in Sen (1976a)). A person below the poverty line may still be among the *relatively* richer in the censured distribution of income with an income above the mean and the median of that distribution. A reduction of his income will in an obvious sense reduce the extent of inequality in the censured distribution, but in an equally obvious sense the community must now be having *more*—not *less*—poverty. So the simplicity of the formulae used by Takayama (1978) and Hamada & Takayama (1977) is achieved at some real cost, viz. failing to establish a monotonic relation between the poverty measure and vector-dominance of deprivation of the poor.

IV. Concluding Remarks

There will be no attempt to summarise the arguments presented in the paper, but a few general remarks will be made to put the discussion in perspective.

(1) There is a good case for viewing the measurement of poverty not, as is often asserted, as an ethical exercise, but primarily as a descriptive one (Section I.1). Furthermore, it can be argued that the frequently-used "policy definition" of poverty is fundamentally flawed (Section I.2). The exercise of describing the predicament of the poor in terms of the prevailing standards of "necessities" does, of course, involve ambiguities, which are inherent in the concept of poverty, but ambiguous description is not the same thing as prescription. Instead, the arbitrariness that is inescapable in choosing between permissible precedures and possible interpretations of standards require recognition and

appropriate treatment, e.g., explicit pointers to arbitrary elements, and use of partial orderings reflecting the intersection of various criteria (Sections I.1 and I.3).

(2) Considerations of "absolute" and "relative" deprivation both enter the concept of poverty. While the so-called "biological approach" of Rowntree (1901) and others may have concentrated too much on absolute aspects and the approach of "relative deprivation" corrects this, still there is an irreducible core of absolute deprivation in the perception of poverty. Attempts at "regarding poverty as an issue in inequality", appealing as it is, is crucially incomplete (Section II.1).

(3) The measurement of poverty can be split into two interrelated exercises, viz. the *identification* of the poor, and *aggregation* of the poverty characteristics of different people into one overall measure, or one ranking. The "direct method" and the "income method" are two different ways of resolving the *identification* exercise. They are not, however, two alternative ways of measuring the "same" thing, but reflect two different conceptions of poverty (Section II.2).

(4) Because of variations of family size, economies of large scale in family consumption, and age-specificity of needs, the problem of converting families into "equivalent adult" numbers involve serious difficulties. But alternative approaches can be considered, providing different *bases* for deriving equivalence of needs. There is the further problem of *weighting* of families of different size in the aggregation exercise. In this the practice of weighting families according to the number of "equivalent adults" rather than according to *actual* numbers reflects confusion, albeit a sophisticated one (Section II.3).

(5) The aggregation exercise is much too crudely performed by the standard measures of poverty such as the "head-count" of the poor and the "income gap" ratio. Some elementary characteristics that any measure of poverty can be expected to satisfy are robustly violated by these measures and by all joint functions of these variables (Section III.2).

(6) An axiomatization of the aggregation exercise using notions of absolute and relative deprivation leads to a poverty measure P, which can be shown to be a function of the "head-count ratio", the "income-gap ratio" and the "Gini coefficient" of income distribution among the poor (eq. 5). While the proof of the theorem has been presented elsewhere (Sen, 1976a), its intuitive content is explored here (Section III.3). It can easily be empirically applied, and has indeed been used to measure and compare poverty in a number of countries, and different states within a country.

(7) The axioms used for deriving the measure P can be varied, yielding other poverty measures, e.g., P_1 to P_6 discussed in the text (Section III.4). An analysis of the rationale of these variants indicate what they are trying to capture *vis-à-vis* what is represented by the poverty measure P. The choice depends largely on the precise motivation underlying the measurement of poverty. Some of these variations, in fact, define *classes* of measures with the

measure P a member of each such class. While P has cartain unique advantages, which its axiomatization brings out, several of the variants are certainly permissible interpretations of the common conception of poverty. There is nothing defeatist or astonishing in the acceptance of this "pluralism". Indeed, as argued earlier (Sections I.1 and I.3), such pluralism is inherent in the nature of the exercise.

References

Abel-Smith, B. & Townsend, P.: *The poor and the poorest*. Bell, London, 1965.

Ahluwalia, M. S.: Rural poverty and agricultural performance in India. *Journal of Development Studies 14*, 1978.

Alamgir, M.: Poverty, inequality and social welfare: Measurement, evidence and policies. *Bangladesh Development Studies 3*, 1975.

Alamgir, M.: Poverty, inequality and development strategy in the Third World. Mimeographed, Bangladesh Institute of Development Studies, February 1976.

Anand, S.: Aspects of poverty in Malaysia. *Review of Income and Wealth 23*, 1977.

Atkinson, A. B.: *Poverty in Britain and the reform of social security*. C.U. Press, Cambridge, 1969.

Atkinson, A. B.: On the measurement of inequality. *Journal of Economic Theory 2*, 1970.

Bardhan, P. K.: On the minimum level of living and the rural poor. *Indian Economic Review 5*, 1970.

Bardhan, P. K.: On the minimum level of living and the rural poor: A further note. *Indian Economic Review 6*, 1971.

Bardhan, P. K.: On the incidence of poverty in rural India. *Economic and Political Weekly*, February 1973; reprinted in Bardhan & Srinivasan (1974).

Bardhan, P. K. & Srinivasan, T. N.: *Poverty and income distribution in India*. Statistical Publishing Society, Calcutta, 1974.

Barten, A. P.: Family composition, prices and expenditure pattern. In Hart & Mills (1964).

Batchelder, A. B.: *The economics of poverty*. Wiley, New York, 1971.

Beckerman, W.: The impact of income maintenance programmes on poverty in Britain. ILO World Employment Programme, WEP 2-23/WP 62, Geneva, 1977.

Bentzel, R.: The social significance of income distribution statistics. *Review of Income and Wealth 16*, 1970.

Bhatty, I. Z.: Inequality and poverty in rural India. In Bardhan & Srinivasan (1974).

Blackorby, C. & Donaldson, D.: Ethical indices for the measurement of poverty. Mimeo, University of British Columbia, Vancover, 1978.

Borda, J. C.: Memoire sur les elections au scrutin. *Memoires de l'Academie Royale des Sciences*, 1781.

Booth, C.: *Life and labour of the people in London*. London, 1889.

Bowley, A. L.: *The nature and purpose of the measurement of social phenomena*. P. S. King, London, 1923.

Brown, J. A. C.: The consumption of food in relation to household composition and income. *Econometrica 22*, 1954.

Butts, R. E. & Hintikka, J. (eds.): *Foundational problems in the special sciences*. Reidel, Dordrecht and Boston, 1977.

Chenery, H., Ahluwalia, M. S., Bell, C. L. G., Duloy, J. H. & Jolly, R.: *Redistribution with growth*. Oxford University Press, London, 1974.

Dalton, H.: The measurement of the inequality of incomes. *Economic Journal 30*, 1920.

Dandekar, V. M. & Rath, N.: *Poverty in India*. Indian School of Political Economy, Poona, 1971.

Drewnowski, D.: Poverty: its meaning and measurement. *Development and Challange 8*, 1977.

Dutta, B.: On poverty in India. *Indian Economic Review 13*, 1978.

Eden, F. M.: *The state of the poor.* London, 1797.

Engel, E.: Die Lebenskosten belgischer Arbeiter-Familien früher und jetzt. *International Statistical Institute Bulletin 9*, 1895.

Engels, F.: *The condition of the working class in England.* 1892.

Friedman, M.: A method of comparing incomes of families differing in composition. *Studies in Income and Wealth 15*, NBER, New York, 1952.

Goedhart, T., Halberstadt, V., Kapteyn, A. & van Praag, B.: The poverty line: concept and measurement. Mimeographed, Economic Institute of Leyden University, March 1976.

Hamada, K. & Takayama, N.: Censored Income distributions and the measurement of poverty. Mimeographed, University of Tokyo, 1977.

Hammond, P. J.: Dual Interpersonal comparisons of utility and the welfare economics of income distribution. *Journal of Public Economics 6*, 1977.

Hansson, B.: The measurement of social inequality. In Butts & Hintikka (1977).

Hare, R. M.: *Freedom and reason.* Clarendon Press, Oxford, 1963.

Hart, P. & Mills, G.: *Econometric analysis for national economics.* Butterworth, London, 1964.

Hirsch, F.: *Social limits to growth.* Harvard U.P., Cambridge, Mass., 1976.

Hobsbawm, E. J.: Poverty. In *International Encyclopaedia of the Social Sciences.* New York, 1968.

Jackson, D.: *Poverty.* Macmillan, London, 1972.

Kakwani, N.: Income distribution: Methods of analysis and applications. World Bank, Washington, D.C., 1977; to be published.

Kakwani, N.: On a class of poverty measures. Mimeographed, 1978: forthcoming in *Econometrica.*

Kolm, S. Ch.: The optimal production of social justice. In *Public economics* (ed. J. Margolis and H. Guitton), Macmillan, London, 1969.

Krelle, W. & Shorrocks, A. F.: *Personal income distribution.* North-Holland, Amsterdam, 1978.

Lal, D.: Agricultural growth, real wages and the rural poor in India. *Economic and Political Weekly 11*, 1976.

Marx, K.: *Capital: A critical analysis of capitalist production*, vol. I. Sonnenschein, London, 1887.

Miller, S. M. & Roby, P.: Poverty: Changing social stratification. In Townsend (1971).

Minhas, B. S.: Rural poverty, land distribution and development. *Indian Economic Review 5*, 1970.

Minhas, B. S.: Rural poverty and minimum level of living. *Indian Economic Review 6*, 1971.

Muellbauer, J.: Testing the Barten model of household composition effects and the cost of children. *Economic Journal 87*, 1977*a.*

Muellbauer, J.: The estimation of the Prais–Houthakker model of equivalent scales. Mimeographed, Birkbeck College, London, 1977*b.*

Muellbauer, J.: Equivalent scales. In Royal Commission on the Distribution of Income and Wealth, *Selected evidence submitted to the Royal Commission for report no 6: Lower incomes.* London, 1978.

Mukherjee, M., Bhattacharya, N. & Chatterjee, G. S.: Poverty in India: Measurement and amelioration. *Commerce 125*, 1972.

Nicholson, J. L.: Appraisal of different methods of estimating equivalent scales and their results. *Review of Income and Wealth 22*, 1976.

Ojha, P. D.: A configuration of Indian poverty. *Reserve Bank of India Bulletin 24*, 1970.

Osmani, R.: Economic inequality and group welfare: Theory and applications to Bangladesh. Ph.D. dissertation, London School of Economics, 1978.

Orshansky, M.: Counting the poor: Another look at the poverty profile. *Social Security Bulletin 28*, 1965.

Orshansky, M.: Recounting the poor: A five year review. *Social Security Bulletin 29*, 1966.

Orshansky, M.: How poverty is measured. *Monthly Labour Review*, 1969.

Prais, S. J. & Houthakker, H. S.: *The analysis of family budgets*. CUP, Cambridge, 1955; 2nd ed. 1971.

Radhakrishna, R. & Sharma, A.: Distributional effects of the current inflation. *Social Scientist 30–31*, 1975.

Rajaraman, I.: Constructing the poverty line. Rural Punjab, 1960–61. RPED Discussion Paper 43, Princeton University, 1974.

Rowntree, S.: *Poverty: A study of town life*. Macmillan, London, 1901.

Runciman, W. G.: *Relative deprivation and social justice*. Routledge, London, 1966.

Sastry, S. A. R.: Poverty, inequality and development: A study of Andhra Pradesh. Sardar Patel Institute of Economic and Social Research, Ahmedabad, 1978.

Scitovsky, T.: *The joyless economy*. Oxford University Press, London and New York, 1976.

Seastrand, F. & Diwan, R.: Measurement and comparison of poverty and inequality in the United States. Presented at the Third World Econometric Congress, Toronto, 1975.

Sen, A. K.: *On economic inequality*. Clarendon Press, Oxford, 1973a.

Sen, A. K.: Poverty, inequality and unemployment: Some conceptual issues in measurement. *Economic and Political Weekly 8*, 1973b; reprinted in Bardhan & Srinivasan (1974).

Sen, A. K.: Information bases of alternative welfare approaches: Aggregation and income distribution. *Journal of Public Economics 4*, 1974.

Sen, A. K.: Poverty: An ordinal approach to measurement. *Econometrica 44*, 1976a.

Sen, A. K.: Real national income. *Review of Economic Studies 43*, 1976b.

Sen, A. K.: Social choice theory: A re-examination. *Econometrica 45*, 1977a.

Sen, A. K.: On weights and measures: Informational constraints in social welfare analysis. *Econometrica 45*, 1977b.

Sen, A. K.: Welfare and rights. Text of Hägerström Lectures delivered at the Philosophy Department of Uppsala University in April 1978a; to be published.

Sen, A. K.: Ethical measurement of inequality: Some difficulties. In Krelle & Shorrocks (1978b).

Smith, A.: *Wealth of nations*. 1776. Everyman's Library, Dent, London, Vol. II.

Stein, S., Susser, M., Saenger, G. & Marolla, F.: *Famines and human-development: The Dutch hunger winter of 1944–45*. Oxford University Press, London, 1975.

Stewart, F. & Streeten, P.: New strategies for development: Poverty, income distribution and growth. *Oxford Economic Papers 28*, 1976.

Stigler, J.: The cost of subsistence. *Journal of Farm Economics 27*, 1945.

Takayama, N.: Poverty, income inequality and their measures: Professor Sen's axiomatic approach reconsidered. Mimeographed; forthcoming *Econometrica*.

Thon, D.: On a class of poverty measures. *Hull Economic Research Paper 39*, 1978.

Townsend, P. (ed.): *The concept of poverty*. Heinemann, H. E. B. Paperback, London, 1971.

Townsend, P.: Poverty as relative deprivation: Resources and styles of living. In Wedderburn (1974).

Vaidynathan, A.: Some aspects of inequalities of living standards in rural India. In Bardhan & Srinivasan (1974).

Wedderburn, D. (ed.): *Poverty, inequality and class structure*. CUP, Cambridge, 1974.

Weisbrod, B. A. (ed.): *The economics of poverty*. Prentice-Hall, Englewood Cliffs, 1965.

Wiles, P.: *Distribution of income: East and west*. North-Holland, Amsterdam, 1974.

POLITOMETRICS OF GOVERNMENT BEHAVIOR IN A DEMOCRACY

*Bruno S. Frey**

Universities of Zürich and Basel, Switzerland

Abstract

One of the major developments in Public Choice has been that of politico-economic models that empirically study the mutual interaction between the economy and the polity ("politometrics"). Government is taken as having a monopolistic position and as maximizing its own utility subject to restrictions, in particular the re-election constraint. Voters evaluate government's performance via elections and popularity surveys, having as their main criterium a satisfactory state of the economy. Politometric estimates for several countries and periods are presented and the politico-economic models' performance is compared to that of traditional econometric models. The research may be fruitfully extended in various directions.

I. The Importance of Empirical Public Choice

Benevolent Dictator vs. Political Economy

In modern economics there are two completely different views on how to improve the welfare of the people in a society:

(1) The *social welfare function approach* assumes that policies optimal from the point of view of society can be derived by maximizing a social welfare function subject to the constraints imposed by the economic system. This procedure is standard even though the maximization is not always explicitly performed. It is most prominently employed in the traditional theory of quantitative economic policy, e.g. Tinbergen (1956) and Theil (1968), as well as in the modern versions applied to dynamic problems, i.e. the normative theory of economic growth, e.g. Shell (1967), and the theory of optimal control, e.g. Chow (1973) and Pindyck (1973). Exactly the same approach is used in the optimal taxation literature, e.g. Diamond & Mirrlees (1971) and *Journal of Public Economics* (1976), to look at efficiency losses arising from distortions brought about by taxes.

The economist's task here is fulfilled once the optimal policies are derived. It is presumed that once derived, these policies will somehow be realized; i.e.,

* I am grateful to Friedrich Schneider for helpful comments, and to Sandra Stuber for improving the English and other suggestions.

that government and the public bureaucracy, functioning as a "benevolent dictator" interested only in the social good, will act in the interests of the social welfare and carry them out.

(2) The *political economy or Public Choice approach* stresses positive analysis. Only when the decision-makers' interaction system and the politico-economic system's function are well understood can one begin to try to influence them. Every decision-maker is assumed to maximize its *own* utility subject to various constraints. Most importantly, it is assumed that government and the public bureaucracy have goals of their own that they pursue, and that they are not interested in furthering the public interest or social welfare. Government is thus considered to be an *endogenous* part of the politico-economic system.

As the behavior of decision-makers is here seen as being determined by the system as a whole, it is not easily influenced by actors exogenous to the inter-action system, i.e. by the economist as policy advisor. The best way to in-fluence the outcomes resulting from the workings of the politico-economic system is to change the rules of the game. These rules are determined by the nature of the particular institutions existent in the system, such as, for in-stance, the way the government is chosen. The political economy approach is thus process-oriented. If the politico-economic process works well, i.e. if it is democratic and takes individual preferences into account, the outcome is considered to be good. It should be noted that this view is analogous to the economist's view of the workings of the ideal market: The *process* of perfect competition leads to Pareto-optimality. Optimality of outcome is here a by-product of the individual actors' behavior, i.e., it results although the common good was not the specific aim of anyone.

The benevolent dictator or social welfare function approach still dominates in modern economics despite the fact that Wicksell had already strongly rejected it in 1896. Since then even more arguments have arisen against it. To name just the most basic ones: It has been proved that no consistent social welfare function can be constructed on the basis of individual preferences; the social welfare function cannot be made operational, i.e. it is not amenable to empirical testing; the policies derived by maximizing the social welfare func-tion are not accepted by practical policymakers as it is not in their interest to behave this way; the approach is methodologically inacceptable because it transfers the concept of individual utility maximization to society as a whole.

Progress in Public Choice

Most economists recognize Downs' (1957) seminal contribution of the idea of vote maximizing parties. They are, however, not fully aware of the subsequent developments in this branch of economics, and especially of the empirical re-search that has been done. So far, the empirical analyses have been relatively limited in scope and have concentrated on special fields such as the median voter model. The empirical work done in other areas of Public Choice has, however, been rapidly increasing over the last few years. One of the major developments has been the construction and empirical testing of politico-economic models that study the mutual interaction between the economy and the polity, especially the government. The use of econometric methods in this area may be called "politometrics".

It is not intended here to give a general survey of either Public Choice, see Taylor (1975), Mueller (1976) and Frey (1977), or politico-economic models, see Frey (1978). The paper concentrates rather on the more limited question of what has been learned about government behavior. It should be noted that this question is not dealt with in isolation, but rather with government included as an integral element of the politico-economic complex.

II. Models of Government Behavior

The Model of Party Competition

Downs and the axiomatic theory subsequently developed following his original idea[1] both assume that there are two parties, that each one attempts to maximize its share of the votes, and that voters' preferences are distributed along a spatial scale representing a particular political issue. Under somewhat restrictive conditions, the following results obtain: Both parties offer the same program and chance decides which one will form the government; both party programs focus on the median of the voters' preference distribution; and the outcome is Pareto-optimal.

The following points of criticism can be raised against this model of party competition:

(*a*) In reality, there are very few countries that have only two parties competing against each other. The extension of the traditional model to more than two parties, however, is confronted with grave difficulties, and so far no satisfactory results have been achieved.

(*b*) It is unclear why a party's only goal should at all times be the maximization of votes. It is easy to think of other goals such as staying in power for as long as possible, or the realization of its ideological preferences.

(*c*) Voters' preferences are left completely unspecified in the basic model. It is, however, well known that voters are strongly influenced by economic conditions. Since Keynes the population has learned—or has been taught—that government can influence the economic process. Most written constitutions give the government the task of maintaining price stability and high employment, and how well it does this is the major criterium on which the voters base their evaluation of the government's performance. The traditional model of

---

[1] A good treatment is in Riker & Ordeshook (1973).

party competition also does not take into account the fact that voters have to make political decisions on the basis of incomplete information.

The Monopolistic Position of Government

Government can be considered to be in a special position of power similar to that of a monopolist. It has various advantages in comparison to the opposition party or parties, the most important of which is the opportunity to influence the course of the economy before elections.

The government's behavior can be analyzed by assuming that it maximizes its own utility subject to various constraints; see Frey & Lau (1968). The utility that government politicians receive by being in power is taken to be their chance to carry out their ideological programs. The most important constraint is political: Government politicians can only stay in power if they are reelected. There are also important economic constraints relating to the structure of the economy which determines how economic policy instruments will affect the economy, as well as the traditional ones of the budget and balance of payments. Government is also restricted in its activity by administrative and legal constraints, in particular by the public bureaucracy which resists structural changes in expenditure programs as much as possible and has an interest in continually increasing public outlays.

The monopolistic model of government behavior sketched above is quite general, and includes as a special case the model of party competition. When the political re-election constraint is very strong (for example, when government popularity is low), the government must maximize votes in order to survive (i.e., to stay in power). It then can only "choose" to act according to its ideology when this falls in line with the voters' wishes. Otherwise, it has no discretionary power. It should be noted that according to this view, vote maximization is seen as being the result of intense competition among parties, rather than an *a priori* assumed goal.

The monopolistic model of government behavior also includes the opposite of party competition: Parties may form a coalition among themselves and stand united against the voters in which case the re-election constraint will have no effect on policy choices; see Wittman (1973).

Neither of the two special cases described seem to be relevant in reality. Government always has some discretionary power, especially in between elections, and thus the model of party competition is too extreme. But government also always depends to at least some extent on the electorate, just as monopolistic firms are still dependent on consumer demand. Thus the idea of a coalition of the parties and the absence of all competition is also too extreme. Within the framework of the monopolistic model of government behavior, empirical research should show what influence the voters' wishes have on government policy, and the actual amount of discretionary power available

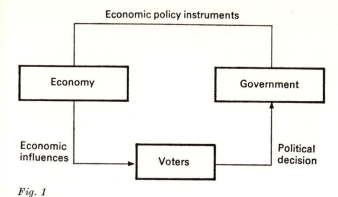

Fig. 1

to the government. Considerable progress has been made here in the past few years. It is no longer necessary to rely solely on impressions of how governments behave, as there are now econometric (or politometric) data available.

III. Politometric Estimation: Some Results

The Complete Politico-Economic System

The overall interaction between the economy and the polity—which is represented here by the government—is shown in Fig. 1. It is, of course, a highly simplified schematisation. The lower loop shows how the state of the economy influences the voters' political decision. The upper loop shows how government reacts and uses its economic policy instruments to influence the economy and therewith reach its ideological goals or increase its re-election chances.

The two loops of the politico-economic system will now be discussed. The economic factors on which the voters' evaluations depend will be treated first, and then the factors that determine government policy. The conclusions will be illustrated with estimates gained from politometric research.

Voters' Evaluations

The way the voters evaluate the government's performance is indicated by two different sets of data. Election results show how voters have decided at discontinuous points in time, usually each fourth or fifth year. Popularity data are collected at much shorter intervals (usually of one month) and on a regular basis. They are collected by survey research institutes such as government or national opinion polls, and reflect the answers to such questions as "If elections were tomorrow, which party would you vote for?"

It is hypothesized that these indicators of the voters' evaluation of government policy depend on economic variables as well as other, non-economic factors, such as long-run influences and autonomous ones not related to the

Table 1. *The influence of economic variables on the vote share of the incumbent, in the United States and the Scandinavian countries*

The parameter estimates may be interpreted in the following way: A one percentage point increase in the rate of inflation decreases the vote share of the incumbent party by -0.49 percentage points in U.S. congressional elections. A one percentage point increase in the rate of unemployment has no significant effect, and a one percentage point increase in the growth rate of real disposable income increases the incumbent's congressional vote share by 0.46 percentage points. The coefficients for the other elections and countries can be interpreted analogously

Dependent variable Vote share of incumbent party (government)	Economic variables		
	Rate of inflation (%)	Change in rate of unemployment (%)	Growth of real (disposable) income (%)
United States			
Congressional elections (1896–1964)	-0.49*	0.001	0.46*
Presidential elections (1916–1976)	-0.55	—	0.88*
Sweden	-0.22	-2.4*	—
	—	—	0.73*
Norway	-0.15	0.05	—
Denmark	-0.43*	0.19	—

* signifies that the respective coefficient is statistically significant at the 95 % level of security. The U.S. estimates for congressional elections are taken from Kramer (1971, Table 1, revised estimates), and those for presidential elections from Fair (1978, Table 2). The Scandinavian estimates are from Madsen (1978, Tables 2–4) and are for 1918–1975. A dash indicates that the respective variable has not been included among the explanatory variables. Kramer and Madsen both exclude the war years in their estimates. For definitions of the variables, sources, and full estimation results, see the original papers.

state of the economy (internal political scandals or foreign policy influences, for example).

The influence of these economic and non-economic variables on popularity and election outcomes can be analyzed by multiple regression.

Elections. In order to have a sufficient number of observations, election function studies must extend over a great number of years. In Table 1, the estimates presented for the United States extend over 68 years, and those for the Scandinavian countries, over 67 years. Table 1 does not present the full multiple regressions but only shows the influence of the economic variables on the incumbent's share of the vote. It is theoretically expected that an increase in the rate of inflation and in the rate of unemployment decreases, and a rise in growth of real income increases, the vote share of the incumbent, i.e., of the party in power.

The results presented in Table 1 only partly bear out the relationship expected. When the rate of inflation rises, the government's share of the vote tends to fall in all four countries, but the negative effect is only statistically significant for United States congressional elections and for Denmark. Unemployment fares even worse: It has the right sign but is only statistically significant for Sweden. In the other three countries it has a positive sign and is either not statistically significant or has not been included at all. A rise in the growth rate of real income has no effect on election outcome in Norway or Denmark. There is a statistically positive effect in Sweden, but this is true only if the other two economic variables are not simultaneously included in the regression equation. It is only in the United States that the theoretical hypothesis holds: The growth of real income significantly increases the incumbent party's share of the vote in congressional and presidential elections beyond the influence of inflation and of unemployment. On the whole, the election function yields somewhat disappointing results. It may be the case that the periods over which the regression results are taken are too long as they may include significant structural shifts in the voters' evaluations of government policy. It may, for instance, be argued that voters have only held the government responsible for unsatisfactory economic conditions since the latter has assumed responsibility for the course of the economy as a result of the Keynesian revolution, i.e. since World War II. It is therefore useful to look at the popularity data.

Government Popularity. The following estimates of government popularity functions are based on quarterly data so that sufficient observations can be had without extending the period covered too far. As governments tend to use current popularity values as indicators of their likely election success, they may also be more relevant for an analysis of government policy in the short- and medium-run.

Table 2 shows the influence of the same economic variables as in Table 1 for the United States, the United Kingdom, the Federal Republic of Germany, and Sweden for the post-war years. The politometric estimates using popularity data perform much better than those using election results. All the coefficients have the theoretically expected signs and are statistically significant. Table 2 shows that an increase in the rate of inflation always decreases the popularity share the government receives, as is also the case with the rate of unemployment. An increase in the growth rate of real disposable income, on the other hand, always increases the government's popularity share. There are some marked differences in the degree to which the change in the macroeconomic variables affects government popularity in the different countries. It should be noted in particular that a rise in unemployment depresses government popularity much less in Germany than in the other three countries. It may in general be concluded that the three major macroeconomic variables of inflation, unemployment, and growth of real income have a strong and significant effect on government's popularity among the voters.

Table 2. *The influence of economic variables on government popularity in the United States, the United Kingdom, Germany, and Sweden, post-war years*

The parameter estimates may be interpreted in the following way: A percentage point increase in the rate of inflation decreases the popularity of the American president by −1.6 percentage points. An increase in the rate of unemployment reduces his popularity by −4.1 percentage points, and an increase in the growth rate of real disposable income increases it by 0.1 percentage points. The coefficients for the other countries can be interpreted analogously

Dependent variable Popularity share of the government	Economic variables		
	Rate of inflation (%)	Rate of unemployment (%)	Growth of real (disposable) income (%)
United States			
President, 1953–76	−1.6*	−4.1*	0.5*
United Kingdom			
1959–74	−0.6*	−6.0*	0.8*
Germany			
1957–75	−1.5*	−1.7*	0.6(*)
Sweden			
1967–73	−0.9*	−5.2*	0.3(*)

* indicates statistical significance at the 90 % level of security. In this table, the rate of unemployment is given as a level and not as a change in level as in Table 1. The estimate for Sweden is based on monthly data and is taken from Kirchgässner (1976, Table 4.9). The estimates for the other countries are based on quarterly data and are taken from various joint publications of Frey and Schneider (see e.g. 1978 a, b, 1979).

The coefficients indicating the effect of economic conditions on government varies over time. Voters' preferences change, their perception of the state of the economy changes, and their evaluation of the government's performance and possibilities changes. This can be seen in the example of Germany. The popularity function has been estimated for 16 years of Christian Democrat dominated government, and for 8 years of Social Democrat dominated government. As may be seen from Table 3, the coefficients of the three variables change in different directions from the first to the second period. The impact on government popularity of rises in inflation decreased; that of increases in unemployment rose; and that of real income growth decreased.

It may be noted that in all countries and all periods studied, a 1 percentage point change in the rate of unemployment had a larger effect than a 1 percentage point change in inflation. A change in the growth of real disposable income of 1 percentage point always had the smallest effect. This can be seen

Table 3. *The influence of economic variables on government popularity in two subsequent periods, in Germany (quarterly data)*

The parameter estimates may be interpreted in the following way: During the period of a Christian Democrat government, an increase in the rate of inflation by one percentage point decreased government popularity by −0.86 percentage points. A one percentage point increase in the rate of unemployment and in the real growth rate of income did not have a statistically significant effect on government popularity. The coefficients relating to the period of Social Democrat rule may be interpreted analogously. For further notes see Table 2

	Economic variables		
Dependent variable Popularity share of the government	Rate of inflation (%)	Rate of unemployment (%)	Growth of real (disposable) income (%)
1950–1966			
Governments dominated by Christian Democrat party	−0.86*	−0.99	0.12
1969–1976			
Governments dominated by Social Democrat party	−0.67*	−1.43*	0.04

in Tables 1, 2 and 3. In Germany in the most recent period covered (1969–76), a 1 percentage point increase in unemployment reduced government popularity by 1.43 %, as compared to −0.67 % in the case of inflation and +0.04 % in the case of real income growth.

The fact that the rate of unemployment has by far the greatest impact on government popularity is of great importance for government behavior. It suggests that an expansionary policy lowering unemployment and raising income growth is an effective policy for raising popularity and thus increasing re-election chances. The positive effect of such a policy will be greater and also much more immediate than the negative effect resulting from any subsequent inflation. As is well known, an expansionary government policy raises the rate of inflation only after a considerable time lag, and it may therefore not show up until the next election period. In modern economies, quantity changes take place before price changes.

Government Policy

The optimization problem faced by the government as sketched above is so complex that it is in general impossible or at least extremely difficult to derive an analytical solution. The problem is, of course, still more difficult to solve in the real world. It may therefore be assumed that government politicians resort to a satisficing strategy, concentrating their attention on the crucial re-election constraint. When current popularity is larger than what they consider to be necessary for winning the forthcoming election, they can allow themselves to undertake policies that raise their own utility. If, on the other hand, their popularity level is so low that they are afraid of losing the next election, they are forced to undertake policies that will increase their re-election chances. They are well aware that their popularity and re-election chances depend heavily on the state of the economy, and will therefore try to bring about what will be perceived by the voters as an improvement in economic conditions. The government must always take into account the constraints imposed on its behavior by the structure of the economic system and by the other economic, administrative and legal constraints, both when popularity is high and when it is low.

The model developed—that government maximizes its own utility subject to various constraints, and that it uses a satisficing strategy to solve this complex maximization problem by differentiating between a state of popularity surplus and popularity deficit—performs quite well in empirical tests. The dependent variables of the policy function thus derived are government expenditures of various types (exhaustive and transfer expenditures, consumption and investment outlays, etc.), taxes, and the use of at least some other instruments such as the wage rate and employment in the public sector. Among the explanatory variables are the size of the popularity surplus and a dummy variable indicating the ideological bias of the party in power when the government is confident of being re-elected; and the size of the popularity deficit and a variable measuring the time left until the forthcoming election when the government is afraid that it will not be re-elected. The budget, balance of payments, and administrative/legal constraints may influence government outlays in both states. The quantitative regression results are not reproduced here for reasons of space; the reader is referred to the original publications. The qualitative results of the politometric estimates with quarterly data for the United States (1943–75), the United Kingdom (1962–74), and Germany (1951–75) can be summarized as follows:

(1) When governments enjoy a popularity surplus, left-wing governments (Labour in the U.K., Social Democrats in Germany) have a tendency to increase government expenditures and taxes, and right-wing governments (Tories in the U.K., Christian Democrats in Germany, Republican presidents in the U.S.) to decrease public expenditures and taxes.

(2) All types of representative governments in the countries and periods up to 1975 studied undertook expandionary policies when they were afraid that they would not be re-elected in the forthcoming election (i.e., when they were in a state of popularity deficit). They tended to increase exhaustive and transfer expenditures, decrease taxes, and increase public employment before elections. This behavior is of course due to the way voters evaluate the state of the economy: Government politicians know that in general an expansionary

policy leads to an increase in government popularity because the decrease in unemployment and the increase in economic growth dominate the lagged increase in the rate of inflation. Other states of affairs are also possible, however. Preliminary research for Switzerland, see Schneider, Pommerehne & Frey (1978), seems to indicate that Swiss voters are most concerned with inflation. Unemployment has not been an issue for the Swiss in the post-war period, partly because of the cushioning effect of a large body of foreign workers, who can be sent back to their home countries. Accordingly, the estimates of the policy functions of the Swiss government indicates that when the Swiss government experiences a support deficit among the voters, it undertakes a restrictive policy to combat inflation by lowering expenditures and increasing taxes as compared to the overall trend.

(3) In a state of popularity deficit all the governments of the countries examined have tended to increase exhaustive and transfer expenditures, decrease taxes, and increase public employment before elections. This is evidence for the existence of a political business cycle in a limited sense: In the approach used here, governments produce a political cycle only when they are afraid of not being re-elected, but have no reason for doing so if they are confident of winning the forthcoming election. The model thus differs strongly from other theories of political business cycles in which government maximizes votes and thus is always producing such a cycle,[1] and from empirically oriented research on political business cycles which looks for regular cycles with the length of one election period; see e.g. Paldam (1977) and McCallum (1978).

(4) The budget and administrative/legal constraints are important determinants of government behavior when re-election expectations are both high and low. In one of the countries referred to, the United Kingdom, the balance of payments as expected has a strong influence on expenditures: The larger the deficit on current account, the smaller are public expenditures on consumption, investment, subsidies and grants; and the higher are taxes.

IV. Evaluation

The model developed and the results sketched constitute only the beginnings of empirical research in political economy, and especially in the study of the interaction between the economy and the polity. In order to try to evaluate the present state and future prospects of this type of research, we shall now discuss its shortcomings and achievements.

Shortcomings

(1) The politico-economic models so far developed do not adequately deal with some of the important decision-makers. It is in particular necessary to integrate

---

[1] See the models by Nordhaus (1975), Lindbeck (1975) and MacRae (1977), as well as the early contribution by Åkerman (1947).

the public bureaucracy, interest groups (business, trade unions), and parliament (the relationship between president and Congress in the United States, for example) more fully.

There is presently research underway in this direction. It has been shown that the model used for the government (utility maximization subject to constraints) is also appropriate for explaining central bank behavior, and therewith monetary policy, with the decisive constraint on the central bank being the possibility of conflict with the government. It has been hypothesized that in the case of conflict, the government is for various reasons in a more powerful position, and the central bank has to yield to its politically motivated demands. The following propositions have been tested in this regard for Germany, with good results; see Frey & Schneider (1978c). In the case of conflict with the government, the central bank follows government policy (with a time lag)—specifically, it undertakes an expansionary monetary policy in accordance with the government's expansionary fiscal policy. In the case of no-conflict with the government, the central bank pursues its own utility by undertaking a restrictive policy, i.e., by increasing interest rates and decreasing credits in order to combat inflation.

Again for Germany, politometric results, see Gärtner (1978), indicate that, before elections, trade unions increase their wage demands to create difficulties for governments of the right, and—*ceteris paribus*—reduce their demands when the party in power is of the left.

(2) The politico-economic models do not allow for the influence of political relations between nations. This aspect is of obvious importance, especially in the age of movements towards economic and political integration, such as the European community. Equally, the interaction of federal units is left out of account. Sub-federal units not only spend a large part of total public expenditures in many countries; they also influence the central government's policy.

(3) In the present models, government activity is reflected only through the budget. There are, however, a great many other policy areas open to the government which it can use substitutively. If the substitution possibilities are heavily employed, the policy function as sketched above may be misspecified.

(4) Informational aspects should receive more attention both with respect to voters and political actors. If, for instance, voters become increasingly aware of the fact that governments voluntarily create business cycles in order to stay in power, they may start reacting adversely to such activity. In that case, it may no longer be worthwhile for governments to create such cycles. The close relationship to the theory of rational expectation should be obvious.

Achievements

The politometric approach to studying the behavior of government in the framework of the macro-interrelationship between the economy and polity

Table 4. *Ex-post forecasts of a politometric model and a "pure economic model"*

Germany, yearly data, 1958–1972. Average percentage deviations per year. Source: Frey & Schneider (1979)

Type of model of government behavior	Economic variables explained			
	Exhaustive government expenditures	Transfers to private households	Nominal GNP	General price level
Politometric	1.80	1.41	2.62	1.80
"Pure" economic	8.34	4.04	4.55	3.66

compares favorably with the early Public Choice models, which had little or no empirical content. The emphasis on the dominant role of government (subject to constraints) seems to be more useful than that of models of party competition, which have become increasing sterile and which, for good reasons, are rarely tested empirically. The politometric approach is also an advance over the systems approaches such as that of Easton (1965), which are quite elaborate but which cannot be quantified with empirical data. The politometric models also seem to be better able to trace past government activity. A comparison of ex-post forecasts for Germany using yearly estimates of a politico-economic model with those of a yearly "pure" econometric model of Krelle (1974) gives the results shown in Table 4.

The traditional or "pure" econometric model explains exhaustive government expenditures simply as a weighted mean of past tax income and gross domestic income; it explains transfers by past income; wages in the public sector, by the general wage level; and employment in the public sector, by hours worked in the public sector. Table 4 shows that the politico-economic model has a consistently lower percentage deviation of predicted from observed values for both policy instruments (exhaustive and transfer expenditures) and for macroeconomic "goals'" variables (GNP, price level). The endogenization of government behavior thus may be expected to improve the quality of ex-ante forecasts; see Schneider (1978).

As was pointed out at the beginning, the fact that government should be considered an endogenous part of the politico-economic system has considerable consequences for the theory of economic policy. The empirical politometric research done so far, even if only in its beginning stages, confirms Wicksell's insight that the benevolent dictator view of government acting in the public interest should be abandoned, and that the political economy view of a democratic government influenced by voters' preferences should be adopted.

References

Åkerman, Johan: Political economic cycles. *Kyklos 1*, 107–17, 1947.

Chow, Gregory C.: Problems of economic policy from the viewpoint of optimal control. *American Economic Review 63*, 825–37, Dec. 1973.

Diamond, Peter A. & Mirrlees, James A.: Optimal taxation and public production. *American Economic Review 61* (March), 8–27, and *61* (June), 261–78, 1971.

Downs, Anthony: *An economic theory of democracy*. Harper, New York. (German edition: *Ökonomische Theorie der Demokratie*. Mohr (Siebeck), Tübingen, 1968.)

Easton, David: *A systems analysis of political life*. Wiley, New York, 1965.

Fair, Ray C.: The effect of economic events on votes for President. *Review of Economics and Statistics 60*, 159–73, May 1978.

Frey, Bruno S.: *Moderne Politische Ökonomie*. Piper, Munich and Zurich, 1977. (English edition: *Modern political economy*. Martin Robertson, London, 1978.)

Frey, Bruno S.: Politico-economic models and cycles. *Journal of Public Economics 9*, 203–220, April 1978.

Frey, Bruno S. & Lau, Lawrence L.: Towards a mathematical model of government behavior. *Zeitschrift für Nationalökonomie 28*, 355–80, 1968.

Frey, Bruno S. & Schneider, Friedrich: An empirical study of politico-economic interaction in the United States. *Review of Economics and Statistics 60*, 174–83, May 1978a.

Frey, Bruno S. & Schneider, Friedrich: A politico-economic model of the United Kingdom. *Economic Journal 88*, 243–53, 1978b.

Frey, Bruno S. & Schneider, Friedrich: Central bank behavior: A positive empirical analysis. Discussion Paper No. 7803. Institute for Empirical Economic Research, University of Zürich, 1978c.

Frey, Bruno S. & Schneider, Friedrich: An econometric model with an endogenous government sector. *Public Choice*, forthcoming 1979.

Gärtner, Manfred: A politico-economic model of wage inflation. Discussion Paper No. 18. Institute for Social Sciences and Institute for Applied Economic Research, University of Basel, April 1978.

Journal of Public Economics (1976): Special issue on "Taxation Theory", 6 (July–Aug.), pp. 1–169.

Kirchgässner, Gebhard: Rationales Wählerverhalten und optimales Regierungsverhalten. Dissertation. University of Konstanz, 1976.

Kramer, Gerald H.: Short-term fluctuations in U.S. voting behavior, 1896–1964. *American Political Science Review 65*, 131–43, March 1971. Revised version in Bobbs-Merrill Reprint Series in Political Science, No. 68877.

Krelle, Wilhelm: *Erfahrungen mit einem ökonometrischen Prognosemodell für die Bundesrepublik Deutschland*. Anton Hain, Meisenheim, 1974.

Lindbeck, Assar: Business cycles, politics and international economic dependence. *Skandinaviska Enskilda Banken Quarterly Review 2*, 53–68, 1975.

Madsen, Henrik Jess: Electoral outcomes and macroeconomic policies: The Scandinavian case. Paper presented at the European Consortium for Political Research Workshop on Formal Political Analysis, Grenoble, April 6–11, 1978.

McCallum, Bennett T.: The political business cycle: An empirical test. *Southern Economic Journal 44*, 504–15, Jan. 1978.

MacRae, Duncan C.: A political model of the business cycle. *Journal of Political Economy 85*, 239–63, April 1977.

Mueller, Dennis C.: Public choice: A survey. *Journal of Economic Literature 14*, 395–433, June 1976.

Nordhaus, William D.: The political business cycle. *Review of Economic Studies 42*, 169–90, April 1975.

Paldam, Martin: Is there an election cycle? A comparative study of national accounts. Institute of Economics, University of Aarhus, Memo 77-8.

Pindyck, Robert S.: *Optimal Planning for Economic Stabilization.* North Holland Publishing Co., Amsterdam, 1973.

Riker, William H. & Ordeshook, Peter: *An introduction to positive political theory.* Prentice Hall, Englewood Cliffs, 1973.

Schneider, Friedrich: Ein politisch-ökonomisches Modell des Zentralbankverhaltens bei endogenem Staat. Paper presented at the meeting of the Verein für Socialpolitik, Hamburg, September 1978.

Schneider, Friedrich, Pommerehne, Werner W. & Frey, Bruno S.: Politico-economic interdependence in a direct democracy: The case of Switzerland. Mimeo. Institute for Empirical Economic Research, University of Zürich, 1978.

Shell, Karl: *Essays in the theory of optimal economic growth.* MIT Press, Cambridge, Mass. and London, 1967.

Taylor, Michael: The theory of collective choice. In *Macropolitical theory* (Handbook of Political Science 3), (ed. F. I. Greenstein and N. W. Polsby), pp. 413–81. Reading, 1975.

Theil, Henry: *Optimal decision rules for government and industry.* North Holland Publishing Co., Amsterdam, 1968.

Tinbergen, Jan: *Economic policy: principles and design.* North Holland Publishing Co., Amsterdam, 1956.

Wicksell, Knut: *Finanztheoretische Untersuchungen.* Gustav Fischer, Jena, 1896.

Wittman, Donald A.: Parties as utility maximizers. *American Political Science Review 67,* 490–98, 1973.

IS THERE AN ELECTIONAL CYCLE?
A COMPARATIVE STUDY
OF NATIONAL ACCOUNTS*

Martin Paldam

University of Aarhus, Aarhus, Denmark

Abstract

This study covers three component series (current growth, real growth and growth in implicit price deflators) for eight main national accounts series for 17 OECD countries. When a government is defined as "stable" if it has a parliamentary majority and if it rules throughout a normal electional period, 49 stable governments are found in the 17 countries between 1948 and 1975. Subsequently, a test is made for all component series in order to see whether each moves in a systematic way during the average stable government period. Data are sufficiently numerous to prove a cycle, even though it turns out to be fairly weak. The cycle does not follow the pattern most often claimed, and to a certain extent it appears to be imported through foreign trade prices. Nevertheless, a policy-generated cycle clearly exists.

I. Theme

It has frequently been claimed that there is a *policy cycle* in the main economic series in typical "Western" economies. A number of theories of political cycles have even been developed, starting with Kalecki (1943), Åkerman (1946). More recently, Nordhaus (1975) and MacRae (1977) have developed formal theories. The central feature of these formal theories is the dynamization of the Phillips curve. Consequently, they are to be analyzed in the context of labor market data. This is done in a closely related paper; see Paldam (1979b) and further in Paldam (1979a). Here we study national accounts data and thus touch upon the formal theories only indirectly.[1] Basically, there are two main types of theories, one which gives a "mismanagement" and the other a "deliberate" kind of cycle. The first type exists in two very distinct versions:

* This study is part of a larger project supported by the Danish Social Science Research Fund through a grant which was used to pay for the able assistance of three students: Kjeld Lumbye Jensen, Henning Gerner Mikkelsen and Erik Strøjer Madsen. The work has benefited greatly from comments on a first version from Jørgen Gelting, Karsten Laursen, Svend Hylleberg, Peder J. Pedersen and Claus Vastrup.
[1] Another reason for keeping down references and formal theory is that the whole area of political cycles has recently been most adequately surveyed by Frey (1976), Dinkel (1977) and Frey (1978). The more general theory of endogenous economic policy has been analyzed by Lindbeck (1976).

Short-run mismanagement. Here the theory is based on the fact that the economy reacts to different policy measures with some time lag (3–18 months). In the meantime, political pressures may cause further actions and, in the end, reactions may consequently overshoot the mark, which may in turn spur excessive countermeasures, etc. This points to a fairly short period of cyclical instability—probably as short as two-three years.

Long-run mismanagement. Here the main idea is that policy-making has a shorter time horizon than its consequences. The most well-known variant is that a successful medium-time (three-six years) policy against unemployment may cause a long-run inflation buildup. The same kind of argument applies to the accumulation of large foreign debts, etc. Such a buildup of a long-term problem may eventually lead to revision of the policy to the opposite side of the long-run "natural" values of the relevant variables. The cycle in this instance must be very long (probably as long as the one proposed by Kondratieff or at least more than 20 years).

It seems unlikely that any of the mismanagement cycles would be very regular. The short-run variant in particular is more likely to produce some kind of erratic movements around the target course than regular movements. However, we do not consider these two kinds of policy cycles here, but concentrate on the deliberate ones:[1]

Electional cycles. Here the argument contains two links. One is that any rational government will try to plan its policy for the full period during which it expects to stay in power. For a "stable" government this period is likely to be an election period. The second—and somewhat more doubtful link—is that *the pattern* at which the planning is aimed, looks fairly similar to most governments. Thus, given high command over the economy, a government will produce an electional cycle in the main variables in the economy.

The pattern most often proposed is a restrictive policy in the beginning of the election period followed by an expansive phase later on—at least until the last three-six months before an election, when campaigning in most countries brings normal decision-making to a halt. The main explanation for this restrictive period is that a rational government will try to make the year before an election a "happy one"[2] in order to be re-elected. It will thus try to carry out its least popular decisions—and the ones most concerned with the long-run—as early as possible.

---

[1] Long-run cycles of the mismanagement type are discussed in Paldam (1979a) and in conjunction with electional cycles in Paldam (1979b) for labor-market data—it appears that there are significant signs of long-run cycles, but that they are as long as about 40 years. Whether, in fact, the economic policies of a government influence election outcomes will be analyzed in a subsequent paper using the same data. This topic has been discussed by Stiegler (1973), Fair (1975) and (78), and many others.
[2] Kindly note that the implicit definition of the word "rational" in this article is not meant to be normative.

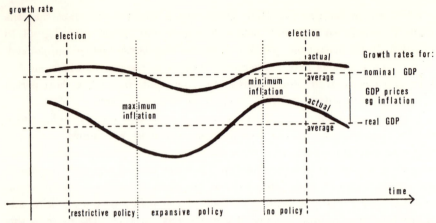

Fig. 1. Illustration of the possible shape of the electional cycle. Note: The figure is purely illustrative; cf. Dinkel (1977), pp. 234–239. In designing the lags the results in Paldam (1973) have been used. Thus, minimum inflation takes place one–two years after the lowest real growth and maximum inflation follows the fastest growth with about the same lag. Compare with the two shapes proposed by Nordhaus (1975) and MacRae (1977).

If the previous government followed the same pattern, then the election period will begin in a sistuation where a (minor) boom has been going on for about a year. Inflation will probably be on the rise, and so will imports. Consequently a restrictive policy may be called for.

In Fig. 1, an attempt has been made to outline the kind of economic movements most people seem to have in mind when they talk about an electional cycle. A prominent feature of this kind of policy cycle appears to be the *election-year effect*, as proposed by Tufte (1975), Dinkel (1977), and, tentatively, by OECD (1977). In the empirical study below we shall see whether the election-year stands out as being somehow "better" than the remaining years.

One main condition has to be fulfilled in order for an electional cycle to emerge. The government has to be sufficiently stable to be able to plan for a certain period. The *stability rules* used to define the political data employed in the study are discussed in Section II.

However stable a government may seem, a great deal may occur to offset its policy planning either in the shape of *external* events such as the two international price waves in 1951 and 1973–75, or *internal* events, unique to the government considered. In fact, every government has a complicated story of its own. Furthermore, most Western countries have had only three-five stable governments in the last 30 years; see Fig. 2. Therefore, it inevitably becomes a highly qualitative undertaking to study the electional cycle in any one country—the results being at best tentative.

The present study has tried to overcome these difficulties by comparing data from as many countries as possible. The three criteria a country has to meet to be included are data availability, a minimum size of one million inhabitants, and a Western-type democracy. This gives a total of 49 stable governments and—as in most comparative studies—has presented considerable difficulties, as will clearly be seen in the following.

II. The Concept of a Stable Government

The countries considered and the governments termed *stable* are listed in Fig. 2. All of these countries have different constitutions, and some have even changed their constitution during the period under study (1948–75). The political structures and many other aspects also differ.[1]

In order to conduct a statistical study some very clear-cut criteria have to be found to decide whether a government is stable. Two rules have been used. They must both be fulfilled:

Rule 1: The government should have a parliamentary majority.
Rule 2: The government remains in power throughout the normal election period.

Rule 1 applies to the party or parties that are members of the government. This means that a minority government will be termed unstable even if it has some kind of agreement with one or more parties in the parliament giving it a "working" majority.[2] Another problem is that most of the countries in the sample have two "houses" in their parliaments. Normally only one of the two houses has real responsibility in economic policy matters—as is the case in the UK and Germany. In these cases only the relevant house is considered. However, there are also cases where both houses have a say in such matters. We have decided to treat the USA as the only true example of a two-chamber system in our sample, so that rule 1 has to be fulfilled for both houses. Third, some countries have an executive "partisan" president who is elected independently of the parliament. In such cases the rule means that the presidential party and other parties in the government should have a majority. In the USA, where the government is the President's government in a very unique way, the rule has been understood as the presidential party having a majority in both houses.[3]

In most countries in the sample the government can dissolve the parliament and call an early election. Here rule 2 is understood to mean that this does not happen earlier than six months before the government is obliged to call an election or nine months if the election period is five years.

In a few countries—notably Japan and Italy—the political system has

---

[1] All data used are documented in Madsen & Paldam (1978), available from the author on request. Some of the many difficulties encountered when applying the two stability rules are also discussed in this "data paper".
[2] This explains the low number of stable governments in Sweden, a country well known for its political stability.
[3] As the two main parties in the USA are very heterogeneous, this rule is of necessity somewhat too simple.

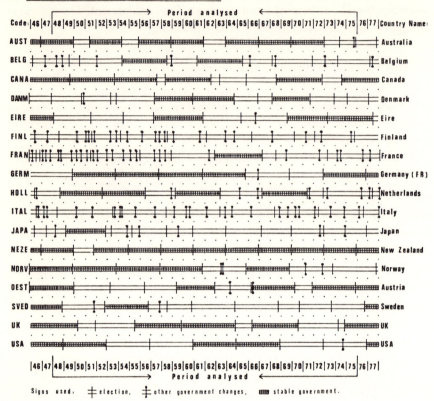

Section A: Data from the individual countries.

Section B: Unweighted cross-country summary of section A.

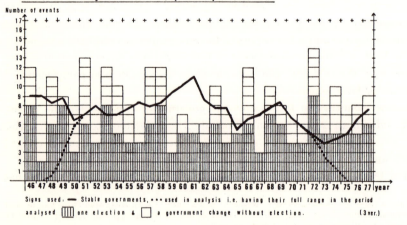

Fig. 2. A graphical exposition of the main political data.

been dominated by one party which, in fact, constitutes some kind of coalition. This means that politics to a certain extent take place as inter-party conflicts between the fractions of the ruling party. In such—and probably other— cases a change in personnel in the leading cabinet posts may more or less amount to a change of government. To be on the safe side, rule 2 is meant to cover only such governments where the prime minister continues or is replaced by a close colleague owing to illness or for a similar reason.

When studying Fig. 2, it is important to note how the governments under analysis—and thus political stability—are distributed over time. This is analyzed in section B of the table and further in Fig. 3 below. The main observation from Fig. 2B is that there are very clear trends in political stability with a peak in stability in 1961 and a fairly consistent and strong decline in stability until 1973 when, once more, development turns towards stability. If we compare this development in political stability with the main economic trends in the OECD-area, some interesting features emerge.

By and large the period from the mid-1950s to 1973 was one of unprecedented high employment and growth. We see that the continuous economic boom led to increasing political stability only in the beginning of the period, after which there was a gradual loss of political stability. This tallies rather well with the predictions made by Kalecki (1943), as discussed by Feiwel (1974) and Paldam (1979b). We further note that as soon as the crisis began in 1973, the trend turned, and stability again increased. While this is once again well in line with some of the (more speculative) suggestions in the theory of long-term political cycles, it is inconsistent with the more popular thesis that there is a simple positive correlation between economic and political difficulties.

III. The National Accounts Figures Used

In order to obtain as comparable data as possible, the study is based on OECD (or OEEC) comparative statistics. All series are entered in the analysis on a *pg* (percentage growth) basis. In addition to the advantages this gives of linking the observations into long series, it facilitates cross-country calculations.

In order to obtain the longest possible series, it was decided to *start in 1948* and *stop in 1975*, which gives a total of 27 observations exept for a few instances where some data were unobtainable.

The starting year was chosen so as to be well before the Korean War price-bubble and still long enough after World War II for the most immediate post-war adjustments to have been completed. Admittedly, 1948 is very close to the War, and this can be seen in some series—particularly in the imports and exports series.

The reason for stopping in 1975 is simply data availability. The major

Table 1. *The 8 main series analyzed*

Name	Definition
(1) GDP	Gross domestic product. For a few countries where only gross national product was available, this concept was used instead. In market prices
(2) GFI	Gross factor income, recognized as our "main" series. In factor prices or purchaser values in the more recent data
(3) Consumption	Private consumption
(4) Government consumption	General government consumption, the OECD definition
(5) Investment	Gross fixed investment. For a few countries, data before 1955 include investment in inventories
(6) Taxes	General government recepits, the OECD definitions (note text, Section III)
(7) Exports	Goods and services
(8) Imports	Goods and services

problems, however, occurred with the data for the first five years of the period. Some of the countries analyzed were not even members of the OECD (OEEC), and others did not have statistical offices in the 1940s. Nevertheless, it turned out to be possible to find most of the data, except with regard to tax pressure (for which data go back to 1951 only in about half of the countries).

All of the series used are listed in Table 1. For all of them except (once again) tax pressure, the analysis is carried out for *three component seies:* nominal growth, real growth and growth in the implicit price deflator. The growth in tax pressure is defined as the percentage by which total tax revenues grow *faster* than nominal GNP.

Finally, it should be noted that Australia's and New Zealand's national accounts reflect the geographical location of the two countries by using a different "year", beginning July 1 and April 1, respectively.

IV. The Main Ideas of the Electional Cycle Test

The main purpose of this paper is to find a reference electional cycle, but not to test whether the electional cycle has an *a priori* given form. Thus the *null hypothesis* is that there is *no* such cycle at all.[1]

The test results appear in Tables 2 and 3. Unfortunately, these two tables are quite difficult to read, as the testing procedure is somewhat complicated. The procedure consists of eight steps to be outlined below. Some of the steps—indicated by an "*"—are discussed in more detail in an appendix. The same procedure is carried out for all the 23 component series:

[1] Another possibility could be to compare the behavior of the stable governments with that of other governments. This has not been tried, as the unstable governments rarely rule a full period, so data do not permit a powerful test. Apart from the basic "existence" test, we try to establish—for the governments most likely to produce a cycle—what this cycle looks like.

(i*) The governmental periods have been standarized by finding the closest matching accounting years of the series. This causes the 49 stable governments to be divided into 35 four-year governments and 14 three-year governments.

(ii*) Data are selected for each government—for the appropriate series— from the data base. Two data-matrices are thereby obtained: a (14×3)-matrix X_1 and a (35×4)-matrix X_2.

Three tests are calculated for each X in order to ascertain whether the columns are different, and thus whether a cycle is present in the data. The tests are all standard *two-way analysis of variance*, and the resulting *"P%"* indicates the probability for the X-columns to be generated from the same distribution. The first two tests are based on the normal distribution and dealt with in steps (iii) to (v).

(iii*) As most of the series are not normally distributed, the X'es first have to be passed through a process of normalization. We use two such processes, thereby giving the two tests mentioned an additive termed *"method A"* and a multiplicative termed *"method M"*. They change matrix X into the two matrices $A(X)$ and $M(X)$.

(iv) The standard test is applied to $A(X)$ and $M(X)$; the resulting"$P\%$" appears in the table under the two relevant headings.

(v) To control that the normality condition is fulfilled X, $A(X)$ $M(X)$ are displayed in probit diagrams. The results are shown next to the test results in the form of a very brief note.

The third two-way analysis of variance is by "ranks" of the matrices and thus a distribution-free test. It is known as the *Friedman-test*, as it was introduced by Friedman (1937).

(vi) A "ranking-matrix" Q is calculated from X, by replacing each row, e.g. governmental observations, by its ranking. If the row in X_1 is (5.91, 4.32, 9.77), the corresponding row in $Q(X_1)$ becomes (2, 1, 3).

(vii*) The Friedman-test is calculated for $Q(X)$, and the resulting *"P%"* entered in the table.

(viii) For easy reference each X is provided with a small graph giving the shape of the average governmental year for the series. To make the graphs immediately comparable, they have been drawn from the $Q(X)$-matrix and thus they have no units of measurement on the ordinate-axis.

The test is carried out for the 23 national accounts series mentioned above. The test has also been applied to a few more series describing the labor markets of the same countries in Paldam (1979*b*, Section III). The results for unemployment are as may be inferred from real GDP and the wage rises give results very similar to other prices.

V. Proving the Cycle

Owing to two disturbing facts, the results in Tables 2 and 3 are not quite as clear as one might have hoped. One is the large difference between the results

Table 2. *Testing for electional cycles in the 3-year governments*

Series as defined in Section III	Tests based on normalization				Distribution-free test	
	Method A		Method M		Friedman's P%	Electional reference cycle
	P%	Comment	P%	Comment		
(1) GDP:						1 2 3
current	74.8	s.	75.6	s.	22.3	
real	41.2	s.o. (2)	36.5	s.o. (2)	42.4	
prices	36.3	l.s.	11.2	s.o. (1)	31.9	
(2) GFI:						
current	61.9	s.	61.4	s.	22.3	
real	65.4	s.o. (1)	60.7	s.o. (2)	60.7	
prices	44.9	l.s.	16.1	s.	39.1	
(3) Consumption:						
current	15.3	l.s.	20.5	l.s.	42.4	
real	6.6	l.s.	7.1	l.s.	30.8	
prices	39.5	l.s.	34.6	l.s.	52.6	
(4) Govt. Cons.:						
current	10.6	l.s.	8.0	s.o. (2)	10.9	
real	10.8	l.s.	10.4	s.o. (3)	25.7	
prices	62.6	l.s.	51.5	s.o. (3)	52.6	
(5) Investment:						
current	86.6	s.o. (1)	64.5	s.o. (1)	83.6	
real	40.8	s.o. (1)	27.2	s.o. (1)	60.7	
prices	32.2	l.s.	24.1	s.o. (3)	75.1	
(6) Taxes:						
current	7.9	l.s.	6.4	s.o. (1)	75.1	
pressure	7.3	s.o. (2)	45.6	s.o. (1)	60.7	
(7) Exports:						
current	61.3	s.	21.5	s.o. (2)	93.1	
real	9.8	l.s.	7.8	l.s.	75.1	
prices	44.1	s.o. (1)	24.1	n.s.	42.4	
(8) Imports:						
current	48.4	s.o. (2)	30.5	l.s.	100.0	
real	38.1	s.o. (2)	24.2	s.o. (1)	75.1	
prices	71.8	s.o. (3)	78.6	n.s.	93.1	

Notes: The statistics underlying the table are explained in Section IV. The comments indicate whether the normalization is successful (s.), successful with n outlying observations (s.o. (n)), less successful (l.s.), or not successful (n.s.).

from the 14 three-year governments where no cycle becomes significant and the 35 four-year governments where most significant cycles appear. The second is that the cycle is strong in foreign trade prices.

The absence of any significant cycle in the three-year governments might be caused by the fact that nearly all of them are in the two unusually politically stable countries, Australia and New Zealand, where re-election may be taken for granted more than elsewhere. Also the relatively low number

Table 3. *Testing for electional cycles in the 4-year governments*

Series as defined in Section III	Tests based on normalization				Distribution-free test	
	Method A		Method M		Friedman's P%	Electional reference cycle
	P%	Comment	P%	Comment		1 2 3 4
(1) GDP:						
current	0.8	s.o. (5)	0.1	s.o. (1)	0.9	
real	32.7	s.o. (6)	35.9	s.o. (3)	55.4	
prices	4.0	l.s.	0.2	s.o. (3)	0.9	
(2) GFI:						
current	1.8	s.o. (2)	0.1	s.o. (2)	0.3	
real	8.9	s.o. (2)	28.4	s.o. (1)	13.3	
prices	5.0	l.s.	11.8	s.o. (3)	3.7	
(3) Consumption:						
current	78.7	s.o. (2)	14.9	s.o. (5)	17.1	
real	34.0	s.o. (3)	23.9	s.o. (3)	20.1	
prices	48.9	s.o. (2)	20.8	s.o. (2)	11.8	
(4) Govt. Cons.:						
current	1.2	s.o. (2)	0.5	s.o. (3)	4.8	
real	24.9	s.o. (3)	21.0	l.s.	23.2	
prices	1.7	l.s.	0.1	l.s.	1.7	
(5) Investment:						
current	59.4	s.o. (3)	68.5	s.o. (3)	86.8	
real	61.1	l.s.	38.5	s.o. (2)	39.4	
prices	1.6	l.s.	2.5	l.s.	0.5	
(6) Taxes:[a]						
current	0.1	s.o. (4)	0.1	s.o. (4)	5.0	
pressure	17.6	s.o. (4)	7.6	n.s.	92.5	
(7) Exports:						
current	22.2	n.s.	10.7	n.s.	3.3	
real	15.8	s.o. (5)	37.1	s.o. (2)	32.2	
prices	0.2	l.s.	22.1	n.s.	0.2	
(8) Imports:						
current	11.8	s.o. (1)	5.1	s.o. (4)	7.0	
real	3.3	s.o. (2)	1.8	s.	45.1	
prices	4.3	l.s.	41.4	n.s.	2.2	

[a] Based on 33 governments only.
Notes: See Table 2.

of governments, the high incidence of government changes in the middle of the year and data problems[1] may explain the negative findings. However, a careful comparison of Tables 2 and 3—as well as the detailed graphical analysis—suggest that if more observations had been available, Table 2 might well have become much more similar to Table 3.

[1] In New Zealand calculations of constant price series for the national accounts were begun in 1954; before that year the consumer price index had to be used to deflate the current series.

Table 4. *Connection between cycles in the prices of government consumption and exports*

Prices	Govt. cons.		Sum
	+	−	
Exports			
+	14	11	25
−	6	4	10
Sum	20	15	35

Note: A hypergeometric test gives the probability of 51 % showing the two cycles to be perfectly independent; see the text for further discussion.

When we turn to the four-year governments in Table 3, more or less clear signs of a cycle are apparent in all of the series. More than half of the series show a significant electional cycle at the 5 % level and as many as eight even become significant at the 1 % level.

At the 1 % level the current and price component of GDP and the current component of GFI become significant. The price component of GFI becomes significant at the 5 % level only.

If the cycle found in the main aggregates originates from the political decision process, we would expect it to be stronger in the more policy-oriented series—that is in the tax and government consumption observations—than in the series for private end uses. The two series for private end uses, consumption and investment, actually turn out to have the least significant cycle, while, as expected, strong cyclical patterns appear in the policy series. However, it is worth noting that here too, the real components become much less cyclical than the nominal or price components (see Section VI).

The strong cyclical pattern in the policy variables and thus in the national product series also explains the cyclical pattern in current imports. However, it is more difficult to explain the cycle in export prices, as discussed below.

A main finding is that the cycle is much stronger in the price than in the real components of the series. Since we know that there is a cycle in the current series, and that there are some connections between prices and real quantities, we may, however (as is done in Section VI) find a weak cycle in the real aggregates.

The cycle does not appear in every government. We can use this fact to whether or not the cycles found in any two series are interrelated. First, we use the small graphs in Table 3 to define a cycle. For instance, the cycle in prices for government consumption is defined by increases below average in the first two years; if we study the rank matrix Q, this translates into the simple rule of $q_1 + q_2 < 5$. This occurs for 20 of the 35 governments. For export prices the criteria become $q_1 < 3$. This occurs for 25 governments. We can decribe this with two strings of 35 pluses and minuses. If we compare the two strings, we obtain a distribution as shown in Table 4.

The same kind of test has been applied to all of the significant or nearly significant component series. It clearly shows that the cycle in current GFI is positively correlated with both the cycles in current government consumption (government consumption prices) and the cycle in export prices.

Consequently, we conclude that the cycle in the large aggregates is caused by government policy as well as export prices—the two explanations being independent of each other.

As government consumption prices are mostly a matter of public sector wages, this independence appears highly reasonable. It also seems likely that increases in the salaries of this large group of voters would be greater as an election approaches.

The argument presupposes that the cycle in foreign trade prices is mainly exogenous, that is, determined by the world market. This presumption is analyzed in Fig. 3. The figure clearly shows that not only are import and export prices rather strongly correlated, but there is also a strong qualitative correlation between the distribution of the government years contributing to the cycle and international trends in prices.[1]

This is a somewhat puzzling finding because *a priori* reasoning indicates that the causal link here must be from prices to the stability of the governments. Consequently, we have to conclude that a certain development in world market prices is more likely to produce stable governments than other developments. The loss of stability due to external chocks may happen more or less deliberately. Quite a large number of the governments examined are coalition governments, and they may have to be dissolved if confronted with too unfavorable international price trends. Also, an early election may be called in order to obtain a full new period if foreign trade prices develop in a way recognized as too unfortunate. In the latter case the eventual outcome might be greater stability later on, but we observe a decrease in stability in the short run.

If this analysis is accepted we may try to infer (from Fig. 3) the pattern in foreign trade prices which is optimal for political stability. First of all, the pattern seems to exhibit fairly small increases and, second, these increases come late in the period.

VI. Quantitative Aspects of the Cycle in GFI

From the preceding section we know that there is a cycle in current GFI. Consequently, this cycle must reappear in the two component series, as we may take it for granted that at least at the most aggregate level there are strong connections between prices and real quantities. The two components of

---

[1] This weak link in the analysis is further treated in Paldam (1978).

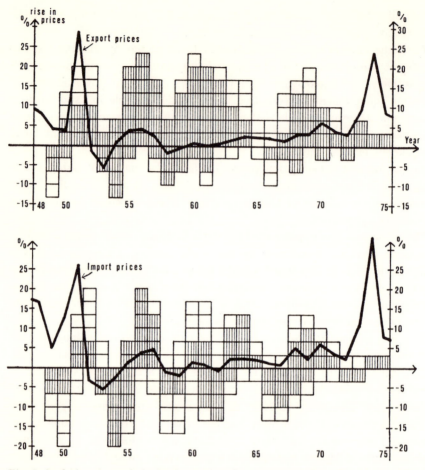

Fig. 3. Analysing the cycle in foreign trade prices. The thick lines show the unweighted averages of growth rates for prices. The "squares" show the distribution of the $35 \times 4 = 140$ years of stable government. Each year is marked by ▥ if it belongs to a government which contributes to the cycle in the relevant price series and by ☐ if it does not. (*a*) *Export prices*. The cycle is defined as having the first year below average. Consequently all first years are shown below the year axis, and the three remaining years above. (*b*) *Import prices*. The cycle is defined as having the first two years below average and is thus drawn below the year axis, and the last two above average, and thus above the axis.

GFI are analyzed in Figs. 4*a* and 4*b*. The most interesting pattern appears in the real component of GFI. Knowing that there is a cycle, we can test the pattern using a one-sided test so that it becomes significant much more easily.

In real quantities, one year stands out very clearly—and it is different from what we expected from the discussion of Fig. 1. The strongest growth occurs in the second year, whereas the other three years are almost impossible to distinguish. The second-year effect is as strong as 1.25 % on the average.[1]

---

[1] Using a one-sided t-test between the second year and the rest, the effect becomes significant on the 1 % level. This also occurs with the data normalized by method M. The second-year effect is equally strong in GDP, but not in private consumption.

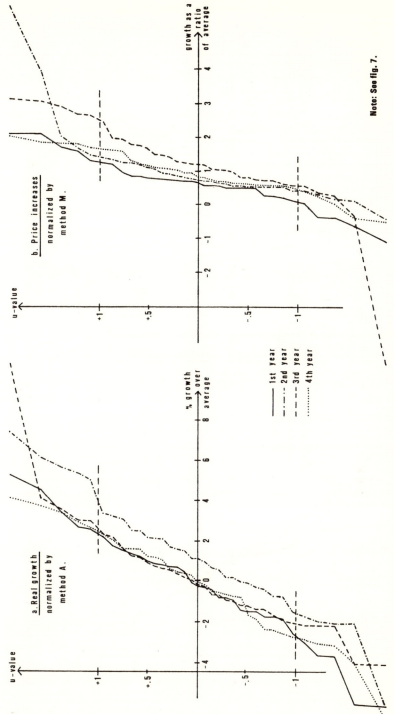

Fig. 4. Probit diagrams for component series of GFI in the 35 four-year governments.

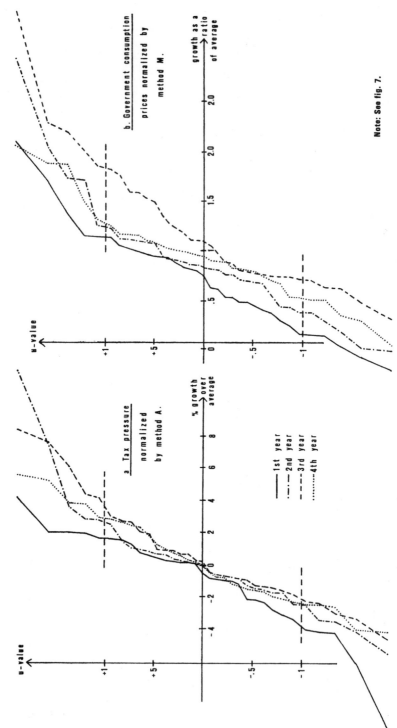

Fig. 5. Probit diagrammes for tax pressure and prices for government consumption in the 35 four-year governments.

Two explanations seem possible. One is that the second-year effect is caused by expansionary measures adopted during the election year, but then the lag must be as long as two years. The second and most likely explanation is that the effect is caused by governments carrying out their election promises. This accounts very well for the lag, and it also explains the fact that the same pattern shows up in real government consumption, which looks almost like Fig. 4a.

The fact that real growth is strongest in the second year helps to explain why price increases are strongest in the third year. This is also explained by foreign trade prices and the cycle in government sector prices.

In order to analyze government policy, we now turn to Figs 5a and 5b. Fig. 5a shows tax pressure. It looks like a "weak" version of the same figure for tax revenue, but is much more easy to interpret as it does not contain the effect of automatic fiscal reactions. If there is any cycle in tax pressure, it is obviously a first-year effect—that taxes increase less in the first year than in the other three years.

Tax rates have to be fixed some time in advance and the rates in the first year then have to be fixed more or less during the election campaign; this probably accounts for the relatively small increases.

Fig. 5b shows the analysis of one of the clearest of the component series, the two last years being significantly higher than the first two.

VII. Conclusions

It is hardly necessary to mention that the cycle found is not really a strong phenomenon as compared with many others in the economy. It becomes highly significant only because of the fairly large amount of data used, and it would provide a very poor basis for forecasting.

If we return to the sketch of rational timing of economic policy in Section I, it does not look much like the pattern actually found. The latter could hardly be explained as a result of successful policy planning aimed at re-election. It has often been claimed that governments have little control over events— and this study seems to give some confirmation to such a claim. This is the case even when the governments studied cover less than 25 % of all governments during the period 1948–75 in the 17 countries analyzed, and are selected as being the ones *most* in control.

In addition to this somewhat negative conclusion we should add another. It was not possible, as expected, to find an election-year effect in the data.[1]

---

[1] For unemployment the election year is the the "best", however, as shown in Section III of Paldam (1979b). The difference between unemployment in the third and fourth years, on the other hand, is barely visible and rather far from significant. The main effect of the electional cycle in unemployment is—as expected from the GDP results—a large fall in the second year.

In none of the diagrams drawn does the last year stand out as the most expansionary, or otherwise as the "best".

In economic policy variables the main cyclical movements are: first, that taxes tend to increase relatively little in the first year, probably because rates have to be fixed during the election compaign. Second, real government activity increases the most in the second year, most likely because governments do carry out electional promises to a fairly large extent. Third, government sector prices increase fastest in the second half of the electional period.

This, combined with world market prices, produces an electional cycle in national income—a cycle where real growth is strongest in the second year after the election, and inflation in the third year.

Appendix: Notes on the Cycle Test

In Section IV above, a short description is given of the 8-step calculation procedure followed in the construction of Tables 2 and 3. We now add a few more comments to some of these steps:

(*A i*). Unfortunately, none of the 49 governments studied ruled from the 1st of January in one year to the 1st of January in another. In fact, the starting and ending months, respectively, of all governments is distributed as shown in Fig. 6. The first step of the analysis is thus to *standardize the government periods*. This is done in the following way. If take-over of the government occurs in the first half of the year, the same year is defined as the first year of the period. If the take-over occurs in the second half of a year, the next year is defined as the first year of the period. The same applies to the termination year. The error committed by this standardization is larger, the more government changes occur in the middle of the year.[1]

When this procedure is applied, the 49 governments are divided into 14 with a 3-year period and 35 with a 4-year period.[2] All of the 3-year governments are in Australia and New Zealand where, furthermore, most of the standardization error is concentrated.

(*A ii*). For each series we thus obtain two matrices X_1 and X_2, having the order $(b \times k)$ of (14×3) and (35×4), respectively. In the X matrix each of the b rows contains the k observations in the standardized period for the relevant series and government. We call the observation $x_{i,j}$. The theory stating that there is an electional cycle then implies that the columns in X are different in some statistically significant way. The appropriate test for this problem is a two-way analysis of variance testing the null hypothesis that the columns in X are from the same distribution. The standard procedures are

---

[1] This procedure solves the problem of how to treat the period between the election and inauguration day in the US. Further, it is to be noted that Australia and New Zealand use a different "year" starting July 1 and April 1, respectively.
[2] Including one with a 5-year period (in the UK) where, however, the last year was disregarded.

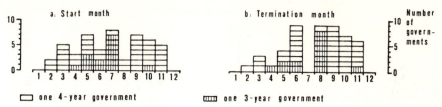

Fig. 6. Beginning and end month of the 49 stable governments. Note the amended definition of the year applied for Australia where month 1 is July, and New Zealand where month 1 is April.

based on the normal distribution. The probit-diagrams for X_1 and X_2 are shown in Fig. 7 for real growth in GFI. The drawings clearly show that the normality assumptions do not apply for real GFI. The same conclusion appears for almost all of the other component series.

(*A iii*). After some experimentation the following simple normalization process was chosen: An extended average $\hat{x}_j$ of each row x_j was calculated, the extension being 4 years to each side of the government. If the row represents a government from 1957 to 1960, the average is thus calculated from 1953 to 1964. If the extension to one of the sides is outside the data collected, the extension to the other side is prolonged to make up for the difference. The advantage obtained by using $\hat{x}_j$ instead of the ordinary average $\bar{x}_j$ is that it is much more stable, and that it does not easily happen to get close to zero for the series analyzed. This extended average is then divided into each observation in the row. We call the matrix obtained from X in this way the multiplicatively normalized matrix M. By subtracting the extended average from the observations we obtain the additively normalized matrix A. To simplify terminology we call the two methods of normalization *methods M and A*.

(*A iv*). We denote the elements at the Q-matrix q. The element $q_{i,j}$ is thus one of the integers from 1 to k, there being one of each in each row. We may call the column sums q_i. For the null hypothesis the mean for all q_i is the same $\bar{q}=b(k+1)/2$. The Friedman test statistics F_q is based on the sum, over all k, of the squared differences between $\bar{q}$ and q_i. F_q is defined as:

$$F_q = 12(\sum_{i=1,k} (\bar{q}-q_i)^2/(b \cdot k(k+1)).$$

It can be proved that under the null hypothesis, F_q is distributed as the $\chi^2(\alpha, f)$ distribution with degrees of freedom $f=k-1$, and α is the probability of obtaining the F_q or a larger one under the null hypothesis.

If the α's calculated are below the reject limit of the reader's preference then the columns are not alike.[1] To get further into the nature of the cycle,

---

[1] The loss of power by using the F_q-statistics instead of the ordinary F-test is—in the case where X is normally distributed—given by the asymptotic relative efficiency of $0.955k/(k+1)$. For such small k's as 3 and 4, this becomes 0.72 and 0.76. The loss of power is thus considerable; see Conover (1971).

200   *M. Paldam*

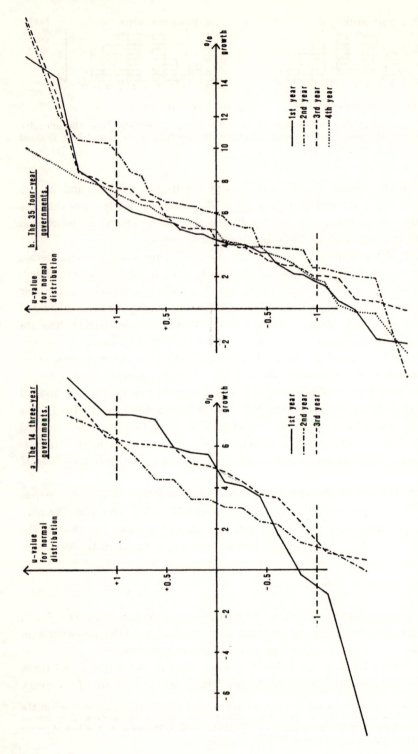

Fig. 7. Probit diagrams for real growth in gross factor income. Note: See text. While *a* is passable for a normal distribution with one outlying observation, *b* is clearly not.

we have to return to the X-matrix, although a clear indication as to how the quantitative results will look may be obtained from the column average in Q. We therefore show these averages as a small graph giving what may be termed *the electional reference cycle* for each component series.

References

Conover, W. J.: *Practical nonparametric statistics*. New York, 1971.

Dinkel, Reiner: *Der Zusammenhang zwischen der ökonomischen und politischen Entwicklung in einer Demokratie*. Berlin, 1977.

Fair, Ray C.: *On controlling the economy to win elections*. Cowles Foundation Discussion, Paper nol 397, 1975.

Fair, Ray C.: The effect of economic events on votes for President. *The Review of Economics and Statistics LX* (2), May 1978.

Feiwel, George R.: Reflections on Kalecki's theory of political business cycle. *Kyklos 27*, 1974.

Frey, Bruno S.: Theorie und Empirie politischer Konjunkturzyklen. *Zeitschrift für Nationalökonomie 36*, Heft 1–2, 1976.

Frey, Bruno S.: *Modern political economy*. London, 1978.

Friedman, Milton: The use of ranks to avoid the assumption of normality implicit in the analysis of variance. *Journal of the American Statistical Association 32*, 1937.

Kalecki, Michał: *Political aspects of full employment, 1943*. Reprinted in: *Selected essays on the dynamics of the capitalist economy*, Cambridge, 1971.

Lindbeck, Assar: Business cycles, politics and international economic dependence. *Scandinaviska Enskilda Bankens Quarterly Review 2*, 1975.

Lindbeck, Assar: Stabilization policy in open economies with endogenous politicians. *American Economic Review, Papers and Proceedings 66*, 1976.

MacRae, C. Duncan: A political model of the business cycle. *Journal of Political Economy 85* (2), April 1977.

Madsen, E. S. & Paldam, M.: *Economic and political data for the main OECD-countries 1948–75*. Memo 78-9, Århus, 1978.

Nordhaus, William D.: The political business cycle. *The Review of Economic Studies XLII* (2), April 1975.

OECD: *Towards full employment and price stability*. Paris, 1977.

Paldam, Martin: An empirical analysis of the relationship between inflation and economic growth in 12 countries, 1950 to 1969. *The Swedish Journal of Economics 75*, 1973.

Paldam, Martin: An empirical study of economic interconnection in the OECD-area 1948–75. Memo 78–12, Inst. of Economics, Aarhus Univ, 1978.

Paldam, Martin: Towards the wage-earner state. A comparative study of wage-shares 1948–75. *The International Journal of Social Economics*, no. 1a 1979a.

Paldam, Martin: Political cycles in the labour market? A comparative study of 17 countries 1948–75. Memo 79-1, Inst. of Economics, Aarhus University, 1979b.

Stiegler, George J.: General economic conditions and national elections. *American Economic Review, Papers and Proceedings 63*, 1973.

Tufte, Edward R.: The political manipulation of the economy. Influence of the electoral cycle on macroeconomic performance and policy. Mimeo, Dep. of Politics, Princeton Univ., 1975.

Åkerman, Johan: *Ekonomiskt skeende och politiska förändringer*. (Also *Kyklos*, Vol. I, 1947.) Lund, 1946.

THE EFFECT OF UNEMPLOYMENT, INFLATION AND REAL INCOME GROWTH ON GOVERNMENT POPULARITY IN SWEDEN

Lars Jonung and Eskil Wadensjö

University of Lund, Lund, Sweden

Abstract

This paper investigates empirically the effects of unemployment, inflation and real income growth on the popularity of the Swedish government by testing various vote functions for the period 1967–1978. Government popularity is measured on the basis of data obtained from monthly opinion polls. The results suggest that unemployment, in particular among workers in manufacturing industry, and inflation exerted a strong influence on the popularity of the Social Democratic Party, which was the ruling party during the period 1967–1976. The effects of real income growth are considerably smaller. The estimations are sensitive to the empirical specifications of the explanatory variables, although the basic conclusions remain unchanged.

I. Introduction

The interaction between macroeconomic events and political developments has been the subject of a large number of econometric studies in the 1970s. One group of studies has considered the effects of economic fluctuations on election outcomes; see *inter alia* Arcelus & Meltzer (1975), Bloom & Price (1975), Fair (1978), Kramer (1971), Meltzer & Vellrath (1975), and Stigler (1973). Other investigations have examined the influence of economic events on party popularity as measured by opinion polls; see e.g. Goodhart & Bhansali (1970), Frey & Garbers (1971), Frey & Schneider (1978a) and (1978b). Another group of studies has constructed and empirically tested models of the mutual relationships between the economic and political spheres. These politico-economic models consist of two equations. The first, the

* The authors are grateful to Hans Zetterberg, director of the Sifo Institute, Stockholm for kindly supplying Sifo data as well as comments on the empirical results. We have also benefited from the suggestions of Tomas Hammar and Daniel Tarschys, Department of Political Science, University of Stockholm, Gunnar Sjöblom, Department of Political Science, University of Copenhagen, Ingemar Ståhl, Department of Economics, University of Lund and from the views of an anonymous referee. The authors wish to thank Sven Norén at the Computer Center of Lund University for his skillful programming assistance and Mark Olson for editing advice on the wording of this article. Financial support from the Bank of Sweden Tercentenary Foundation is gratefully acknowledged.

evaluation function, describes the effects of macroeconomic developments on government popularity; the second, the policy function, depicts the policy measures taken by the government to influence its popularity standing and thus its re-election prospects; see *inter alia* Frey (1978), Frey & Schneider (1978a) and (1978b).

Most of the empirical work on the interdependence of economic and political events has dealt with the American record. A few studies of the experience in various European countries have also been published. As yet, Swedish economists have not developed and tested models of this kind for Sweden, although they have discussed the interaction between the economy and the polity, in particular Johan Åkerman and some of his students, as well as Assar Lindbeck.

The purpose of this paper is to construct a small model for examining the relationship between macroeconomic changes and the popularity standing of the Swedish government in power, as measured by opinion poll data. The effect of unemployment, the rate of inflation and changes in real disposable income on government popularity is empirically measured for the period 1967–1978.

II. Earlier Swedish Studies

Johan Åkerman has examined the interaction between economic and political developments in a number of books and articles. His great interest in this field—a field he regarded as the "synthesis of economics, statistics, history and political science"[1]—grew out of his work on business cycle fluctuations. His major contribution dealt with the experience of the United Kingdom, the United States, Germany and Sweden during the period 1850–1940; see Åkerman (1946).[2] Here he adopted a rather impressionistic approach, comparing cabinet changes with business cycle fluctuations. Several time series were used as measures of the influence of economic changes such as data on unemployment, stock prices, construction activity, emigration and railroad construction.

In his analysis of the Swedish record, he suggested three conclusions: (1) one-third of the 33 cabinet changes between 1866 and 1940 were due to downturns in the business cycle, (2) booms had a tendency to improve political support for conservative parties, while depressions strengthened the political power of the Social Democrats, and (3) structural changes in the political system were caused by long-term economic changes, that is, various stages of industrialism eventually gave rise to political democracy. Later, when considering the experiences of the United States and the United Kingdom in greater detail, Åkerman (1947b) and (1948) argued that as a rule, economic

---

[1] Åkerman (1946, p. 2).
[2] A good summary in English of Åkerman's views on political business cycles is found in Åkerman (1947a).

204 L. Jonung and E. Wadensjö

events had significantly stronger effects on political outcomes in these countries than in Sweden.

Kurt Rydé (1950), one of Åkerman's students, investigated the relationship between short-term economic conditions and the election outcomes in Sweden during the period 1896–1948 using Åkerman's approach. He applied three indices: one describing the economic status of Swedish industry, a second measuring the business situation in the agricultural sector and third, an index of political outcomes. His method was based on tabular comparisons, although he also made some computations of correlation coefficients. He found the correlation between the industry index and that of election outcomes to be 0.73, while the corresponding value for the index of the agricultural business situation and election outcomes was 0.06.[1] Rydé presented three conclusions; (1) a causal effect originating from the economic situation in Swedish industry had affected the outcomes of all elections except the election of 1928, when "ideological" events predominated, (2) all elections during wars were influenced by non-business cycle developments, and (3) effects stemming from the economic situation of the farming community and influencing the elections were either weak or completely absent.

Another student of Åkerman's, Sven Grönhagen (1951), studied the relationship between parliamentary elections and economic events in Great Britain during the period 1850–1950. He used several economic indicators such as changes in wholesale prices, in imports, in industrial production, in employment, in stock prices and in total employment during various time periods before the election dates. Grönhagen concluded that a considerable number of the elections between 1852 and 1950 were influenced by economic developments. He employed roughly the same approach as Åkerman and Rydé.

The work of Åkerman and his students was not continued by either economists or political scientists in Sweden. Recently, however, Assar Lindbeck has studied the incorporation of political behavior into macroeconomic models. Lindbeck (1976) discussed the problem of endogenous politicians in general terms. He also made an attempt to bring the discussion to bear on the Swedish record. Employing a Phillips curve framework, Lindbeck (1975) considered the relationship between the dating of election years, the rate

---

[1] Rydé calculated simple correlation coefficients for the independent variables and the dependent variable in his study. An estimation, using his data, with regression analysis gives the following result:

$$P = 27.528 + 0.395I + 0.237A$$
$$\quad (24.950) \quad (0.188) \quad (0.166)$$

Standard errors in parentheses
$R^2 = 0.312$ \qquad DW = 1.871 \qquad $N = 18$

where P = index of political outcomes, I = industry index, A = index of the agricultural business situation. Both coefficients have the expected signs but only the coefficient of the industry index differs significantly from zero, when tested at the five per cent level using a t-test.

of inflation and the level of unemployment in postwar Sweden in reference to a number of charts. He stressed the policy option of manipulating the temporal allocation of inflation and unemployment through stabilization policy in such a way as to enhance re-election chances. Considering the work by Åkerman and his students, and that of Lindbeck, as well as the policy-oriented research carried out by Swedish economists, it may seem surprising that Swedish economists have not carried the empirical study of politico-economic interdependence further.[1]

III. The Model

Recent work on the interaction between the political and economic spheres revolves around two functions. The first, the evaluation function, depicts the effects of economic events on the political situation as measured either by election outcomes (the vote function) or by opinion polls (the popularity function). The second basic function, the policy function, describes the effects of changes in the political market on the use of various economic policy instruments and/or economic aggregates.

This paper focuses on the first type of relationship. The empirical study of evaluation functions has been based on two sets of data, either time series on election outcomes or data from public opinion polls. Poll data are used in this study for a number of reasons. Such data have been available for Sweden on a monthly basis since March 1967. Consequently, a large number of observations exist for a fairly short period of time. Due to considerable changes in the Swedish constitutional system, it is difficult to utilize data on elections in studies covering long time spans. Furthermore, consistent data on several economic indicators are available for 1967–1978, facilitating an investigation of various relationships during this period.

Several macroeconomic indicators may be assumed to influence the popularity standing of the party in power. Econometric studies generally indicate that the rate of unemployment, changes in the price level and changes in the growth of real disposable income are important determinants of government popularity; see e.g. Frey (1978) for the evidence from the United States, Great Britain and West Germany. These three variables will thus be included in the popularity function to be examined for Sweden.

The model to be tested can now be expressed in the following way:[2]

$$S = a + b \cdot U + c \cdot P + d \cdot Y + \varepsilon \tag{I}$$

---

[1] Outside of Sweden, Kirchgässner (1976), Madsen (1978) and Paldam (1977) have considered the Swedish politico-economic experience in comparative studies.

[2] The vote function postulated here may be regarded as a reduced form equation. The derivation of this function from a microeconomic to a macroeconomic level is a problem hardly touched upon in the politico-econometric literature. The vote function is as a rule tested in a linear form in empirical work.

where S represents the popularity of the Social Democratic Party in Sweden, the ruling party prior to October 1976, as measured by opinion surveys; U, the rate of unemployment; P, the rate of inflation; Y, the rate of growth in real disposable income; ε is an error term that is assumed to be normally distributed. The coefficients of the unemployment and inflation terms are expected to be negative.[1] Real income growth, however, is expected to influence government popularity positively, producing a positive coefficient for income changes. The choice of the proper empirical measures of the explanatory variables in eq. (I) will be discussed in connection with the empirical results.

IV. The Empirical Results

The estimation period is limited by the availability of data. In March 1967, the Swedish Sifo Institute began continuous opinion polls among a representative group of Swedish voters. In these polls, which have generally been made on a monthly basis, the following question was asked: "Which party do you think is the best one today?" In parliamentary election months, the question was: "Which party are you going to vote for in the election?" The Sifo polls are regarded as a reliable estimate of the popularity standing of the various parties as well as of the election outcomes. The divergence of the Sifo gallup poll results from the actual election outcomes may be regarded as small.[2]

The Social Democratic Party was in power in 1967—when the first poll was taken—until October 1976. Since then the Social Democrats have remained in the opposition. For this reason, two estimation periods are used: 1967:03–1976:09 and 1976:10–1978:08. The latter period covers the rule of the non-socialist three-party government before this coalition was dissolved. The estimates covering the opposition period of the Social Democrats are expected to give rise to a change in the signs of the coefficients of unemployment and inflation.

A number of empirical measures of the explanatory variables in eq. (I) may be suggested. The consumer price index, P^c, is used as one measure of the behavior of prices. Considering the political weight given to the behavior of food prices and the attempts made by the government to influence food prices, the food price index, P^f, is also adopted as an indicator of the rate of inflation.

---

[1] This model suggests that unemployment and inflation reduce the re-election chances for the party in power. However, voters may have a greater dislike for unemployment than for inflation. In that case, the government may try to choose a combination of unemployment and inflation that maximizes its re-election chances, by reducing unemployment prior to the election at the expense of a higher rate of inflation, which—given time-lags—may not be noticeable until after the election. As analyzed in the literature on political business cycles, such short-run vote-maximizing behavior may induce election cycles or political business cycles. See Lindbeck (1975) for a discussion of the Swedish record.

[2] The difference between the Sifo polls and the election outcomes declined from 2.1 percentage points in the 1950s (as an average for three elections), to 1.4 percentage points in the 1960s (as an average for five elections) and to 0.7 percentage points in the 1970s (as an average for three elections).

Regarding the rate of unemployment, a time series is used including all categories of insured unemployed, U. As workers in manufacturing and industry are regarded as the core of the Social Democratic Party, the rate of unemployment among this labor group, U^m, may be expected to exert an influence on the party's popularity standing which differs from the general measure U. U^m is also less influenced by changes in the coverage of the unemployment insurance system and less affected by seasonal variations than U. Changes in disposable real income, Y, are adopted here as the measure of income growth.

It is reasonable to assume that unemployment, inflation and changes in real income do not immediately influence the popularity standing of the government. It takes time for voters to collect information about the behavior of various macroeconomic indicators and to change their political attitudes. Furthermore, data on various macroeconomic time series are not calculated and reported until at least one month after the data have been collected. For this reason a lag of one month is used in the regressions.

A number of regression estimates of the popularity function are reported in Table 1. The first three regressions in the table cover the period 1967–1976 when the Social Democrats were in power. The first and second estimates show that the effect of unemployment among industrial workers on the polls was larger than the effect of unemployment including all categories. The difference is considerable; a one-percentage point increase in U^m reduced government popularity by 4.1 percentage points while the corresponding decline is only 2.4 percentage points for U.

The influence of inflation as measured by the consumer price index is significant. The third regression in Table 1 shows that changes in food prices also exerted a significant influence on the popularity standing of the government, although much smaller than that exerted by the consumer price index. The sign of the coefficient of the growth in disposable real income in the first three equations reported in Table 1 is positive as expected. A one per cent rise in the growth rate increased the popularity of the Social Democratic government by about 0.3–0.4 percentage points.[1]

---

[1] Two measures of the relative importance of the different explanatory variables have been employed, beta-coefficients and elasticities at the point of means. See e.g. Hanushek & Jackson (1977), pp. 78–79.

Variable	Beta-coefficient	Elasticity at the point of means
U^m_{-1}	0.430	− 0.167
P^c_{-1}	0.443	− 0.083
Y_{-1}	0.237	0.020

According to both measures, the influence of growth in real disposable income is much less than the influence of the other variables.

The equations in Table 1 display a high positive autocorrelation judging from the Durbin-Watson statistic. One explanation for the high autocorrelation may be that economic events as well as other events occurring in a given month influence government popularity not only in the month immediately following, but also in subsequent months. A Koyck-lag is introduced in Table 2 to capture a lagged influence on the popularity of the government. Eq. (5) including the lagged dependent variable shows that the coefficients of both unemployment (U^m_{-1}) and the rate of inflation (P^c_{-1}) still have the expected signs and that they differ significantly from zero when tested at the five per cent level using a t-test. The coefficient of the growth in disposable real income (Y_{-1}) does not, however, have a predicted positive sign and does not differ significantly from zero. Excluding real income growth, as done in eq. (6), the coefficients of the remaining explanatory variables are practically unchanged. The autocorrelation is reduced in comparison with eq. (1) and is negative instead of positive.

Eq. (6a) shows the steady state solution of eq. (5). The coefficients of unemployment (U^m_{-1}) and inflation (P^c_{-1}) are somewhat higher than in eq. (1). An increase in the rate of unemployment by one per cent reduced government popularity by 5.8 percentage points as compared to 4.1 in eq. (1). The corresponding values for the coefficients of inflation are 0.8 and 0.6, respectively.[1]

The size of the Koyck-lag suggests that the effects of changes in the explanatory variables on government popularity are concentrated to the first year. After 12 months the effect is about 20 per cent of the original impact, and after three years (the electoral period since 1970) it is only about one per cent.

Two residuals of eq. (5) are exceptionally large. For October 1968, the actual value for government popularity is 3.99 percentage points larger than the fitted value. The explanation is that the events in Czechoslovakia sharply increased political support for the Social Democrats.[2] In April 1976,

---

[1] The beta-coefficients and the elasticities at the point of means for unemployment and inflation in eq. (6a) are shown below.

Variable	Beta-coefficient	Elasticity at the point of means
U^m_{-1}	0.617	− 0.236
P^c_{-1}	0.629	− 0.117

The above numbers are in accordance with the results shown in the preceding footnote.

[2] If a dummy is introduced for the events in Czechoslovakia ($T = 1$, October 1968; $T = 0$, all other months), the estimates in eq. (6b) are obtained:

(6b) $S = 6.802 + 0.884S_{-1} + 4.168T - 0.643U^m_{-1} - 0.074P^c_{-1}$
       (2.036) (0.035)   (1.129)   (0.305)   (0.040)
   $R^2 = 0.917$ $h = -1.379$ $N = 114$

Durbin's h-statistic shows that the autocorrelation problem is less than in eq. (6). As the value of $|h|$ is less than 1.645, the hypothesis of zero autocorrelation cannot be rejected.

Table 1. *The effect of unemployment, inflation and real income growth on the popularity standing of the Social Democratic Party. Monthly data, 1967–1978*

S = popularity standing of the Social Democratic Party, U = rate of unemployment including all categories of insured unemployed, U^m = rate of unemployment among insured industrial workers, P^c = rate of inflation as measured by the consumer price index, P^f = rate of inflation as measured by the food price index, Y = rate of growth in disposable real income

---

The Social Democrats in power. 1967: 03–1976: 09.

(1) $S = 54.729 - 4.116 U^m_{-1} - 0.565 P^c_{-1} + 0.299 Y_{-1}$
     (1.404) (0.670)   (0.088)   (0.088)

Standard errors in parentheses
$R^2 = 0.474$ DW = 0.389 $N = 115$

(2) $S = 52.170 - 2.440 U_{-1} - 0.713 P^c_{-1} + 0.364 Y_{-1}$
     (1.424) (0.596)   (0.100)   (0.094)

Standard errors in parentheses
$R^2 = 0.388$ DW = 0.357 $N = 115$

(3) $S = 52.548 - 3.830 U^m_{-1} - 0.265 P^f_{-1} + 0.246 Y_{-1}$
     (1.479) (0.751)   (0.073)   (0.098)

Standard errors in parentheses
$R^2 = 0.355$ DW = 0.269 $N = 115$

The Social Democrats in opposition. 1976: 10–1978: 08.

(4) $S = 33.852 + 2.844 U^m_{-1} + 0.294 P^c_{-1} + 0.394 Y_{-1}$
     (4.211) (1.183)   (0.292)   (0.301)

Standard errors in parentheses
$R^2 = 0.278$ DW = 0.554 $N = 23$

(4a) $S = 43.559 + 1.985 U^m_{-1} + 0.039 P^c_{-1}$
     (2.242) (1.003)   (0.022)

Standard errors in parentheses
$R^2 = 0.212$ DW = 0.464 $N = 23$

Comments: The rate of inflation and the rate of change in disposable real income are expressed as yearly percentage changes on a monthly basis as $100(X_t - X_{t-12})/(X_{t-12})$.

the actual value is 3.67 percentage points lower than the fitted value. This residual is probably due to some events in the spring of 1976 called *affärerna* (literally "the affairs"). These, including the fact that film director Ingmar Bergman was taken into custody and that a high-ranking trade union official made a trip to the Canary Islands during a tourist boycott of Spain, reduced the popularity of the Social Democrats.

A slightly different picture emerges when the popularity function is estimated for the period 1976–1978, when the Social Democrats were in opposition. As expected, the signs of the coefficients are reversed for inflation and unemployment. This does not hold, however, for the growth in disposable

210 L. Jonung and E. Wadensjö

Table 2. *The effect of unemployment, inflation and real income growth on the popularity standing of the Social Democratic Party. Monthly data 1967–1978. Estimations including a lagged dependent variable*

The Social Democrats in power. 1967: 04–1976: 09.

(5) $S = 7.479 + 0.877 S_{-1} - 0.726 U^m_{-1} - 0.099 P^c_{-1} - 0.005 Y_{-1}$
     (2.221) (0.040)   (0.322)   (0.043)   (0.040)

    Standard errors in parentheses
    $R^2 = 0.907$ $h = -1.752$ $N = 114$

Excluding real disposable income

(6) $S = 7.550 + 0.875 S_{-1} - 0.727 U^m_{-1} - 0.100 P^c_{-1}$
     (2.139) (0.037)   (0.321)   (0.041)

    Standard errors in parentheses
    $R^2 = 0.907$ $h = -1.733$ $N = 114$

Steady state solution $(S = S_{-1})$

(6a) $S = 60.400 - 5.808 U^m_{-1} - 0.800 P^c_{-1}$

Comments: See Table 1. h denotes the Durbin h-statistic.

real income. Only unemployment differs significantly from zero at the five per cent level. One possible explanation is that in the months immediately following the change of power in October 1976, the public still judged economic conditions as a result of the policy of the former government. This view is confirmed by using eq. (1) and eq. (6) to calculate the popularity standing of the Social Democratic Party in the period 1976:10–1978:08 when the Social Democrats were in opposition. The actual and fitted values of both equations follow each other closely in the last quarter of 1977 and in January 1978. But from then on they differ substantially. The non-socialist government presented its first budget in January 1978. This was perhaps a decisive event that made the public regard macroeconomic developments from then on as the result of the policies of the new government, although the budget did not go into effect until July 1978.

The regressions in Tables 1 and 2 reveal that unemployment and inflation exerted a significant influence on the popularity standing of the Social Democrats. The estimations are, however, sensitive to the empirical specifications of the explanatory variables. The results are also sensitive to the estimation period used, although this choice does not change the basic results of the calculations. Estimations using concomitant changes, that is, without the one-month lag, do not improve the results.[1]

---

[1] Kirchgässner (1976) used Sifo data in a number of estimations of popularity functions for Sweden covering the period March 1967 to March 1973, that is a shorter time period than in this study. His results are fairly similar to the regressions reported in Tables 1 and 2 for the period 1967–1976.

V. Conclusions

The rate of unemployment, and inflation exerted a significant influence on the popularity standing of the Swedish government during the period 1967–1978. Unemployment and inflation had a considerably larger effect on government popularity than real income growth during the time periods examined.

List of symbols, definitions and sources

S Popularity, in per cent, of the Social Democratic Party as measured by the opinion polls of the Sifo Institute. Monthly data. Data have been constructed through linear interpolation for months when no polls were made, generally 1–3 months a year. Source: *Väljarbarometern 1967–1978*. Sifo, 1978.

U The rate of insured unemployed. Monthly data. Source: The National Labor Market Board.

U^m The rate of insured unemployed in manufacturing industry. Monthly data. Source: The National Labor Market Board.

P^c Consumer price index. Monthly data. Source: *Allmän månadsstatistik* (Monthly Digest of Swedish Statistics).

P^f Food price index. Monthly data. Source: *Allmän månadsstatistik* (Monthly Digest of Swedish Statistics).

Y Real disposable income. Quarterly data. Monthly data constructed through linear interpolation. Source: National Central Bureau of Statistics.

References

Arcelus, F. & Meltzer, A. H.: The effect of aggregate economic variables on congressional elections. *American Political Science Review 69*, 1232–1239, 1975.

Bloom, H. S. & Price, H. D.: Voter response to short-run economic conditions: The asymmetric effect of prosperity and recession. *American Political Science Review 69*, 1240–1254, 1975.

Fair, R. C.: The effect of economic events on votes for president. *The Review of Economics and Statistics 60*, 159–173, 1978.

Frey, B. S.: Politico-economic models and cycles. *Journal of Public Economics 9*, 203–220, 1978.

Frey, B. S. & Garbers, H.: 'Politico-Econometrics'—on estimation in political economy. *Political Studies 19*, 316–320, 1971.

Frey, B. S. & Schneider, F.: A model of politico-economic interaction in the U.S. *Review of Economics and Statistics 60*, 174–183, 1978*a*.

Frey, B. S. & Schneider, F.: A politico-economic model of the United Kingdom. *Economic Journal 88*, 243–53, 1978*b*.

Goodhart, C. A. E. & Bhansali, R. J.: Political economy. *Political Studies 18*, 43–106, 1970.

Grönhagen, S.: *Ekonomiskt förlopp och allmänna val i Storbritannien 1850–1950* (Economic Changes and General Elections in Great Britain 1850–1950). Gleerup, Lund, 1951.

Hanushek, E. A. & Jackson, J. E.: *Sta-*

tistical methods for social scientists. Academic Press, New York, 1977.

Kirchgässner, G.: Rationales Wählerverhalten und optimale Regierungsverhalten. Dissertation. University of Konstanz, 1976.

Kramer, G. H.: Short run fluctuations in U.S. voting behavior, 1896–1964. *American Political Science Review 65*, 131–143, 1971.

Lindbeck, A.: Business cycles, politics and international economic dependence. *Skandinaviska Enskilda Banken Quarterly Review 4*, 53–68, 1975.

Lindbeck, A.: Stabilization policy in open economies with endogenous politicians. *American Economic Review 66*, 1–19, 1976.

Madsen, H. J.: Electoral outcomes and macroeconomic policies: The Scandinavian case. Paper presented at the European Consortium for Political Research Workshop on Formal Political Analysis, Grenoble, April 1978.

Meltzer, A. & Vellrath, M.: The effects of economic policies on votes for the presidency: Some evidence from recent elections. *The Journal of Law and Economics 18*, 781–798, 1975.

Paldam, M.: Is there an election cycle? A comparative study of national accounts. Institute of Economics, University of Aarhus, memo 1977-8, 1977.

Rydé, K.: Ekonomi och politik: konjunkturer och allmänna val till riksdagens andra kammare i Sverige 1896–1948 (Economics and politics: business cycles and general elections in Sweden 1896–1948). *Statsvetenskaplig tidskrift 53*, 323–336.

Stigler, G. J.: General economic conditions and national elections. *American Economic Review, Papers and Proceedings 63*, 160–167, 1973.

Åkerman, J.: *Ekonomiskt skeende och politiska förändringar* (Economic conditions and political changes). Lund, 1946.

Åkerman, J.: Political economic cycles. *Kyklos 1*, 107–117, 1947 a.

Åkerman, J.: Ekonomi och politik. Ekonomiska konjunkturer och politiska val i USA 1868–1944. (Business and politics. Business cycles and political elections in the USA 1868–1944. *Ekonomisk Tidskrift 49*, 239–254, 1947 b.

Åkerman, J.: Genmäle (Reply). *Ekonomisk tidskrift 50*, 23–28, 1948. This is a reply to a critical comment to Åkerman (1947 b) raised by E. Ruist and J. Wallander.